D0413440

OCR GCSE
Sociology

Jannine Jacobs-Roth
Lynn Taylor
Bruce Viveash
Karen Waterworth
Consultant: Lynn Taylor

080022

Official Publisher Partnership

OCR AND HEINEMANN ARE WORKING TOGETHER TO PROVIDE BETTER SUPPORT FOR YOU

Heinemann is an imprint of Pearson Education Limited, a company incorporated in England and Wales, having its registered office at Edinburgh Gate, Harlow, Essex, CM20 2JE. Registered company number: 872828

www.heinemann.co.uk

Heinemann is a registered trademark of Pearson Education Limited

Text © Pearson Education Limited 2009

First published 2009

14
10 9 8

British Library Cataloguing in Publication Data
A catalogue record for this book is available from the British Library

ISBN 978 0 435807 57 3

Edited by Lucy Dickinson
Designed by Pearson Education Limited
Typeset by Phoenix Photosetting, Chatham, Kent
Original illustrations © Pearson Education Limited 2009
Illustrated by Julian Mosedale and Phoenix Photosetting
Cover design by Dickidot Limited
Picture research by Helen Reilly
Cover photo © Mitchell Funk/Getty Images
Printed in China (CTPS/08)

Acknowledgements
The author and publisher would like to thank the following individuals and organisations for permission to reproduce photographs and copyrighted text/realia:

P1 Shutterstock/Elena Elisseeva; P3 Debbie Rowe/Pearson Education; P4 Mary Evans Picture Library; P22 Getty Images/Anne Frank Fonds; P29 Pres Panayotov/Shutterstock; P30 Photodisc/Pearson Education; P39 T Getty Images/Kristian Dowling; P39 B Shutterstock/Maria Weidner; P49 Shutterstock/Elena Elisseeva; P51 Alamy/Pearson Education; P57 Corbis/Dex Images; P59 Panos/Karen Robinson; P75 Pearson Education/Studio 8 Clark Wiseman; P90 Pearson Education/Rob van Petten; P103 Shutterstock/Andriy Rovenko; P104 L Rex Features/Brian Rasic; P104 R Rex Features/Sipa Press; P119 Mary Evans Picture Library; P123 Pearson Education/Ben Nicholson; P127 Still Pictures; P143 KPT Power Photos/Pearson Education; P146 Rex Features/Geoff Wilkinson; P158 Corbis/Sean Justice; P167 Clarke Wiseman/Pearson Education; P173 Dreamstime/Photoeuphoria; P185 Shutterstock/Elena Elisseeva.

P12 Extract from 'Headhunters Unmasked' by Nick Lowles from Searchlight Magazine (December 1999), reproduced with kind permission of the author and Searchlight Magazine; P22 Extract from 'The Diary of a Young Girl: The Definitive Edition' by Anne Frank, edited by Otto H Frank and Mirjam Pressler, translated by Susan Massotty (Viking, 1997) © The Anne Frank-Fonds, Basle, Switzerland, 1991. English translation © Doubleday (a division of Bantam Doubleday Dell Publishing Group Inc.) 1995; P31 'Girl survived tribe's custom of live baby burial' by Jemima Wright, The Daily Telegraph, 22 June 2007. Reproduced by permission of the Telegraph Media Group Limited; P34 Extract from 'Subculture: the meaning of style' by Dick Hebdige, 2002 Routledge. Reproduced by kind permission of Taylor & Francis Books (UK); P35 Extract on feral children from http://listverse.com, reproduced by kind permission of Jamie Frater; P60 Table 2.1.1 © Crown Copyright, reproduced by permission of the Controller, Office of Public Sector Information (OPSI); P63 Table 2.1.2 and 2.1.3 © Crown Copyright; P67 Adapted extracts from 'The Symmetrical Family' by M Young and P Willmott, 1973, Routledge & Kegan Paul reproduced by permission of Taylor & Francis Books (UK); P70 Table 2.1.5 © Crown Copyright; P83 '£40m waste of the 'Mickey Mouse' degrees by Steve Doughty, The Daily Mail, 20th August 2007. Reproduced by permission of Solo Syndication on behalf of The Daily Mail; P89 Figure 2.2.1 © Crown Copyright; P92 Figure 2.2.2 © Crown Copyright; P94 Figure 2.2.3 © Crown Copyright; P107 Extract from 'A False Wikipedia Biography' by John Seigenthaler, USA Today, November 2005. Reprinted by permission of the author; P111 Extract from 'Investigating Mass Media' by Paul Trowler, 1996, Collins. Reprinted by permission of HarperCollins Publishers Ltd © Paul Trowler 1996; P114 Extract from www.tibet.org, reproduced by permission of www.tibet.org; P117 Extract from 'Grand Theft Auto withdrawn in Thailand after copycat killing' by Jonathan Richards from The Times, August 4 2008. Reproduced by permission of NI Syndication; P128 Extract from 'The Real Toy Story' by Eric Clark, reproduced by permission of Random House Group; P129 Adapted extract from 'The £30m Man' by Andrew Norfolk, The Times, June 9 2008. Reproduced by permission of NI Syndication; P132 Table 2.4.2 © Crown Copyright; P133 Table 2.4.3 © Crown Copyright; P134 'Plenty to smile about working underground' by Roland Gribben, The Telegraph, 7 October 2008. Reproduced by permission of Telegraph Media Group Ltd; P134 Table 2.4.4 © Crown Copyright; P135 Table 2.4.5 © Crown Copyright; P136 Tables 2.4.6, 2.4.7 and 2.4.8 © Crown Copyright; P151 Table 2.5.3 © Crown Copyright; P172 'Youth escapes charge over 'happy slap' attack', The Daily Mail, 20 June 2005. Reproduced by permission of Solo Syndication on behalf of The Daily Mail; P177 'Twisted world of Britain's gang kids' by Jon Kirk from The People, 22 July 2007, reproduced by permission of Mirrorpix; P191 Extract from 'Magistrates take the hood off young offenders' by John Elliott, The Sunday Times, 14 November 2004, reproduced by permission of NI Syndication.

Every effort has been made to contact copyright holders of material reproduced in this book. Any omissions will be rectified in subsequent printings if notice is given to the publishers.

Websites
There are links to relevant websites in this book. In order to ensure that the links are up to date, that the links work, and that the sites are not inadvertently linked to sites that could be considered offensive, we have made the links available on the Heinemann website at www.heinemann.co.uk/hotlinks. When you access the site, the express code is 7573P.

Contents

How to use this book

The book is divided into three parts as follows:

Unit 1 is made up of the two sections you will study in the specification for the exam 'Sociology Basics'. The first section covers some of the basic ideas and concepts used in sociology and the second section deals with how sociologists use research methods to find out about society.

Unit 2 deals with the six topics in the specification. You will need to study three of the topics for the exam 'Socialisation, culture and identity' to answer one question on each.

Unit 3 will give you guidance on how to study the two investigations which make up the pre-release material and apply your knowledge of research methods to the investigations to answer the questions in the exam, 'Applying sociological research techniques'.

The **Exam Café** within each part will provide help and guidance on how to tackle the questions in the exams.

Pause for thought

The chapters in Units 1 and 2 begin with a 'Pause for thought'. This is made up of some questions or short activities to get you thinking about some of the issues in the section or topic. You will be able to use your own experience of the social world as a starting point to studying society in a sociological way. By sharing ideas with your classmates you will be able to start seeing society and social life from different viewpoints.

Main text

The text is written at an appropriate level for GCSE students and contains the key concepts used in sociology, studies carried out by sociologists and contemporary examples to help your understanding of the topic or section. In some chapters you will find some sociological theory to show how different sociologists see the same aspect of society in different ways. The content of each chapter links directly to the OCR specification and you will need knowledge of the topics and sociological concepts.

Activities

Within the main text there are activities which will help you to understand and apply what you have read and also help you to develop the skills you need to answer the question in the unit exams. The activities vary from studying photographs and matching concepts with definitions to practising using statistical evidence. Some activities will be done individually but some involve discussing and sharing ideas and experiences with your classmates. Each chapter also includes research links to tell you how you can find out more information for yourself through for example, useful websites.

Key concepts

A glossary of key concepts is included in each chapter of Units 1 and 2 to help you to have an overview and as a check for revision. As Unit 3 is to help you develop skills, there are less key concepts in this chapter.

KEY CONCEPTS

Non-participant observation – where a researcher watches a group without getting involved in what they are doing.

Participant observation – where a researcher joins the group being studied and acts as they do whilst completing the observation.

Covert observation – where the researcher does not let the group being studied know that they are being observed.

Overt observation – where the researcher tells the group under study that they are being observed or does not attempt to hide their presence from them.

Objectivity – studying topics and people with an open mind and not allowing your own views and opinions to influence the findings.

Exam Café

At the end of each chapter in Units 1 and 2 there is an Exam Café section to help you prepare for your exams.

Exam**Café**

The Exam Café includes sample questions, together with students' answers and comments. These questions are the same type as those you will have to answer in your final unit exams. All the questions can be answered using the information in the chapters but if you use the research links and collect additional information, you may be able to improve your answers. If you study the comments carefully you will gain an understanding of the difference between a good and a poor answer. Unit 3 does not have a specific Exam Café section as most of the unit deals with how to apply the knowledge of research methods you gained in Unit 1 to answer exam questions on the pre-release material.

What is sociology?

Sociologists want to understand the behaviour of people in terms of the age, gender, social class and other groups they belong to. They try to find and explain patterns of behaviour common to the people in these groups. Most chapters start with a section on identity to help you to understand how people see themselves in terms of their membership of a particular group and in 'Sociology Basics' you will study the identity people have as male or female in depth and how this identity has been created by the society a person lives in.

Sociologists are keen to study different societies to see how expected behaviour varies. Sometimes you will be very surprised to find out that in some cultures people have several marriage partners or see adulthood as beginning at the age of 12! You will find interesting examples of cross-cultural behaviour in the book.

Sociology is not just common sense as sociologists must provide evidence to support the claims they make. Studying research methods in Unit 1 will help you to understand how sociologists collect their evidence in a systematic and scientific way, putting aside their own views about how people should behave.

Different types of sociologists see society in very different ways, for example Marxists see the gap between rich and poor as unfair but functionalists see this as useful to help society work well. For GCSE you do not need to know about the different theories in depth, but you will gain some understanding of these and it will help you to

prepare for studying sociology at AS level should you choose to do this later.

Is sociology easy? Not really as people are complex beings! You will need to learn the language of sociology and develop skills to answer questions. However, human behaviour is fascinating and you will find class discussions interesting. Also, there are suggestions in the book as to how you can learn the research techniques through practical activities. Remember, you are a member of society and you can bring to your lessons a range of personal experiences and knowledge which will be useful in helping you to understand social behaviour.

What is OCR Sociology?

OCR Sociology is made up of three units and you will have an exam for each one.

Unit 1: Sociology Basics (25% of GCSE)

This unit is divided into two sections:-

- Research methods
- Basic key concepts in Sociology and links between the individual and society (with a specific focus on gender identity)

Assessment is through one 60-minute examination with two compulsory structured questions, one based on research methods and one based on key concepts.

Unit 2: Socialisation, Culture and Identity (50% of GCSE)

This unit offers a choice of topics through which the themes of culture, socialisation and identity are developed. It builds upon the knowledge and skills acquired in Unit 1.

This unit offers six optional sections from which candidates must study **at least three**:

- **Family**
- **Education**
- **Mass Media**
- **Work**
- **Crime and deviance**
- **Youth**

Assessment is through one 90-minute examination comprising four structured questions per section. There are six sections in this paper and you must answer **all** questions from any **three** of the sections.

Unit 3: Applying Sociological Research Techniques (25% of GCSE)

In this unit you will need to apply your knowledge and understanding of the research techniques learned in Unit 1, to two investigations given to you before the exam as pre-release material. The investigations will be on a different topic area each year but you do not need to have studied the topic. You will study the investigations in your class and will be given a copy of them in the exam.

Assessment is through one 60-minute examination comprising three sections.

Section A of this unit will consist of a set of questions on Investigation 1.

Section B of this unit will consist of a set of questions on Investigation 2.

Section C of this unit will consist of **one** essay type question in which you might need to evaluate all or part of one or both of the investigations or be asked how they could be compared or developed further. You will be given some guidance in the question as to what to focus your answer on, with a list of bullet points.

Sociology basics

1

Unit 1
Part A: Investigating society and collecting and using information and evidence

What have CSI, The Bill and The X Files all got in common? They are all about investigations: people and teams searching for answers amidst a sea of possible outcomes. You will soon discover that sociologists undertake a very similar role.

The key areas you will study in this unit are:

- The basics of sociology, including research methods and evidence
- How research is carried out
- Different types of evidence
- How to develop the skills necessary to evaluate collected evidence.

PAUSE FOR THOUGHT

1 If money was no object, what social issues would you personally like to research and find out more about? 'I'd love to know more about whether people think capital punishment should be re-introduced,' for example.

2 If you wanted to find out whether the media affects girls' body image, how would you go about doing this?

3 If you were questioning people as part of your research, how would you know whether you could believe what they said?

4 Casual sex, drug dealing, prostitution and violent gang crime have all been investigated in the name of sociology. Are there any topics in society that you don't think should be researched? Why?

Investigating society

Primary methods

ACTIVITY 1

Leeper's Lady

What can you see in this image? Are you certain? Remember that a real investigator would make sure all angles were covered, so check again!

There are no simple answers when it comes to sociology; things are often not as they may seem! Examine evidence that you are presented with, or that you find out for yourself, with caution. Always be critical and do not just accept what someone tells you as being true.

You are now going to start learning about the main methods used in sociology. This will allow you to complete investigations of your own as well as to gain a better understanding of research that has already been done by other sociologists.

Questionnaires

What are they?

A questionnaire is a list of written questions which are completed by a number of respondents. They are normally handed out or posted for **self-completion** but occasionally they are read out to respondents instead. When this occurs they are known as **interview questionnaires**. There are two main types of questions that can be used in a questionnaire and most questionnaires will include examples of both.

Firstly, there are **closed questions** which are often fixed choice and tick box. The respondent might be presented with a list of possible options and they have to tick the one that they most agree with. For example, 'What do you think about the amount of violence on television? – far too much; a little too much; about right; not enough.' Alternatively, a closed question may be 'two-way', meaning that there are just two answers to choose from. A common option for two-way questions is 'yes/no'. An example of a closed question that could be asked like this is 'Will you vote in the next general election? – yes/no.'

If you want to gather more in-depth answers from your respondents, then **open questions** will work better. These give no preset answer options and instead allow the respondents to put down exactly what they think in their own words. An example of an open question would be 'Why do you think young people join gangs?'

What are they used for?

Questionnaires are typically used to find out information from a large number of respondents. They can investigate people's opinions, attitudes and behaviour and so can be used to analyse **trends** in society. They are used by a wide range of different researchers – from the government, to market research teams, to students – and are a very popular means of research.

What is good about them?

Firstly, questionnaires are relatively cheap, quick and easy to use. Because you just need to post or hand them out, you can reach large numbers of people in any geographical location you want. This allows you to find out a wide range of opinions from lots of different respondents. Using closed questions in a questionnaire will allow the researcher to generate statistics and so be able to measure trends. The use of **standardised questions** with all respondents also means that you can compare findings over time or between social groups. Finally, because there doesn't have to be any face-to-face contact between the researcher and the respondents, you might get more truthful answers. This is particularly the case when asking personal or embarrassing questions about, say, sexual or criminal behaviour.

What is not so good about them?

Probably the biggest problem when it comes to questionnaires is that people get fed up with them and often cannot be bothered to fill them in. This means that you may not get them all back, meaning that you will have what is known as a **low response rate**. You may also find that people do not take them very seriously and just rush their answers. Another factor to consider is that if a large number of closed questions are used you are not really finding out what people think or do because of the lack of detail in their responses. Finally, the fact that there is no researcher present can also cause a number of problems. How do you know that the person you wanted to fill in the questionnaire actually did so? The answer is that you don't! Also, there's no one there to help out if any of the respondents don't quite understand the questions. All of these issues basically mean that you need to treat any data gathered from questionnaires with caution.

What kind of evidence can you get from them?

Closed questions will generate short answers that allow you to measure and compare people's responses. These kinds of answers can be turned into **statistics** and are referred to as **quantitative data**. Open questions, however, will get you very different evidence. Since respondents have a completely free choice when they are answering, responses will be very varied and therefore difficult to put into statistical form. What you will get, though, is in-depth information, otherwise known as **qualitative data**.

ACTIVITY 3

There is a lot to take in here, so before we move on it is important that you review and refresh your understanding of the good and bad points of using questionnaires as a research device. Copy and complete the following table with the title 'Questionnaires'.

GOOD POINTS	BAD POINTS

KEY CONCEPTS

Self-completion questionnaires – respondents complete the questionnaire themselves and then return it to the researcher.

Interview questionnaires – questions are read out to the respondent by the researcher, who then records the respondent answers.

Closed questions – respondents are presented with either a list of options or a two-way choice and have to select the response with which they most agree.

Open questions – respondents are free to answer the question in any way that they like; there are no preset options.

Trends – patterns of behaviour or attitudes seen in evidence.

Standardised questions – all respondents are asked the same questions in the same order, allowing for comparisons to be made.

Low response rate – not everyone that you want to participate in your research may do so, meaning that your respondents may no longer be typical of the population under study.

Statistics – data presented in a numerical form as a percentage.

Quantitative data – numerical data, often presented as statistics.

Qualitative data – in-depth data usually presented in a written form.

GradeStudio

In the examination you will be expected to have an in-depth understanding of the pros and cons of using questionnaires. You will also need to know what they can be used for, what kind of data they produce and the kind of questions that can be asked in them. A possible examination question could ask you to **describe one advantage and one disadvantage of using questionnaires as a research method**. To do this well you would need to use accurate sociological language to make your points clearly and concisely.

How do you do this kind of research well?

The best advice is to keep things simple. As the researcher is not typically present when the research takes place, you have got to be sure that everyone taking part can understand the questions being asked of them. So questions need to be as clear and straightforward as possible.

- Do not be too personal in the questions you ask.
- Try to keep your own ideas and opinions out of the questions. You do not want to influence the way that your respondents answer.
- Keep the questionnaire as short as possible, but make sure that you ask enough questions to find out what you need to know.
- Include a brief introduction to explain the purpose of the questionnaire and always end by thanking your respondents.
- Think carefully about who you give your questionnaires to, as you will be drawing all of your conclusions from these respondents.

Example and evaluation

Have a look at the questionnaire opposite that was given to office workers to find out about their experiences in the workplace. Answer the following questions about it:

1. What is wrong with the introduction? Can you write a better one?
2. Which questions do you think work well? Why?
3. Which questions are not so successful? Why?

Questionnaire for Office Workers

Hi, my names Ash, how ya doin? This is to help me with my coursework so make sure you fill it in proper.

1. Age: under 18 ☐;   18–30 ☐;
        30–45 ☐;   45–60 ☐

2. Gender: Male ☐   Female ☐

3. What job do you do?

    Type ☐   Answer the phone ☐

    File ☐   Make tea ☐

4. How long have you been in your job?

    Less than a year   ☐

    1–5 years   ☐

    More than 5 years   ☐

5. Do you like your job?

    Yes ☐   No ☐

6. Have you ever stolen anything from your workplace? ....

7. Do you think that your job affects what you do in your free time? Please explain ....
    ....
    ....
    ....
    ....

8. How many hours do you work per week?

    Under 20 ☐   20–37 ☐   Over 37 ☐

9. Would you like to change your job?

    Yes ☐   No ☐

    Why or why not? ....
    ....
    ....
    ....

10. How much do you earn in your job?

    Under £10,000   ☐

    £10,000–£25,000   ☐

    over £25,000   ☐

    Thanks for helping me.

RESEARCH TASK
Now that you are an expert when it comes to questionnaires, it's time to put all of this new-found knowledge into practice. You need to design your own short questionnaire to investigate attitudes in your school to violence in the media. Once you've finished, give the questionnaire to ten people and analyse your findings. What would you need to do to improve the quality of your research? Summarise your conclusions as a PowerPoint or a podcast and present them to the rest of your class.

Interviews

What are they?

There are two main types of interview: **structured** and **unstructured**, with **semi-structured** falling somewhere in-between.

Structured interviews are the same as the interview questionnaires that you have already learned about. Just to remind you, this basically means that they are a list of questions that the researcher reads out to the respondent in a particular order. They typically contain closed questions and so produce largely quantitative data.

Unstructured interviews, however, are very different. Instead of having a set of pre-planned questions, the interviewer will just have some ideas and topic areas to cover. This should make the interview less formal and more like a conversation. It is also likely to take place in a relaxed environment where the researcher tries to put the respondent at ease.

KEY CONCEPTS

Structured interview – a set of standardised preset questions is read out to the respondent by the researcher.

Unstructured interview – a very flexible interview, more like a conversation. Instead of a list of questions to answer, the researcher is more likely just to have general topics or ideas to discuss.

Semi-structured interview – somewhere in-between a structured and an unstructured interview, meaning that the researcher can have preset questions but also has the flexibility to follow up on interesting answers given by the respondent.

Focus group – several respondents are interviewed at once and are allowed to discuss the questions being asked of them.

As an unstructured interview is so informal, the researcher is able to be flexible and follow up on interesting points raised by the respondents. This means that no one interview will be like another.

A semi-structured interview falls somewhere in-between structured and unstructured interviews. Questions are likely to be preset, but the researcher does not have to read them all out in the same order and, instead, has the flexibility to miss out or add in questions depending on what the respondent has said. They are also able to follow up on any interesting points raised if they wish to.

A final type of interview that can be used is known as a **focus group**. This is basically a group interview where respondents discuss something together, with the researcher present to listen, ask questions and make notes.

Have a look at the five situations described below and decide which would be best investigated using structured interviews and which would be better suited to unstructured. Are there any where you think a semi-structured interview might work better?

1. an investigation into how many teenagers have committed criminal acts
2. an investigation into why so many young people do not vote
3. an investigation into what subjects students choose at A Level and why they choose them
4. an investigation into married women's experiences of domestic violence
5. an investigation into how often people exercise.

Unstructured and semi-structured

We will be focusing on unstructured and semi-structured interviews from now on. (You can look back at the 'Questionnaire' section on pages 4–6 for information on structured interviews.) An interview is typically used to find out people's attitudes and opinions on particular issues. They are also useful if you want to find out why someone behaves or thinks in the way they do. Since they are conducted face-to-face, a relationship is built up between the researcher and the respondent, so they are thought to be particularly good for investigating sensitive and personal topics.

What is good about them?

The first thing is that the response rate for interviews is far higher than for questionnaires, as this is a personal experience and we all know that it is much harder to say 'no' to someone than it is to throw a piece of paper in the bin. Also, you can get a lot more depth and detail from respondents, allowing you to find out what they really think. All the answers will be in their own words, so there will be no problems with them being obliged to simply select an option that is closest to what they think. If the respondent does not understand a question properly then the interviewer is able to rephrase and explain it to make sure that the respondent is able to answer. Finally, many people believe that respondents are more likely to open up and tell the truth if they have developed a bond with the researcher.

What is not so good about them?

The success of the interview rests on the skills of the interviewer. If the interviewer does not do a good job in getting the respondent to relax and open up, then the amount and quality of data produced will not be good. This takes time and costs money. As interviews take far longer to complete than questionnaires, you cannot interview large numbers of people so you always need to consider how typical the people you've spoken to actually are of your **research population**.

There is also a difficulty in deciding how best to record the interview. When maintaining eye contact you cannot make detailed notes, but a lot of people feel uncomfortable if they are being recorded. When interviews are unstructured each one is unique, a one-off. This means that you cannot go back and check anything and it becomes very difficult to compare findings when each interview may have featured completely different questions.

Probably the biggest issue with interviews, though, is **interviewer bias**. This refers to the ways that the interviewer may influence the respondent to answer in a particular way. We all like to please, and so may find ourselves just subconsciously giving answers that we think the researcher wants to hear. Sociologists call this **social desirability**. For instance, an interview about racism may produce very different answers depending on the ethnicity of the interviewer. Interviewers must consider their body language, facial expressions and choose their words carefully so as not to influence the answers given.

KEY CONCEPTS

Research population – the group(s) of people relevant to the study being completed.

Interviewer bias – where the interviewer influences the answers that the respondent gives.

Social desirability – where the respondent gives the kind of answer that they think the researcher wants to hear.

ACTIVITY 6

Look at the following scenarios and suggest how interviewer bias could occur. What could be done to help reduce any bias that you spot?

- a black interviewer asking respondents from a variety of ethnic groups about their attitudes to racism
- a teacher interviewing students about truancy rates
- a middle-class researcher asking the homeless about their lifestyle
- an adult interviewer researching teenage attitudes to the legislation of drugs.

What kind of information can you get from them?

The kind of evidence that you get depends upon the type of interview. The more structured the interview, the more quantitative the data gathered will be, whereas unstructured interviews will generate lots of qualitative data. Semi-structured interviews will give you a mixture of the two. If you want answers to things you can measure, such as 'how many' or 'how frequently', then a structured interview will work best. If, however, you are looking for reasons to explain something, then you should use a more unstructured format.

GradeStudio

You will need precise and accurate knowledge of all the research methods if you are going to score highly in the exam. Mind maps are really useful for summarising information and are great revision tools.

How do you do this kind of research well?

The key to being a successful interviewer is being prepared and organised. You should make sure you have made appointments with all of your respondents before the interview date. Never just turn up, presuming it will be OK to do the research. You will also need to do the following.

- Book a quiet interview room and organise how you are going to collect your findings. If this involves any recording, make sure you have got permission to do so.
- Think carefully about how you dress and how you speak and present yourself during the interviews.
- Explain at the start what you are doing and why. Consider including some 'warm-up' questions so your respondents can settle down and feel more comfortable with you before the 'proper' interview begins.

- Try to maintain as much eye contact as possible and look interested in what's being said.
- Follow up on anything interesting that your respondents tell you, as long as it is relevant to your research, of course!

Example and evaluation

As you can probably imagine, interviews have been used extensively by researchers to investigate attitudes and behaviour and to try to understand what motivates people to act and think as they do. Sue Sharpe (1994), for instance, used in-depth interviews to draw conclusions about what it meant to be a girl in contemporary society and Stephen Frosh et al. (1997–1999) looked at how masculine identities were constructed for boys aged 11–14 using both individual and group interviews. You will also see and read interviews regularly in the media, for example, with politicians, actors, the police or the latest *Big Brother* evictee.

You are now going to read some adapted extracts from the transcript of Donal MacIntyre's interviews with two teenage drug dealers (Patrick Butler, 2005):

AMBITION

Donal MacIntyre: Do you want to be the biggest drug dealer in Manchester?

Ryan: Yeah, I want to be the biggest drug dealer in the world.

Wayne: It might not happen but you can always try.

Ryan: We're going to try. Guaranteed. If I'm still here in six years' time, guaranteed, we'll own about a quarter of Manchester . . . It will be ours, which means you will not be able to set foot on it, 'cos it will be ours, and if you want to come and sell on it, you have to pay me.

ECONOMICS

Ryan: We've tried getting jobs, innit? We get laughed at.

Wayne: I had a couple of jobs. I've done building, I've done labouring, I've done plumbing. It's all petty money though.

Ryan: We're just not the sort of people to work. We like the easy money, we like the lifestyle.

Wayne: You don't get the kind of money we do doing a job. We can sit on our backside all day doing f**k all and make twice as much money as someone working a full week.

ETHICS

Ryan: We really don't care. We'll rob you or shoot you, anything.

DM: Would you shoot?

Ryan: Yeah.

Wayne: Yeah.

DM: Why don't you care? Normal people care, I think.

Wayne: You can't care. If you care, then you can't get about in life.

ACTIVITY 7

1. What kind of interviews do you think MacIntyre has used with the teenage criminals? Why?
2. Do you think the respondents told MacIntyre the truth in the interviews?
3. What does the researcher find out about teenage criminals?

Observation

What is it?

Observation is a research method typically used by those sociologists who believe that the best way to understand people and their actions is to see them in their daily lives doing what they normally do. There are several different ways of observing and you will need to make sure that you can discuss all of these.

- **Non-participant observation** – the researcher is completely separate from what is being observed and plays no part in what is going on. Sitting at the back of a classroom and noting down what you see is a good example. In other words, it is like a 'fly-on-the-wall' observation – you can see what is going on but you do not get involved in it.

- **Participant observation** – this time the researcher acts like the members of the group under study and basically does whatever they do.

- **Covert** – this is the name for a secret observation. The group being studied is not aware that the research is taking place.

- **Overt** – the group being observed knows that the research is happening, either because the researcher has explained what they are doing or because of their visible presence.

What is it used for?

Observation can be used for any kind of study, particularly those where you want to collect qualitative data. It is thought by many researchers to be particularly useful for investigating people in deviant or criminal groups, where other methods such as questionnaires would not work. So you tend to find sociologists using observation for rather more taboo topics. For example, James Patrick (1973) used it to study gang behaviour, Laud Humphries (1970) used it to study male homosexuality and Eileen Barker (1984) used it to investigate what made people join the religious cult known as the 'Moonies'.

What is good about it?

Probably the biggest advantage of observation is that you get to see what is going on with your own eyes. You do not have to rely on anyone else's memory or opinion, so the data you gather should be more accurate.

A big advantage of observing as a non-participant is that you will always be a step apart from your research subjects. This means that you are less likely to be influenced because of particular feelings you may have about members of the group, and that you remain **objective**.

Researchers would argue that there are many benefits to using participant observation. The main benefit is that because you are acting as part of the group under study, you are going to really understand things as they do and see things from their point of view.

The main advantage of covert observation is that you can be confident that what you are seeing is real and natural behaviour. If the group does not know it is being observed then you can reasonably presume that it is not changing its behaviour.

Overt observation also has its good points. Its big advantage over covert research is that there is no deception involved – everything is out in the open, so no one feels compromised.

What is not so good about it?

Probably the biggest disadvantage of non-participant observation is that you always remain an outsider, so how can you really claim to understand what is going on? With participant observation there are a number of potential problems. Firstly, it can often be difficult to gain access to the group you want to study. Eileen Barker took two years to gain access to the 'Moonies', for example. That is a lot of time and effort! Also, how do you go about recording your findings? Taking notes would be very difficult, meaning researchers often have to rely on their memories and write up their findings later. Obviously they can forget things or remember them inaccurately. Many researchers find that they become too involved with the group they are studying and hence start to lose their objectivity. This can introduce elements of bias into the research findings.

- Overt observers always have the worry that they are not actually seeing true behaviour, that the group is changing its behaviour, either consciously or subconsciously, because of the researcher's presence. This is known as the **observer effect**.

- Covert observation, despite all of its advantages, is ethically unsound. It is difficult to justify spying on people in the name of research. Ethically this throws up a number of issues. You will learn all about **ethics** later on in this chapter on pages 19–20.

later on in this chapter on pages 19–20.

KEY CONCEPTS

Non-participant observation – where a researcher watches a group without getting involved in what they are doing.

Participant observation – where a researcher joins the group being studied and acts as they do whilst completing the observation.

Covert observation – where the researcher does not let the group being studied know that they are being observed.

Overt observation – where the researcher tells the group under study that they are being observed or does not attempt to hide their presence from them.

Objectivity – studying topics and people with an open mind and not allowing your own views and opinions to influence the findings.

Observer effect – when the presence of an observer affects the actions of the group under study, preventing the observer from seeing natural behaviour.

Ethics – ideas about what is morally right and wrong.

ACTIVITY 9

For each of the investigations described below, decide what kind of observation you would use and why:

- investigating why young people join subcultures
- investigating whether girls and boys are treated differently by their teachers in schools
- investigating the amount of illegal drugs taken by teenagers.

What kind of evidence can you get from it?

If you use an observation grid where you simply mark down the frequency with which particular things take place, then you will gather quantitative data. If you write notes and descriptions of what you have seen, then this will give you qualitative, in-depth data. Many researchers will want both kinds of data for their investigation and so will take this into account when planning how they will carry out their observations.

How do you do this kind of research well?

Preparation cannot be emphasised enough here.

- If the research is overt, then you will need to schedule all of your observations carefully and gain permission to complete them.
- If it is covert, then you will need to gain entry into the group under study and think about how best to record your findings.
- For observations where you want to acquire quantitative data, you will need a pre-prepared observation grid.

Example and evaluation

You read some of Donal MacIntyre's work in the 'Interviews' section on page 9. He is actually probably better known for the varied and often dangerous observations he has done. You are now going to read some information about his participant observation on football hooliganism when he infiltrated the notorious Chelsea Headhunters gang. The information at the top of page 12 is adapted from a report entitled 'Headhunters unmasked' by Nick Lowles in *Searchlight Magazine* (December 1999). Go to *www.heinemann.co.uk/hotlinks* and enter express code 7573P. Click on the *Donal MacIntyre website* for more details on all of his research.

Over the whole of the last football season, BBC journalist Donal MacIntyre spent time in the company of some of Britain's most violent hooligans. MacIntyre, and several other BBC journalists, secretly filmed football violence, the organising of fights and the boasting afterwards. MacIntyre befriended Jason Marriner, 32, a long-time hooligan. Through Marriner, he was to meet some of the most violent hooligans around: Andy Frain, nicknamed Nightmare, who boasted while on the way up to Scotland of cutting up an off-duty policeman; the twins, David and Ian Sim, who were later to be sent to prison for attacking Spurs fans; Stuart Glass, who was filmed on camera snorting cocaine off a pub table; and Tony Covele, one of the country's best-known hooligans. While most of the Chelsea hooligans MacIntyre met were in their thirties, he also crossed paths with the Reading Youth Firm, a younger group of hooligans in their late teens and early twenties who follow Reading Football Club. They too were involved in drug-dealing, violence and Nazi politics.

Adapted from Nick Lowles, *Searchlight Magazine*, December 1999

ACTIVITY 10

You should prepare your answers to these questions in small groups, ready to discuss with the rest of your class.

1. How easy do you think it was for Donal MacIntyre to observe the football hooligans?

2. Why do you think he chose to do covert participant observation?

3. What sort of problems do you think MacIntyre may have had when conducting his observation?

4. Would you have been able to do this kind of observational work as successfully as MacIntyre?

Many other interesting and exciting observations have been carried out by such researchers as Terry Williams (1989) 'Researching cocaine kids', Andrew Parker (1998) 'Trainee footballers in a professional football club' and Irving Spergel's (2007) work on youth gangs. You will find lots more information on observations like these on the internet, so why not have a look?

ACTIVITY 11

RESEARCH TASK

Observation is the research method that most students really want to have a go at but, like anything, it will only be successful if you plan and prepare it properly. You are going to start by completing a non-participant observation in a classroom, looking at whether boys behave differently from girls. You should aim to collect mainly quantitative data, so take this into account when you are planning your observation chart. Secondly, you are going to take part in a participant observation. This one you will do at home, covertly, where you will be focusing on gender roles and expectations. Both observations should last for approximately one hour. Your teacher will help you set them up and once you have completed them you will then be able to discuss what went well and any problems you encountered with the rest of your class.

Content analysis

What is it?

This is a method used by sociologists to study the content of the media. Any form of media can be analysed in order to see how a social group, issue or event is represented. This is done by preparing relevant categories and then going through the specified media and recording the number of times items in each category appear. All terms used should be **operationalised** so that there can be no confusion about what the researcher is looking for in each category. So, if studying stereotyping in films, there might be such categories as 'ethnic negative', 'male provider' and 'youth as troublemakers', amongst others.

What is it used for?

Content analysis is a way of studying media content and has been used to research topics such as media violence, stereotyping and bad language. Probably the best-known study that has used content analysis in sociology is the work completed by the Glasgow University Media Group, who have looked at bias in news and war reporting.

What is good about it?

This is a relatively cheap and easy method to use, as all you really need is the media to analyse. The growth of the internet has made the whole process even easier, as newspaper articles, adverts and television shows are now archived and thus access is simple. This also allows researchers to make comparisons over time. Completing research is straightforward, as you just need to tally up the number of times each category in your chart is shown. As long as the categories have been clearly operationalised there should be no confusion for the researcher when doing this. This quantitative data can then be turned into statistics, so comparisons between different media and different categories are easy to make. It is really the only method to use if you want to study the actual content of the media rather than what people think about it.

What is not so good about it?

The media itself is often very **biased**, so a researcher using content analysis needs to be aware that any results gained may also be biased. The success of a content analysis is clearly dependent on the quality of the categories that have been drawn up. If important points are missed out, then these will also be missing from the final results. Similarly, if the terms used in the categories are not clearly operationalised, then there will be no consistency when completing the research. This would be a real problem if research was being conducted by a team of researchers, as they would all be recording different information in different categories. Content analysis typically produces quantitative data. This could be a problem as it will not be detailed or in-depth, so some would question just how useful it actually is. Finally, results are often based on the thoughts, judgements and opinions of one person. This is likely to make any conclusions biased.

ACTIVITY 12

The following categories were included in a content analysis to study the use of bad language on television:

- words that cause mild offence
- words to do with genitalia
- words to do with mental illness or disability
- words to do with sexuality
- words that cause serious offence.

Have a look at them to see if you can work out what problems there may have been. Next, try to improve the categories by making changes and operationalising terms where necessary. Discuss with the rest of your class and see if they agree with your changes.

What kind of evidence can you get from it?

As most content analyses simply count the number of occurrences of something in the media – for example, the number and type of ethnic minorities in a soap opera – then this will give you quantitative data. However, were you to describe in detail the content of, say, crime stories in the tabloid press, then this data would be qualitative.

How do you do this kind of research well?

Just looking at, or reading, something in the media and then writing down what you see is not really the best way to do a content analysis, as it would be very vague and unfocused.

- It is better to produce an analysis table or grid that categorises all the factors you should be considering during the analysis.
- Operationalising what you mean will also be crucial, especially if there is more than one person completing the research.
- Finally, you need to carefully consider and select your media sample before beginning the research.

GradeStudio

When doing a content analysis of a topic in the media, it helps to give each category a colour. You can then highlight the textual evidence of each category in its own colour on printouts of articles. This really helps to pick out the different strands of your research clearly. For audio-visual materials, try to get hold of printouts of the transcripts.

Example and evaluation

A good example of content analysis comes from the Glasgow University Media Group, who has a long tradition of working with this research method. In a chapter from the book *Message Received* entitled 'Media and Mental Illness' by Greg Philo (Longman, 1999), Philo describes a content analysis that was completed on press and television output. Television news, press reporting, popular magazines, children's books and fictional television, such as soap operas, films and drama, were analysed for a period of one month. The researchers were looking to see how mental illnesses were represented and found that the 562 items analysed fell into five main categories:

- violence to others
- harm to self
- advice
- criticism of accepted definitions of mental illness
- 'comic' images.

Overall, the category of 'violence to others' was by far the most common representation. The researchers concluded from this that inaccurate beliefs regarding mental illness can be traced directly to media accounts.

ACTIVITY 13

1. What areas of the media did Greg Philo focus on for his research?

2. He carried out his research for one month. Can you think of any problems with limiting the research to this timescale?

3. Are there any problems with placing media content into five main categories?

KEY CONCEPTS

Research device – the research method that you will use for your investigation, such as a questionnaire or interview questions.

ACTIVITY 14

RESEARCH TASK

As you know, content analysis is all about researching the content of the media. You are going to focus on two national news programmes to see if the way the news is presented is biased. For this to work you will need to prepare your content analysis grid as a class, thinking carefully about what factors could show bias and how you are going to record the data. Possible factors to consider could be the amount of time devoted to a story or to one side of a story, words used to report the 'facts' or perhaps the images that are chosen to accompany the news report.

When you are all ready you will need to watch the two news programmes and fill in your grids.

When you have finished the research try to analyse your own findings and draw conclusions about whether there is bias in national news programmes. Finally, evaluate the **research device** with the rest of your class.

- Is there anything that did not work?
- What would you do differently if you were going to repeat this piece of research?

Conducting research

Now that you understand the main methods used by sociologists when completing their research, we are going to have a look at a few more ideas and issues that every good researcher should be aware of.

The main stages of social research

Research in sociology refers to the process of investigating a topic to find out relevant information and then analysing it in order to be able to draw conclusions and make comparisons. There are several stages that a researcher will go through in order to do this successfully.

Creating aims and hypotheses

This is where you start to identify exactly what it is that you are going to research. Be realistic with your aims – three or four will be about right – and make sure that they are straightforward and clear. Your hypothesis is basically a prediction of what you think you will find out from your research. This can be based on previous studies and findings, media reports or simply common sense.

ACTIVITY 15

Here is an example to illustrate what you have read above:

> **TOPIC:** Youth subcultures
>
> **AIMS:**
>
> 1. to find out which subcultures young people join
>
> 2. to find out what influences young people to join subcultures
>
> 3. to find out how being in a subculture affects young people's attitudes, behaviour and dress.
>
> **HYPOTHESIS:** I predict that the chav subculture will be the most popular because it is seen so much in the media and is popular with many celebrities. I also think that chavs will mainly wear sports labels and fake Burberry, listen to dance music and hang around in gangs.

You are now going to have a go at doing this for yourself. Your topic is 'Marriage'. Your job is to come up with three or four realistic aims for the study and a hypothesis.

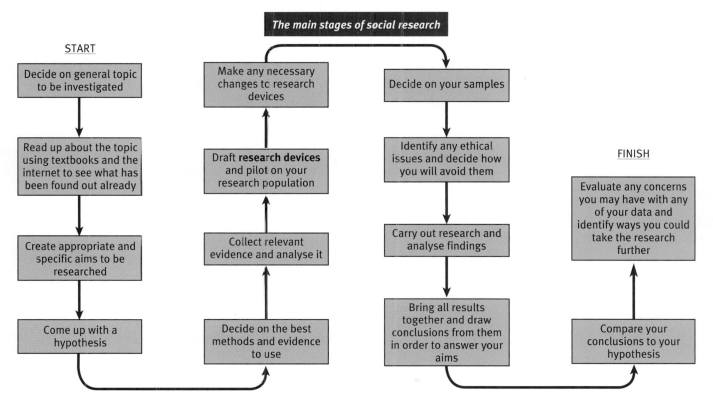

The main stages of social research

START

Decide on general topic to be investigated

→

Read up about the topic using textbooks and the internet to see what has been found out already

→

Create appropriate and specific aims to be researched

→

Come up with a hypothesis

Make any necessary changes to research devices

Draft **research devices** and pilot on your research population

Collect relevant evidence and analyse it

Decide on the best methods and evidence to use

Decide on your samples

→

Identify any ethical issues and decide how you will avoid them

→

Carry out research and analyse findings

→

Bring all results together and draw conclusions from them in order to answer your aims

FINISH

Evaluate any concerns you may have with any of your data and identify ways you could take the research further

Compare your conclusions to your hypothesis

Practical issues

Before starting any research a sociologist will think carefully about any practical issues that may cause problems in the study. These will typically be to do with time, cost and access.

- **Time:** unfortunately, we do not have unlimited time for our research, so what a researcher wants to do will have to fit into a reasonable timescale. For example, it would not be possible to interview everybody in, say, Wales – you would never have time. And, however interesting it may be, you would not have time to watch every episode of *Friends* in order to complete a content analysis on the representations of age in sitcoms.

- **Cost:** this is related to the issue of time, since time, as they say, is money! As a researcher you would not be able to afford not to work for a year just to complete your study. Similarly, there may be issues with wanting to investigate gender roles in a tribal society as it would cost rather a lot to travel and stay there. Even when doing relatively small-scale research in your local area, there may still be costs involved. For example, it is often very difficult to get people to actually take part in research projects, so many market research companies now have to pay both the researchers and the participants in order to generate results.

- **Access:** this basically means how you would get hold of the people on whom you intended to do your research. So if you planned a research study into criminal gangs, how would you access enough criminal gangs and members to produce any kind of meaningful research? It is a similar story when it comes to other taboo topic areas such as prostitution and abuse.

Sampling

With approximately 60 million people living in the UK, research would be extremely difficult if you ever tried to study them all! The government do actually do this in a survey called the census, but even with all their resources it is such a big job that they only do it once every ten years. With this in mind, sociologists will study a smaller number of people. As long as this group is **cross-sectional** this is not really a problem, as results from it should represent the opinions of the rest of society, meaning **generalisations** can be made. Researchers have to think very carefully about a range of social factors such as gender, ethnicity, social class and age when drawing up their sample to best represent their research population. This small group of people being studied is known as a **sample**. But where do you actually get them from? You might choose names from a class register, names from the electoral roll, every tenth person walking down the street or even names from the phone book. All of these are sources that you can draw your sample from and are called a **sampling frame.**

ACTIVITY 16

Can you spot what is wrong with the following samples and sampling frames? How would you improve them?

1. **SAMPLES**

   i) Matt is studying behaviour in schools across the UK and has decided to observe in four schools which are all in the same town in Scotland.

   ii) Olga is researching changing attitudes to religion in the UK and has asked her friends and family to be her sample group.

   iii) Luca wants to investigate employment opportunities for women and has made contact with a local **feminist** group who are willing to help him out and be his sample.

2. **SAMPLING FRAMES**

   i) GROUP TO BE STUDIED : adults

   SAMPLING FRAME: people who look over 18

   ii) GROUP TO BE STUDIED : homosexuals

   SAMPLING FRAME: people who look 'camp'

   iii) GROUP TO BE STUDIED : school students

   SAMPLING FRAME: everyone in your sociology class.

Types of sample

There are several different kinds of samples that sociologists can use in their research. Let us have a look at the ones you will need to know about for the exam.

Random sampling

This is the simplest of sample types and so is relatively cheap and easy to organise. The easiest way to imagine it is that it is just like pulling names out of a hat or lottery numbers out of a machine. Most sociologists do not actually use a hat though! Instead they use a computer to select the names of their sample at random. This means that everybody in the sampling frame has an equal chance of being selected so it is a fair method to use. However, a big problem with any **random sample** is that it is unlikely to be **representative** of your research population. This will probably mean that a random sample will not be cross-sectional and so generalisations are unlikely to be accurate.

Stratified sampling

Stratified random **sampling** was developed to try to solve some of the problems with random sampling. Instead of leaving everything to chance, this time the sampling frame is divided into different groups of people that are appropriate to what is being studied. So, if your sampling frame was nurses and earlier research told you that approximately 90 per cent of nurses were female, then you would also want 90 per cent of your research sample to be female. Although you would be controlling the number of men and women in the sample, you would still pick the actual males and females to take part in the research at random. You could similarly take into account other relevant factors such as age and ethnicity. You should, therefore, end up with a sample that represents your research population and so allows you to make generalisations.

Systematic sampling

This is a form of non-random sampling and is a simple way of selecting a sample for research. All the researcher does is decide on a pattern for the selection of the sample and then follows this in order to select those people who will become the sample group. So this could mean choosing every fifth name from the sampling frame until the required sample size is reached.

Snowball sampling

A final type of sample worth considering is one known as a **snowball sample**. This is another non-random sample but this time does not involve any sampling frame. It is normally used when investigating sensitive or illegal activity, such as prostitution or benefit fraud, where there is not going to be a handy list available of potential people to ask to take part in your research. To get a sample the researcher makes contact with one member of the research population willing to participate and then uses this contact to acquire more participants. They will put you in touch with their friends, acquaintances or family members who are relevant to your research. You then go on building up your sample to the required size by asking all these people for further contacts. This ensures you end up with a relevant sample for your study but, as everyone has come through just one contact, it is unlikely to be a representative one.

Cross-sectional – if a sample is cross-sectional, then it will be made up of a range of different people to best represent the research population.

Generalisations – results from a study can be applied to the whole of the research population.

Sample – a small group of people, usually cross-sectional, on whom research will be carried out.

Sampling frame – the source from which a sample is drawn.

Feminist – someone who thinks that women are disadvantaged in society and wants to make them equal with men.

Random sample – the sample group is chosen completely at random.

Representative – when the data can be said to accurately represent the research population in terms of, for example, gender and age composition.

Stratified sample – the research population is divided up into relevant groups, such as by gender and age, and a random sample is then taken from each of these groups to generate more representative data.

Systematic sample – selecting every nth name from the sampling frame, therefore not random at all.

Snowball sample – another non-random sample where a researcher makes contact with one relevant respondent and then asks them to put them into contact with further respondents. Often used when studying a topic with no sampling frame, for example, gang members.

ACTIVITY 17

Copy the following terms and match them with the correct definitions.

	TERM		DEFINITION
1	STRATIFIED SAMPLE	a)	The group being studied
2	GENERALISATIONS	b)	The researcher makes contact with one person and builds up their sample from there
3	RESEARCH POPULATION	c)	Results from the study can be applied to the whole of the research population
4	SNOWBALL SAMPLE	d)	A range of different people's views to represent the research population
5	SAMPLE	e)	The place or list from which the sample is drawn
6	SAMPLING FRAME	f)	Selecting every nth name from the sampling frame
7	REPRESENTATIVE	g)	The group of people on whom the research is completed
8	RANDOM SAMPLE	h)	Typical of the group under study
9	CROSS-SECTIONAL	i)	Dividing up the research population into relevant smaller groups to best represent the research population
10	SYSTEMATIC SAMPLE	j)	Everybody in the sampling frame has the same chance of being included in the research

Using more than one method

Most sociologists will typically use more than one method or piece of evidence when completing their research. This means that any weaknesses in one of the methods used can be compensated for by the use of another method. So if you have doubts about people's honesty in your questionnaires, then you could also complete some interviews to give you a better chance of gaining more truthful information. The sociological name for using more than one method to complete research is **triangulation**. Another way a researcher can triangulate their research is to use more than one researcher, which clearly has several benefits. Firstly, more research can be completed and, secondly, it may allow you to reduce the possibility of interviewer bias or researcher effect.

KEY CONCEPTS

Triangulation – using more than one research method or researcher in order to complete the investigation.

 Grade**Studio**

Mix and match activities like the one on page 17 are a really good way of testing your sociological knowledge and understanding. You will find questions like this in the examination, so completing these regularly during your sociology course is great preparation for you. Have a go now at the activity that follows.

Source A: Behaviour in Schools

'I conducted unstructured interviews with 50 school students; 25 male and 25 female. The students were of different ages and from different schools across the UK. Each interview lasted about 20 minutes and took place in a school office with a member of staff present.'

This is an extract from one boy's response:

'In my English class it's definitely the girls that behave the worst. They're always chatting and putting on make-up, all my mates would agree with me. But it's unfair because they never seem to get in trouble for it. That winds me up.'

(Adapted from a university student's research, 2005)

Using **Source A** to help you, state whether the following statements (a–d) are **true** or **false**. Circle the correct answer.

(a) The method used in Source A is an interview.

TRUE   FALSE   [1]

(b) The data gained from this method would be quantitative.

TRUE   FALSE   [1]

(c) The researcher asked a stratified sample.

TRUE   FALSE   [1]

(d) People were researched from all over the UK.

TRUE   FALSE   [1]

Social surveys

A survey is where information is gathered from a group of people in the research population by asking them questions. Probably the best example of this is an opinion poll. These are done regularly to measure public opinion on a variety of different issues. Results of these can be found everywhere, from newspapers to online sources to television news shows. You will probably have seen them around election time when researchers try to predict voting results, for example.

Whilst surveys help us to see what people think on a subject or issue, it is important that they are given to a cross-section of the population if the results are to be accurate. So social factors such as age, gender, ethnicity, social class and religion all need to be accounted for. A problem with surveys, though, is that they only tell us what somebody thinks at one moment in time. Opinions change, often from day to day, and a survey cannot really show this.

Pilot studies

Doing a **pilot study** is good practice in sociological research as it can often save you both time and money later and help to ensure that you get the best data possible. A pilot study is a mini version of your research that you complete before the final project in order to spot any potential problems with either the research plan or the research device(s). By piloting a questionnaire, for example, before the research itself you will be able to check that all your questions can be easily understood and, if not, make any adjustments necessary.

Case studies

A **case study** is the detailed and in-depth study of one particular group or situation to find out as much information as possible. Student research is often case study based. An example of a case study is a student who is studying peer pressure but only investigates their own school. Case studies are also used a lot by professional sociologists and a famous example of this is James Patrick's case study of gangs, *A Glasgow Gang Observed* (1973). If you want to find out more details on this particular case study, then have a look on the internet or in your sociology library. In terms of understanding why certain things happen, or how people think, this is a great method to use as you have the depth of information needed to do this. It does have some disadvantages, though, the main one being that

because a case study only looks at one situation or group you cannot really generalise from it.

Longitudinal studies

These are studies that go on for a long time. A good example of such a study in sociology is the British Household Panel Survey that has been interviewing families since 1991. A similar example that you may have heard about or seen on television is Robert Winston's *Child of our Time*. This 20-year project is following 25 children from across the UK who were born in 2000 and looking at how their social circumstances affect their lives. **Longitudinal studies** are good in that they allow researchers to build up a picture of social life that recognises change and does not go out of date. However, they are quite difficult to manage as people's circumstances are constantly changing. Therefore, researchers have to cope with people dropping out of the study, moving away and even dying.

KEY CONCEPTS

Triangulation – using more than one research method or researcher in order to complete the investigation.

Pilot study – a small-scale study completed before a piece of research to identify any possible problems.

Case study – a detailed and in-depth study of one particular group or situation.

Longitudinal study – a study completed over a long period of time.

Ethical issues

Here we take a look at the moral obligations that all researchers have as developed by the British Sociological Association. Researchers have a responsibility to themselves and to everybody else involved in the research. Nobody should be put in a position where they could come to any emotional or physical harm. People should never be made to feel uncomfortable, embarrassed or threatened. To ensure that this happens, the performance of the sociologists will be crucial. They need to be well trained and skilled in the role of researcher and to conduct themselves professionally at all times. Another important ethical consideration is to make sure that everyone who is involved in the research has consented to do it. Researchers also have a responsibility not to discuss anything that respondents say or do. All research participants need to be assured that any information they give will be kept confidential. Finally, a researcher has a duty to make sure that what they are studying is actually suitable. Upsetting topics, such as paedophilia and abuse, must be dealt with carefully.

ACTIVITY 18

Have a look at the scenarios that follow and see if you can spot any ethical considerations that a researcher would have to be aware of. What could be done to make each piece of research more ethical?

1. Ollie intends to study drug abuse in his local area. He is in Year 11 so for ease has decided just to focus his research on that year group in his school. He is planning to use interviews to ask his sample about what drugs they take and what they think about drugs. He would also like to interview local drug dealers so he is going to ask his respondents for some names so he can contact the dealers and see if they will take part.

2. Mike wants to investigate women's experiences of domestic violence. He is going to use women of different ages and ethnic groups to see if they have different views. His sister works for a charity that helps abused women so he is going to get access to his sample there. He has decided to use questionnaires as his method.

3. Tariq is very concerned about the amount of bullying in his school. He has decided to investigate it by using covert observation so he can prove to teachers what really goes on. As well as watching out for things himself he is going to rig up a video camera in the toilets as this is one of the main places that bullying occurs.

Collecting and using information and evidence

Different types of data

There are several different types of information that can be generated from any sociological investigation. The key ones that you will need to know about are primary, secondary, quantitative and qualitative, some of which you have already learned about earlier on in this chapter.

Primary and secondary data

Primary data is information that has been gathered directly by the sociologist by using observations or interviews. Although you know exactly where the information has come from, how true it is and who has been researched, it is not without its problems, for example interviewer bias or the observer effect. **Secondary data**, on the other hand, already exists and so has been collected by somebody else. It is still a popular source of evidence for sociologists, however, and is often used in research studies. Examples of secondary data include statistics, documents and media materials. It is a good way of building up a bigger picture than an individual sociologist could ever do and allows researchers to look at things from the past and include them in their research. However, a big problem with any piece of secondary data is its accuracy. You do not always know why the evidence has been collected, whether it contains bias or whether you can actually trust the author's words. In terms of using it for research, approach it with caution!

Qualitative and quantitative data

We have covered this already (see page 5 for more details) but here is a quick reminder. Qualitative data is presented as words and is detailed and in-depth. Quantitative data is presented in a numerical format and allows researchers to measure amounts and make comparisons. Both primary and secondary data can be either qualitative or quantitative, depending on the evidence or method being used.

Quantitative evidence

In this section you are going to be introduced to two examples of secondary evidence that can be used to collect numerical, quantitative data.

KEY CONCEPTS

Primary data – information that researchers have gathered themselves.

Secondary data – information that has been collected by somebody else and then used by the researcher.

Statistics: official and non-official

Official statistics are produced by the government and other official bodies. These can be on a range of different topics but are mainly used to measure an amount or frequency of something. Some that you might have seen yourself are births, marriages and deaths; crime rates; GCSE pass rates; divorce and unemployment rates. The census is a big source of official statistical data for the government and is carried out every ten years, aiming to gather information from every household in the UK. The Office for National Statistics (ONS) publishes *Social Trends* every year, which is another large and well-known source of official statistical data. Non-official statistical data are simply statistics that have been produced by non-official sources. So they could have been generated by university researchers, sociologists or students, for example.

Statistics are popular with researchers for a number of reasons. Firstly, they cover a wide range of areas of social life, are cheap and are easily available. So on this practical level they are clearly useful. Typically, official statistics have been compiled from large, national samples, to which sociologists would never get access themselves. Since the information used to produce official statistics is gathered so frequently, another big advantage is that they are up to date. This is not so true for non-official statistical data from organisations which are unlikely to have access to such resources.

ACTIVITY 19

Go to *www.heinemann.co.uk/hotlinks* and enter express code 7573P. Click on the *UK National Statistics website* to investigate a wide range of official government statistics on various topics.

It is not all good news, though! When using official statistical information for research you should always remember that the definitions used may not be those that a sociologist would have used or may not have been clearly operationalised. The unemployment statistics are a good example of this, as any statistics on the number of unemployed people in society will depend entirely on how 'unemployment' has been defined. So does it include people on training schemes or women looking after their children, for example? The government knows that its performance will be judged by the amount of unemployment in society and so any statistics that it has generated on this may be rather biased, as it will want to look as good as possible. This should not be so much of a problem with non-official statistics, but these have the problem of not being so large scale and are, therefore, less likely to be representative. The other big issue with any kind of statistics is that they are simply a number – they do not give you reasons or explanations for any of the trends seen.

Qualitative evidence

Historical documents and evidence

Historical documents and evidence can be anything from the past from which we can draw information. Sometimes this is the only way to find things out if, say, we want to research something from so long ago that all the people alive at the time are now dead. In this sense, historical documents add an important element to the research process. A big drawback with them, though, is that you can never be sure how truthful they actually are, as there is no way to go back in time and check.

ACTIVITY 20

Think of examples of historical documents or evidence that sociologists would find useful when investigating the following topic areas?

- changes in the role of women in the family
- changing trends and tastes in fashion
- whether football hooliganism is a modern problem.

Personal documents and diaries

Letters and diaries are the personal documents most often used in sociological investigations. They could range from a household budget to a school report to a photograph. Any kind of document, whether written or visual, can prove to be a good source of information. You need to consider whether the document was intended to be read or seen when assessing its usefulness. If it is a private document never meant for publication, then it could well be a very truthful source that gives you a real insight into a person's thoughts. However, you might also want to question some of the information found in the document. Think back to diaries you kept when you were younger. For example, was that 'love affair' you had with some famous film star really going on or was it more a figment of your imagination? Documents written with the intention of being published should also be treated with caution. The writer will have wanted to present themself in the best possible light and so truth might not have been top of the agenda.

ACTIVITY 21

Probably one of the most famous personal documents used for research purposes is Anne Frank's diary, telling her story of hiding from the Nazis during the Second World War. (See the extract and photograph below.) How do you think this could be useful for researchers?

'My father, the most adorable father I've ever seen, didn't marry my mother until he was thirty-six and she was twenty-five. My sister Margot was born in Frankfurt am Main in Germany in 1926. I was born on June 12, 1929.'

Anne Frank

Anne with her friends: (from left to right) Hanneli Goslar, Anne Frank, Dolly Citroen, Hannah Toby, Barbara Ledermann and Sanne Ledermann.

Taken from the *Anne Frank website* which you can access through *www.heinemann.co.uk/hotlinks* (enter express code 7573P).

Media material

The mass media provides sociologists with a great deal of material that can be used for research. One way that media materials can be used is as a source of background information on the topic you are researching. Whilst the media is readily and easily available, you should always bear in mind that it may be either biased or not an accurate picture of reality. The media, after all, is not particularly well known for its truthfulness!

Evaluation

We now move into the final section of this chapter, where you will be encouraged to be critical of any data you are presented with. The skill of evaluation that you will develop is vital to success in your examinations.

Strengths and weaknesses of information collected by different sociological methods

All of the methods and evidence that you have been learning about in this part of the course have had their good and bad points. You need to make sure that you are clear about all of these: firstly, because you are going to be asked about them in the exam and, secondly, because if you ever complete your own piece of research you will need to weigh up which methods and evidence would be the best ones to use. Knowing the strengths and weaknesses of particular methods will allow you to do this.

Exaggeration, distortion, selection and bias

These four terms are all important ones to consider whenever you assess a piece of evidence. Let us have a look at each one in turn.

1. **Exaggeration** – this means to stretch the truth. The media is often accused of doing this. Think of those sensationalist tabloid headlines for a start!

2. **Distortion** – if you distort something you change the way it looks. So when researchers write up notes from a participant observation and have perhaps lost a little of their objectivity, they may distort what they have actually observed.

3. **Selection** – this refers to how researchers decide which parts of their data to select for their study and which to get rid of. Imagine all the data you would collect from unstructured interviews – there would be no way you could include it all in your findings. As a researcher you therefore must select the most relevant parts. But can you be sure that other people would agree with you?

4. **Bias** – this is where your personal views affect either your interpretation of the data collected or the way that you carry out your research.

Fitness for purpose

How useful something is depends on a number of different factors, so you should always look at the specifics of the research scenario before making any decisions. For example, questionnaires have lots of good points. But what if you want to research how people feel, how they make sense of things in their day-to-day lives? Instead of quantitative data, qualitative responses would be needed, and so what have been identified as the advantages of questionnaires suddenly become negatives. This is what is meant by 'fitness for purpose', that is making sure that the methods and evidence you choose for any piece of research are the ones that give you the best chance of completing your investigation accurately and meeting your aims.

Making generalisations

To be able to generalise from your research findings means that you are confident in applying them to the whole of the research population. Whether or not you can do this is largely dependent on the size, composition and type of sample that you have used. You need to be sure that your sample is representative of the wider research population to be able to generalise from it. So, if you are carrying out research in a sample of different secondary schools to investigate why girls do better in exams than boys, you will need to account for the following factors. Firstly, you will need to use schools from all over the country: some in rural areas, others more urban; some in middle-class areas, others working-class. You will also have to include both state and private schools in the sample, in the right kind of proportions. Students used for research will need to reflect all different ages, genders, ethnicities, religions, etc. A stratified, cross-sectional sample is most likely to provide you with representative data and is therefore your best bet when it comes to making generalisations.

GradeStudio

In the examination you are likely to be asked about the usefulness of a piece of data for **all** students/voters/workers, etc. So this will essentially be a question about representativeness and whether generalisations can be made. When deciding which points to make, the best advice is to look closely at the sample and evaluate it. Is it big enough? Is it cross-sectional? Does it account for all relevant social factors? Be particularly cautious of small-scale, qualitative data when it comes to generalisations.

Reliability of research methods

Reliability refers to whether research can be replicated in order to check its findings. For data to be reliable, it should not matter who has collected it; the findings should be the same. So the key question to consider is: if someone else did the research in the same way would they get the same or similar results? If the answer to this question is 'yes', then you can say that the research is reliable. People are influenced by others and by their surroundings, and so may give quite different answers to different researchers. If you suspect that this has happened, then you should question the reliability of any findings. In sociological research this is most likely to occur with methods and evidence that produce qualitative data.

Validity of the data

For data to be **valid** it needs to give the researcher accurate and truthful information. So if, in a questionnaire, the respondent just ticks any option box without thought or perhaps lies, then

the validity will suffer. By and large, it is the methods and evidence that give you qualitative data which are most likely to provide you with valid information, as they allow you to form a relationship with your respondent and probe their answers.

ACTIVITY 22

In the following scenarios Yvonne is trying out a number of different research methods:

- using official crime statistics to measure how much crime goes on in society
- using unstructured interviews to find out about teenagers' use of contraception
- using an observation to study equality in the workplace
- using a closed question questionnaire to investigate how healthily people eat.

Have a look at the scenarios and try to advise Yvonne on which method or piece of evidence will get her the most valid data.

KNOW YOUR STUFF?

Check your understanding by discussing these questions.

1. Name and describe three research methods that can give you primary data.
2. What does it mean to do research covertly?
3. Which would be more likely to get you qualitative data – questionnaires or interviews?
4. What might the problem be in using school statistics for unauthorised absence to investigate whether males or females truant more and why?
5. What is the term to describe the use of more than one research method in an investigation?
6. What type of sample would you use if you wanted to make your sample as cross-sectional and representative as possible?

Exam**Café**

Welcome

Welcome to your first Exam Café. There will be an Exam Café at the end of every chapter in the book which will help you to put your new-found sociological knowledge into practice in an examination context. We all know how stressful preparing for exams can be and this is why we have designed these sections for you. There is no need to panic and plenty of time to get sorted. So come in, sit down and prepare to relax!

All the Exam Café sections in this book will focus on different topic areas that you can be tested on in the exam room. Each Exam Café is different – it will specifically prepare you for exam questions that could come up in that particular topic. There are different ways of using these sections, which means you will be able to decide what will work best for you. You can use them to really see how much you have learned at the end of a topic. As well as the content, you will also be able to try out your exam technique. Alternatively, you could use the Exam Café once you enter your exam preparation and revision phase after the teaching of the course has finished. Either way you should find them invaluable in terms of helping you feel better prepared for the exam. Feeling and being prepared are the keys to success.

Revision

We are going to start off your revision with a reminder of all the possible content you could be asked about in the examination. Do not let this scare you; it is all material you have covered during your course. Now is the time to check off what you are feeling confident with and what you know you need to do more work on.

A really good tip is to use this as a starting point for producing your own revision mind maps. So use all the key terms from the specification and then add on to these with your own notes, definitions, examples and explanations. Set them out on A3 paper or on the computer and use plenty of bright colours to really make this an appealing revision document. Stick it on your bedroom wall and get revising!

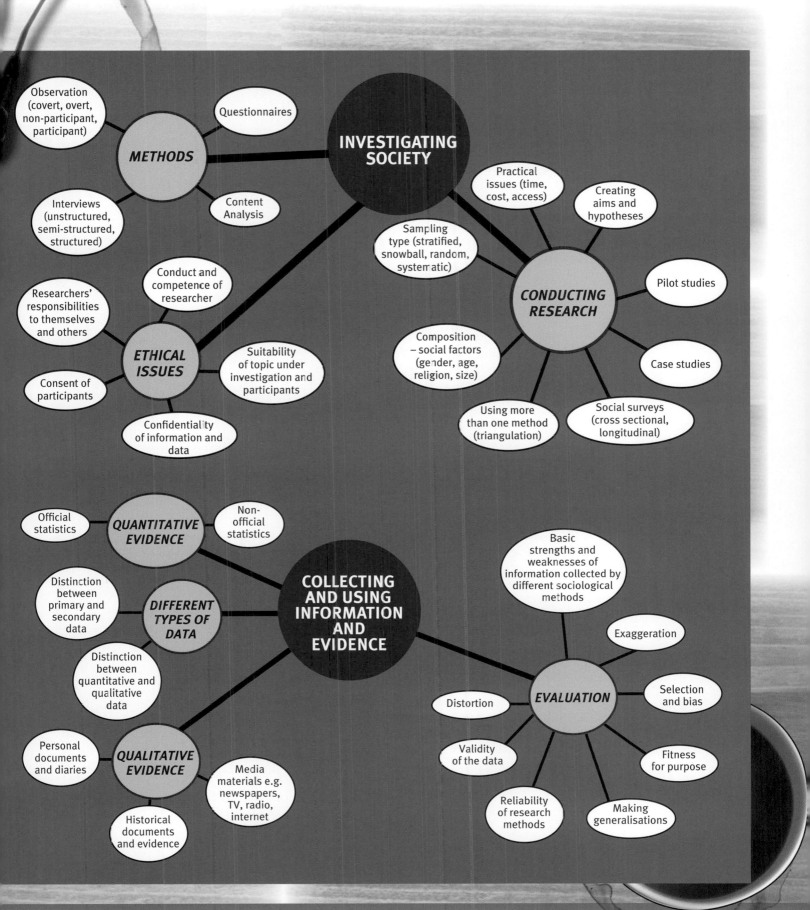

INVESTIGATING SOCIETY

METHODS
- Observation (covert, overt, non-participant, participant)
- Questionnaires
- Content Analysis
- Interviews (unstructured, semi-structured, structured)

ETHICAL ISSUES
- Conduct and competence of researcher
- Researchers' responsibilities to themselves and others
- Consent of participants
- Suitability of topic under investigation and participants
- Confidentiality of information and data

CONDUCTING RESEARCH
- Practical issues (time, cost, access)
- Creating aims and hypotheses
- Sampling type (stratified, snowball, random, systematic)
- Pilot studies
- Case studies
- Composition – social factors (gender, age, religion, size)
- Social surveys (cross sectional, longitudinal)
- Using more than one method (triangulation)

COLLECTING AND USING INFORMATION AND EVIDENCE

QUANTITATIVE EVIDENCE
- Official statistics
- Non-official statistics

DIFFERENT TYPES OF DATA
- Distinction between primary and secondary data
- Distinction between quantitative and qualitative data

QUALITATIVE EVIDENCE
- Personal documents and diaries
- Media materials e.g. newspapers, TV, radio, internet
- Historical documents and evidence

EVALUATION
- Basic strengths and weaknesses of information collected by different sociological methods
- Exaggeration
- Selection and bias
- Fitness for purpose
- Making generalisations
- Reliability of research methods
- Validity of the data
- Distortion

25

ExamCafé
Exam preparation

Examiner's tips

There is a lot you can do to improve your performance in the exam. Follow the 'ten top tips' below and you are well on your way…

1. This part of your exam will always start with source material, so make sure you have got a highlighter handy – read the source very carefully and highlight any important points.

2. Your first question will be structured, something like 'true or false' or 'fill the gaps'.

3. If you are asked to 'identify' more than one point in any question, then make sure you number the different points that you are making. This will make it clear what your different points actually are – a simple but useful tip.

4. When asked to 'explain or describe' something, try not to waffle. Focus on saying what it is, giving an example and why/how it occurred.

5. A 1-mark question does not require you to write very much. In fact, in many cases one word will do!

6. When asked to use your 'wider sociological knowledge' try to include sociological theories, concepts, statistics and/or studies.

7. A question about 'accuracy' is one where you should be focusing on such issues as the date of the research; the source; the researcher's abilities; how the research was conducted, etc.

8. A question about the usefulness of a piece of evidence for **all** members of a research population should prompt you to focus more on the sample and on whether generalisations can be made and the representativeness of the sample.

9. In the final 12-mark question you need to write more. This is where you can really show off your knowledge of methods.

10. Always keep an eye on the time – from experience this is probably the best piece of advice. Good luck!

Structuring your answers

Here we are going to focus on the 12-mark question in Section A of the exam. To be successful there are a number of things you can do when it comes to structuring your answer:

*   Firstly, what is it that you will be researching? What are your aims and hypothesis?

*   Next, simply identify two primary methods and samples that you would use to investigate the title.

*   Follow this by identifying what secondary evidence you would use.

*   Now it is time to go into more detail. You need to describe how you would actually do the research, including sampling decisions.

*   Also remember to explain why you would do it in this way.

- Do not forget to consider any possible problems with your chosen methods and evidence.

- Why have you chosen this particular combination of methods and evidence to investigate the given claim?

- Always keep focused on the specific topic area you are researching and the specific aims you are investigating.

This is the question that will really stretch you, so make sure you get plenty of practice before the exam. Ask your teacher and classmates to read your answers for feedback.

Practice questions

Below you will find some examples of the kinds of questions you can expect to meet in the exam to test your knowledge of methods and evidence. Read them carefully and then give them a go. Use the marks for each question as a guideline for how much to write – the basic rule is a mark a minute. If you are feeling really confident, try them in exam conditions and see how good your time management is. This is just as important as your sociological understanding if you want to do well, so get some practice in now.

Source B : Behaviour in the classroom

'I carried out non-participant observation in Year 8 Maths lessons at a school in Leeds. I observed four lessons, sitting at the back and making notes. Each observation lasted 45 minutes.'

This is an extract from the findings:

'Boys were seen to be worse behaved than girls in the classroom. They were more likely to swear, mess about and shout out answers. Girls sat at the side of the classroom quietly and were quicker to settle to their work. They were less likely than the boys to ask the teacher for help. The boys were told off and sent out more than the girls.'

Adapted from a university student's research, 2008)

1. a) Identify the research method and size of the sample used in **Source B**.

   i) Method [1]

   ii) Size of sample [1]

b) Identify and explain **two** reasons why the evidence in **Source B** might **not** be useful as evidence of **all** behaviour in the classroom. [4]

2. 'Boys behave better at school than girls.'

   Identify and explain the methods and evidence you would use to investigate this hypothesis.

   - What would your first primary method and sample be?

   - What would your second primary method and sample be?

   - What secondary evidence would you use?

   - Explain your research design.

   (Explain and justify your methods and evidence; sampling choices; why you have chosen this research design; how the methods and evidence will work together; how your research design will allow you to meet the aims of the research.) [12]

Exam**Café**

Sample student answers

Take a look at the student answer by Vicky and the examiner's comments for the following question:

Describe one advantage and one disadvantage of using questionnaires as a research method.

Vicky

One advantage of a questionnaire is that it wouldn't cost much to do which is great because students don't have much money. But not everyone would fill it in.

Now have a look at Danny's answer to the same question. He has read the comments and has tried to put that into practice.

Danny

A good point of using a questionnaire is you can include closed questions. A closed question can be either a tick box or a two-way response. Whichever you choose you're going to be able to identify any trends in your data by turning your findings into statistics. This will mean you can compare answers from different social groups. A disadvantage, though, is that closed questions don't get much detail in their answers as people are not required to write freely in their own words. This may mean that the researcher doesn't really find out what the respondents really think if closed questions are used in the questionnaire.

Comments

'This candidate clearly knows something about the good and bad points of questionnaires but the answer is not clear or detailed enough to score full marks. Cost is a relevant point to make but the follow-on point about students is irrelevant and adds nothing to the answer. The second point is not labelled as a disadvantage and is far too brief. Vicky is making a good point that not everyone would fill in a questionnaire but she does not go on to explain why this is a problem or why it happens.'

Comments

This is a very good response that clearly identifies and describes both an advantage and a disadvantage of using questionnaires. The points are accurate and well explained. Danny has made both his points well without waffling and writing too much.

Unit 1
Part B: Culture, socialisation and identity

The key areas you will study in this unit are:

- **Culture:** How does society function? How do we all learn the rules?
- **Socialisation:** How are we made into the person that we are today? What is it that actually influences us to behave and think in particular ways?
- **Identity:** How are we socialised into our gender identity? How does social control help to maintain and reinforce these identities? What stereotypes exist about men and women? What is meant by femininity and masculinity?

PAUSE FOR THOUGHT

1 How do we learn the rules of our society?

2 Are we born or made human?

3 What does it mean to be male or female?

Culture

Concepts

To help to explain human behaviour and lifestyle, sociologists have developed a range of terms and ideas. All of us have been born into a culture, the whole way of life of a group of people. We live by the rules of our culture and mix with other people living in it; this is what makes us human. So let us have a look at some of the key ideas that will help you to better understand the culture you live in and the social groups within that culture. Social groups are those people we meet in our day-to-day lives – our families, peers, teachers in schools and colleagues in the workplace, for example.

Norms

Norms are the unwritten rules of behaviour that tell us what is appropriate and acceptable in particular situations. We are learning norms from the moment we are born to the moment we die; they are all around us. They can be explicitly taught to us or can be something that we see and try out. Norms create order in society as they ensure that we all know what is expected of us and that we know we are likely to be punished if we do not conform to them. So, in the supermarket when we want to pay for our goods we join a queue – this is the norm. Anyone who tries to push in will be criticised and probably prevented from doing so. Similarly, walking down the street naked or shouting out obscenities at a wedding would meet with very negative reactions as this behaviour is quite simply not what is expected; it is not the norm. We must remember, however, that norms are not the same for everyone. They will differ depending on the social group involved, the society the group belongs to and the era, for example. This is known as **relativity**, meaning norms are very specific to particular situations.

KEY CONCEPTS

Norms – the unwritten rules of society that determine acceptable behaviour.

Relativity – specific to a particular situation, social group or society, not general.

ACTIVITY 23

1. What would the norms of behaviour be for the following people?

   • patients sitting in a dentist's waiting room

   • teenagers at a party

   • a gang member

   • a children's television presenter.

2. Look at the extract at the top of the next page, written by Jemimah Wright (2007). Using this and your own ideas, explain how norms are relative.

Girl survived tribe's custom of live baby burial

Babies born into some Indian tribes in the Amazon are being buried alive.

The tradition is based on beliefs that babies with any sort of physical defect have no souls and that others, such as twins or triplets, are also 'cursed'.

Babies who are girls, who have some disability or who have unmarried mothers are all in danger of an early death in a shallow grave in the rainforest. Others are suffocated with leaves, poisoned or simply abandoned in the jungle.

According to Dr Marcos Pelegrini, a doctor working in the Yanomami Tribe Health Care District, 98 children were killed by their mothers in 2004 alone.

Born in 1995, Hakani – which means Smile – was still unable to walk or talk by the age of two, prompting tribal leaders to conclude she had no soul and to order her parents to kill her.

Her parents committed suicide – by eating a poison root – rather than obey the order. Hakani's 15-year-old brother was then told he had to kill her. He dug a hole to bury her next to the village hut, which is where the tribe usually buries animals, and hit her over the head with a machete to knock her out.

However, she woke up as she was being placed in the hole and the boy found he could not go through with the killing. Hakani's grandfather then shot her with an arrow. He was so upset he tried to commit suicide, too.

But Hakani survived, although her wound became infected and she was left to live like an animal in the forest for three years.

Adapted from J. Wright, *Daily Telegraph*, 22 June 2007

Values

Where norms refer to the specifics of social behaviour, **values** are more about general guidelines and ideas. They refer to what is seen as correct behaviour, beliefs about what is right and wrong and the idea that something is important and worthwhile. So, in Britain, common shared values might include the importance of privacy and the idea that it is wrong to hurt another person. You will learn values from the people around you, but often they are also enforced by the law – stab a person and you face a prison sentence, for example. The law here reinforces our shared value that we should not hurt fellow human beings.

As with norms, however, values are not the same for everyone. Again they are relative; they depend on the period in history, the society and the social group involved. So you could argue that the tribe featured in the passage above does not place the same value on human life that Western cultures do. Similarly, whereas we value material possessions such as getting the latest mobile phone, the best car and designer labels, the Cheyenne and Apache Indians value giving away possessions. When a family member dies they inherit nothing; instead they give it away to others to show that they feel nothing but sadness that the person has died. Examples of different values can also be found by looking at British society. In the West we value falling in love, whereas a lot of Muslim people believe in the tradition of arranged marriages.

KEY CONCEPTS

Values – general ideas about what is right and wrong, the correct ways of behaving and what is considered important and worthwhile.

ACTIVITY 24

1. Take a look at the values that Bill Rammell has suggested become part of the school curriculum (see extract below by Jayne Dowle from the *Yorkshire Post*, 18 May 2006). Discuss each one in turn and consider whether you think they are important values for young people to learn about.

   '... Bill Rammell, an Education Minister, has suggested that "core **British values**" become part of the school curriculum for 11- to 18-year-olds. Teaching "the **British values** of freedom, fairness, civic responsibility and democracy" would be incorporated into the existing compulsory curriculum.

2. Look at following list of additional values:
   - educational success
   - privacy
   - not hurting others
   - earning your place in society
   - respect for your elders/people in authority
   - helping others
   - buying more and more material possessions
   - being honest and telling the truth
   - respecting human life.

Which do you think are valued in Britain today? Can you think of any other values that we have in society? Give reasons for all your answers.

Identities

Here we need to consider what sociologists mean when they refer to an **identity**. You might be thinking that it is simply to do with who we are, and this is not too far from the truth. Identity is also about who we want to be like and the choices we make in order to fulfil this. So if we think about the Olympics, we will think about the identity of Team GB. To show that we identify with 'our' team we fly the Union Jack, paint our faces, cheer and wave our banners. We feel British, and to those looking on we can clearly be identified as such through our very public support of the team. This is a crucial part of identity – how we see ourselves but also how others see us. There are lots of factors that help to make up our identities, such as:

- lifestyle
- age
- social class
- gender
- ethnicity
- nationality
- job
- family position
- hobbies
- supporting a particular football team.

Identities today are in a constant state of movement. As society moves on with increasing technological developments and changing attitudes, so our identities start to alter. **Postmodernist** sociologists believe that today we have greater choice in our identities than ever before, as they become less and less fixed. Take women, for example. In the not too distant past a female's identity was defined as a housewife and mother. Some women still choose this identity today, but the point is that now they have a choice. Many women now create different identities through their choice of career or decision to remain childless. It is the same with ethnicity; few of the old rules apply. So today it is not unusual to see an Asian female dressed in jeans and a baseball cap, or a Geordie-speaking Sikh, wearing a turban and a sovereign ring.

Status

When we talk about a person's **status** we are referring to their position in society and the amount of prestige that this position gives them. So you as a student in a school or a college have a particular status. When you go home you move into different statuses – a son, a daughter, a sister or a brother, for

example. There are many sources of our status in society. Some of the most common are jobs, family, education, social class and gender.

There are two main types of statuses in society: ascribed and achieved. An **ascribed status** is that fixed at birth by our social characteristics and is something that we cannot change easily. **Achieved status** is down to a person's own achievements and efforts. This is typically done through gaining educational qualifications and a professional career. In a society based on this kind of status it will be relatively easy to change the position you have been born into and there will be lots of opportunities for movement between status groups.

ACTIVITY 25

Discuss with a partner whether the following people's status has been ascribed or achieved.

1. Prince Charles
2. David Beckham
3. Pete Burns
4. Amy Winehouse

Explain your thoughts in discussion with the rest of your class.

Roles

Along with every status that a person has there is an accepted set of norms. So in the status position of a teacher, certain norms of behaviour are expected. All the norms that are associated with a particular status position are called a **role**. A role is a part that we play which has expected and acceptable behaviour associated with it. Let's look at an example to try and make things easier.

Consider the role of a doctor. A person playing this role is expected to act in a particular way, to follow expected norms of behaviour. These are linked to the fact that this role is high status. So we expect a white coat, an air of authority, the ability to listen to patients and to speak knowledgeably and politely. We do not expect someone to swear or burp, or listen to an iPod when they are playing the role of a doctor! We do not just play one role in an average day; most of us have many roles that we regularly switch between, each one bringing with it its own set of norms. This playing of more than one part is known as having **multiple roles**. Sometimes, however, things do not go quite as smoothly as all of this might suggest, as the roles that a person plays may start to clash. So consider a boy's typical day in which he might play the roles of son, brother, boyfriend, student, part-time waiter, friend and footballer. These are his multiple roles. But what happens when he gets in from school and has homework to do, a girlfriend who wants to go to the cinema, a football match to play, a shift in the local restaurant, a mother who wants him to babysit for his little sister and a group of friends who want him to go down to the local youth club? He clearly cannot do everything and so has decisions to make because the roles that he plays have come into conflict with one another. When this happens it is simply called **role conflict**.

ACTIVITY 26

1. List all the roles that you play in a typical day. Have you ever experienced role conflict? What did you do?

2. Your teacher will provide you with a card with a role written on it. Your job is to try to get your classmates to say the word on your card. They can ask you up to ten questions – your response can only be either 'yes' or 'no'!

KEY CONCEPTS

Identity – how we see ourselves and how others see us.

Postmodernism – a sociological theory associated with changes in society from the 1990s onwards.

Status – the amount of prestige a person's position in society gives them.

Ascribed status – your position in society that is based on the social characteristics you were born with and is difficult to change.

Achieved status – your position in society that is earned by your own efforts and achievements.

Role – a part you play that is associated with particular norms and expectations.

Multiple roles – playing more than one role.

Role conflict – where the demands of one role clash with the demands of other roles played.

Culture – the whole way of life of a society.

Cultural diversity – differences between cultures.

Subculture – a smaller culture within a culture with its own set of norms and values.

ACTIVITY 27

RESEARCH TASK

In Unit 1 Part A you learned about covert participant observation as a sociological research method (pages 10–12). You are going to put this into practice in order to see for yourself how ingrained role expectations are in our day-to-day lives. In your next lesson today take five minutes to act the role of a teacher with your friend, instead of that of a student, and when you get home from school adopt the role of a parent instead of that of a son or a daughter. See what kind of reactions you get when you do not play the expected roles. Discuss all your findings with your teacher and classmates in your next Sociology lesson.

Culture

When talking about a **culture**, sociologists are referring to the whole way of life of society. This involves all those things that are shared by the members of a society that teach us how we should behave and act. This incorporates norms, values, language, education, food, knowledge and behaviour. All these common and shared experiences combine to give us our culture. However, culture is not a fixed thing; it varies according to the time and the place. Consider time, for instance. In modern Britain it is illegal to smoke in many different places, but not so long ago smoking was a norm – and not just for rebellious teenagers behind the bike sheds! It was legal in clubs, pubs, aeroplanes and even the teachers' staffroom. Adults smoked, movie stars smoked, everyone did it. Another example is attitudes to food in different places. In France people regularly eat duck heart and snails, in Japan eating raw fish is a norm and in Peru people eat roast guinea pigs. These are not foods we would tend to associate with British culture! In fact we may find them odd, a little bit repulsive and certainly not a cultural norm. Sociologists would refer to these variations as examples of **cultural diversity**. So we come to recognise both what is a part of our culture and what makes us different from other cultures.

Subculture

Cultures are not always as similar as the paragraph above might suggest. Within every culture there will be groups with different values, lifestyle or dress. These smaller groups are known as **subcultures**. They will share many similarities with the wider culture whilst also having differences.

Take a youth subculture such as punks, for example. They eat with a knife and fork, wear clothes when out in public and go to school where they study for exams. However, they dress very differently, have distinctive hairstyles and colours and are sometimes anti-authority and rebellious in their attitudes.

ACTIVITY 28

Have a look at some comments about punk subculture made by Dick Hebdige, a famous researcher in this field (Dick Hebdige, 1979).

'The most unremarkable and inappropriate items – a pin, a plastic clothes peg, a television component, a razor blade, a tampon – could be brought within the province of punk (un)fashion ... Objects borrowed from the most sordid of contexts found a place in punks' ensembles; lavatory chains were draped in graceful arcs across chests in plastic bin liners. Safety pins were taken out of their domestic "utility" context and worn as gruesome ornaments through the cheek, ear or lip...fragments of school uniform (white bri-nylon shirts, school ties) were symbolically defiled (the shirts covered in graffiti, or fake blood; the ties left undone) and juxtaposed against leather drains or shocking pink mohair tops.'

1. What examples can you find in the text to illustrate how the punks' appearance was different to that of mainstream culture?
2. Why do you think punks dress and look the way that they do?
3. Go to *www.heinemann.co.uk/hotlinks* and enter express code 7573P. Click on the *wikiHow website* to find out more about punks as a subculture.

GradeStudio

Your knowledge of these key concepts will be tested in Section B of the Sociology Basics examination. One way this may be done is through a structured question such as the one below. Have a go and see how you do.

ACTIVITY 29

Copy the key sociological concepts and definitions and match them with an arrow. (The first one is done for you.)

	Key concept		Definition
1	NORM	a)	Accepted and expected behaviour in a specific situation
2	SUBCULTURE	b)	When the part you are playing clashes with another part that you are expected to play
3	VALUES	c)	A small group of people with their own distinct norms and values
4	ASCRIBED STATUS	d)	The position we are born into, which is by and large fixed
5	ROLE CONFLICT	e)	Things that we consider to be important and correct

Socialisation

All of the things that you have read about so far in this chapter have to be learned, since nobody is born knowing about their culture's norms and values. This learning process is called **socialisation** and refers to all the different ways that a person learns how they should behave and act in society. There is nothing natural about what we do; sociologists believe that it is all learned behaviour. A useful way to illustrate this is to consider the examples of children who have not been socialised.

ACTIVITY 30

The extract below (taken from the *List Universe website*) details the case of a young girl who had not been socialised and so had not learned how she was expected to behave in her culture.

'Oxana Malaya (Оксана Малая) (born November 1983) was found as an eight-year-old feral child in Ukraine in 1991, having lived most of her life in the company of dogs. She picked up a number of dog-like habits and found it difficult to master language. Oxana's alcoholic parents were unable to care for her. They lived in an impoverished area where there were wild dogs roaming the streets. She lived in a dog kennel behind her house where she was cared for by dogs and learned their behaviours and mannerisms. She growled, barked and crouched like a wild dog, sniffed at her food before she ate it, and was found to have acquired extremely acute senses of hearing, smell and sight.'

Answer the following questions.

- What examples of non-human behaviour did Oxana display?
- Why did she not act like a 'normal' child?
- Is loving a child natural or learned behaviour?
- Oxana was found aged eight. Do you think she will have been able to learn how to be human?

KEY CONCEPTS

Socialisation – the process of learning the correct behaviour, norms and values in a society; this can be either primary or secondary.

Agents of socialisation – the places or groups of people responsible for teaching individuals correct norms, values and behaviour.

Process of socialisation

Primary socialisation

Sociologists typically think of socialisation as a two-stage process. The first stage is known as primary socialisation and refers to children learning the basics during early childhood from their families. Much primary socialisation is now also taking place outside the home in institutions such as nurseries, as increasingly both parents are working full time. Children are taught how to eat, what to eat and what not to eat, how to use the toilet, that they must wear clothes in public, not to use rude words, to be polite and so on. Remember, though, that what is learned as a norm will vary from culture to culture and over time. Much of what children learn is by imitation of their adult role models, copying what they see and hear. They also learn from the reactions of others, so when they get praised for a particular action they are likely to repeat it and so learn that it is acceptable and expected behaviour. When they do something wrong they will be told off and punished and so start to learn that this kind of behaviour is not desirable.

Secondary socialisation

This stage of the socialisation process begins around age five and continues into adulthood, lasting until the day we die. Here all the basics that we have learned during primary socialisation are further developed and reinforced to ensure that each individual learns the norms and values that collectively make up their culture. The main sources of this process of socialisation are the media, the peer group, the education system and the workplace. These are known as **agents of socialisation** and also include the family, which is a primary agent.

Agents of socialisation

Agents of socialisation are the places or social groups where we are taught about our culture and learn how we are expected to behave. There are rewards for acting appropriately and punishments if we fail to conform to the norms.

Family

Families are the key agent of primary socialisation, teaching young children the skills and behaviour necessary to live in society. Children are like sponges, ready to soak up everything that their families show and tell them. This makes the family a very influential agency of socialisation. Parents are often seen as role models, as children at this young age tend to accept without question the norms and values presented to them, so these soon become their own guidelines for life. A famous study that looked at the role of the family in terms of socialisation was conducted by Ann Oakley in 1981. She found that children were clearly being taught how to be girls and boys by their parents through a number of different means.

The first of these is called **manipulation** and refers to the ways that parents will encourage certain behaviour seen as normal for either a girl or a boy, and discourage any behaviour associated with the opposite sex. So, for example, girls might be encouraged to play with dolls and boys will not.

The second method of socialisation that she discovered is called **canalisation**. This is when parents push their children into either male or female roles. This is typically done through the toys which the children receive and the activities they engage in. A good example would be little girls playing with toy kitchens, preparing them for their future role cooking for a family. The way that parents talk to their children will also reinforce gender norms and expectations, with such phrases as 'little princess' and 'brave little soldier'. Oakley's study emphasises just how important the family can be in socialising children into their expected gender roles.

ACTIVITY 31

Working in small groups, think about your own experiences of primary socialisation. What were you taught in this process? How were you taught? Were you manipulated and/or canalised into behaving like a girl or a boy and, if so, in what ways?

Mass media

Media products are an increasingly important part of modern life and so are thought to have a lot of influence over us when it comes to learning our culture. You do not have to look very far to see just how important the media is when it comes to socialisation. Take rap music; it is no coincidence that the gold jewellery ('bling'), baseball caps, baggy jeans and visible underwear shown regularly on channels such as MTV have become an everyday part of today's urban youth culture. How males and females are represented is also thought to be an important part of the media's role in secondary socialisation.

ACTIVITY 32

Your teacher will provide you with a selection of media materials for analysis. These will be set up as a carousel, giving you time to visit each one, see what you can find out and collect your results. Your task is to find evidence of different ways that the media can socialise people in society.

Peers

Your peers are those people who share a similar social position to you in terms of age, lifestyle, status and/or job. These are people that you are with regularly – work colleagues, friends or classmates, for example – and so can play a big role in the socialisation process. Young people can be very influenced by their peer groups and often feel pressure to conform to their norms and values. It is through this shared behaviour that they feel accepted and part of the group. Peer group pressure can be both positive and negative. A peer group that values education is likely to encourage its members to work hard at school, whereas one that holds more anti-school values may pressurise young people into truancy, smoking or being cheeky to the teacher.

Education

It is in schools that most formal education takes place. These institutions have been set up with the intention of socialising the students who attend. They are taught about their history, their culture and its norms and values during many lessons. However, this is not the only learning that takes place in education. There is also a **hidden curriculum** in place that continually socialises students into the acceptable ways of behaving in our society. So we learn how to get on with other people, the importance of punctuality and the normality of doing what someone else tells us without question.

ACTIVITY 33

Work with a partner to make a list of all the ways that your school socialises you into the norms, values and expectations of society. Try to include examples from both the formal and the hidden curriculum in your answer.

Workplace

You may already have had experience of the workplace as an agent of socialisation, either through a part-time job or by listening to your parents talking about their work. In the future, this will undoubtedly be an important place in which society's norms and values will be reinforced for you. Adults spend such a large amount of time in their job that the importance of the workplace's influence in the socialisation process should not be underestimated. In the workplace, you will soon learn what is expected of you in terms of appearance, punctuality, behaviour and language. This learning could be through any formal rules that are in place or informally via chatting with work colleagues, for example.

Social control, rewards and sanctions

All the agents of socialisation that you have read about teach people what is expected of them in society. However, exposure to these influences does not necessarily mean that people will conform. Therefore, society has to develop ways of making people do what is considered the right thing. The process that ensures that this happens is known as **social control**. One way of doing this is by having a system of rewards and punishments ready for use. Sociologists refer to punishments as **negative sanctions** and these are intended to deter people from doing the wrong thing in society. So sending a criminal to prison would be an example of a negative sanction, as it is a punishment used to control a person's behaviour that also sends out a clear message to the rest of us that crime is unacceptable. Rewards are the opposite of this process and are called **positive sanctions**. This time the aim is to encourage certain acceptable and desired behaviours to continue. A teacher who gives out praise, stickers and sweets for good work is using positive sanctions to try and make sure that this good work carries on.

ACTIVITY 34

Working with a partner, think back over a recent school day. Make a note of all the negative and positive sanctions you received that day from any of the different agents of socialisation. What were these sanctions trying to get you to do? Were they successful?

Sanctions can be applied by an official group of people, such as a court or a person in authority. When this happens we call it **formal social control**. These agents typically have a lot of power and influence and are backed by written rules and laws. Key agents of formal social control are the police force, the courts, the prison service and the army. The main purpose of these agents is to control and regulate social behaviour.

Not all sanctions are applied formally, however. In fact it is probably true to say that most social control occurs informally. This is referred to as **informal social control**. Here there are unlikely to be written rules and instructions; instead the control is far more likely to happen as a normal part of everyday life. Imagine that your best friend has done something that you really do not approve of; you are going to let them know about it. Your body language is likely to be negative and closed, you might argue, you might ignore their calls and criticise them on MySpace. All of this informal social control is going to send out a very clear message to your friend that what they have done is not OK. This is likely to affect them and will probably result in an apology and no repetition of the unacceptable behaviour. In this way you have socially controlled your friend using informal methods.

KEY CONCEPTS

Manipulation – parents encourage children to behave in a way that is seen to be appropriate for their gender.

Canalisation – parents give children gender-specific goods that are considered the norm for their gender, dolls for girls and not for boys, for example.

Hidden curriculum – the norms and values that schools teach students through day-to-day school life, not part of the formal timetable.

Social control – the methods used during the socialisation process to make sure individuals conform to the expected and acceptable norms and values in society.

Negative sanctions – punishments used to prevent unacceptable behaviour.

Positive sanctions – rewards used to encourage acceptable behaviour.

Formal social control – written rules and laws enforced by powerful agents such as the police and courts.

Informal social control – controlling people's behaviour using informal methods in everyday situations.

Below is a typical examination question on this topic area. Imogen and Emma have both had a go at answering it. Read through their responses and, working with a partner, decide whose answer would work best in the exam and why. Remember – in terms of timings work on the 'mark a minute' rule for guidance.

QUESTION: Using your wider sociological knowledge, identify and describe **one** formal agent of social control. **[2]**

<u>Imogen:</u> 'One formal agent of social control is the police force. This is an official agent where rules are written down allowing them to control us. The police can control people through laws and force, for example they can arrest or handcuff a criminal.'

<u>Emma:</u> 'The media is a good example of an agency of social control. In the media we learn about society and culture and, according to Postmodernists, it is a very important source of our identity. There are several ways the media can control us. We might copy what we see or change our attitudes or believe something to be the norm all because of the media. A good example of this is the size zero models that are seen particularly in magazines. These representations make women anxious about their own bodies so that they begin to think being thin is normal. They are therefore being controlled by the media.'

Identity

This final section of the chapter returns to the concept of identity with an in-depth focus on gender. This is something that is relevant to all of us; we cannot escape the fact that we have a gender identity. It is, therefore, an important part of how we see ourselves and how others see us.

ACTIVITY 36

Discuss the following statements with the rest of your class and teacher. Try to give reasons to support your points of view.

a. Women with children should not be allowed to work.

b. It does not make any difference if you dress a baby boy in blue or pink – he will be treated and act exactly the same regardless.

c. Boys are born knowing how to be boys; girls are born knowing how to be girls.

Gender identities

Males and females will always be thought of in terms of their gender. Just think about a newborn baby; the first thing we all want to know is whether it is a girl or a boy! Along with the biological differences between males and females, there is also a whole host of assumptions made about a person just because of their gender. Go back to that image of a newborn baby again. Dress it in pink and we talk softly, covering it in kisses and presenting it with cute teddy bears. Our presumption is that this baby is a girl. But if we dress the baby in blue, suddenly very different assumptions can be seen. Now we presume that this little baby likes to be bounced around or flown in aeroplane swoops and to play with toy blocks and bricks. From an early age our assumptions about male and female identities are very different. These ideas have changed over time, though. For example, in the not too distant past women were seen primarily as homemakers and mothers whose role was to look after and nurture their children and husbands. This role is still very much in evidence today but is increasingly being accompanied by the newer identity of high-flying career women.

Gender identities are also different in different cultures and societies. A famous study by Margaret Mead (1935) investigated three different tribes in New Guinea, looking at their gender roles. The first tribe she studied was the Mundugumar where males and females both demonstrated typically masculine characteristics (typical to our culture, that is), such as being aggressive and not enjoying spending time with or rearing children. The next tribe she visited were the Arapesh who all displayed characteristics associated with femininity. For example, they were very gentle and caring and both males and females got fully involved in the process of child rearing. Finally, she looked at the Tchambuli where there were clear differences in gender roles. However, what was interesting was that it was the men who did the shopping, wore make-up and preened themselves. Women, on the other hand, took responsibility for the trading, were aggressive and competitive and made all of the sexual advances to the menfolk.

This is the opposite of traditional gender roles in the UK. All of this goes to show that there are different gender identities for males and females and that these are relative to time and place.

ACTIVITY 37

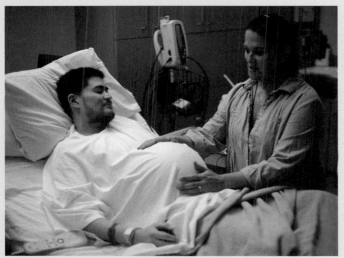

Thomas Beatie, the world's first pregnant man.

A male tranvestite.

Look closely at the photographs above. For each image, discuss what gender identity can be seen.

How gender identity is constructed via the socialisation process

All of the agents of socialisation have important roles to play in terms of teaching males and females their gender identities.

ACTIVITY 38

What is a female? What does it mean to be female? Have a look at the following definitions and then come up with your own definition.

Female: a member of the human race with breasts and a womb, able to conceive, carry and give birth to babies. The opposite to a male.

Female: drinks alcohol to excess at the weekend, may flash her breasts at passers by, wears revealing clothes and sometimes engages in sexual activity with men she meets in nightclubs.

Female: attends university after doing well in her GCSEs and A Levels, wants to be a lawyer, currently in a relationship with another woman.

Female: likes to gossip, is good at ironing, enjoys cooking and cleaning.

Family

We have already looked at how families can manipulate and canalise children into their gender roles earlier in the chapter. Alongside this, there are many everyday things that parents do in order to teach their children the expected norms of behaviour for their gender. This typically starts with the assumption that boys and girls are very different beings and thus need to be treated differently. As Oakley commented, this can show itself in the toys the children are given to play with. Boys are kept active with their sports equipment, cars and pretend guns, whilst girls are already being placed in the domestic sphere with their tea sets, colouring books and prams. The purpose of a toy is obviously for it to be played with and when you watch children playing, it is immediately obvious that much of what they do is to imitate adult gender roles. So we see little girls performing pretend domestic tasks, cooking meals and dressing up and little boys becoming the latest superhero or wrestling one another to the ground.

When they get older, boys and girls are often allocated quite different household chores; again many researchers believe that these are divided along gender lines. So girls may be asked to help out with housework, whilst boys may have responsibilities for gardening or washing the car.

Similarly, parental social control of girls and boys can be quite different. Girls are more likely to be given earlier curfews, more likely to be dropped off and picked up from outings and less likely to be allowed to play outside than boys. All of this leaves boys and girls in no doubt that expectations of their behaviour are different depending on their gender. Imitation is probably the main way that children learn what is expected of them. So if they see their dad occupying the breadwinner role and their mum bearing the main responsibility for housework, it is hardly surprising if they grow up believing that this is normal.

ACTIVITY 39

1. Get hold of a copy of a children's toy catalogue. Have a look at the toys that girls and boys are shown playing with and how this might link to their future gender roles. Present your findings on A3 paper, including both visual images and written analysis.

2. Try to complete some observation of young children in their home environments – brothers and sisters, family members or neighbours' children would be perfect. Make sure you ask permission from the children's parents before doing this. See if you can find any evidence that families are socialising boys and girls into different gender roles through such things as toys, clothes, language and behaviour.

Mass media

In the postmodern world the media is everywhere and is likely to play a big part in our gender role socialisation. Although there are undoubtedly more women involved in the modern media than there have ever been before, there are still big issues when it comes to equality. Research indicates that males are more likely to occupy the stronger, independent and more dominant roles, whilst females are shown as emotional, pretty and caring. This kind of unequal representation is particularly prevalent in television adverts, although it can also be found in other areas of the media. However, things are starting to improve, and you will not struggle to find examples of powerful, strong, lead females and more emotional, family-driven males now, alongside the more traditional representations.

Education

Children spend a great many years in the education system, so it is hardly surprising that sociologists feel that this is a very important agent in gender role socialisation. Gender roles can be transmitted and learned through the unofficial hidden curriculum inside schools. Evidence suggests that some teachers still have different attitudes to male and female students. At the back of their minds there may still be the assumption that males are destined to be breadwinners, whilst girls are destined for domesticity. This may lead to different careers advice and work experience placements. Boys are still more likely to be found in practical, computing and financial work and girls in office jobs, caring for others and health and beauty.

Behaviour in the classroom may also be treated differently depending on whether the student involved is male or female. Boys are almost expected to be a little disruptive in class, to need nagging to do their work and to engage in a bit of playground fighting. This may mean that teachers are more tolerant of such behaviour in boys than they are in girls, so if girls do this they will be punished more harshly than a boy would.

Since equal opportunities legislation has been introduced, sexism in school books has declined rapidly. However, representations of girls and boys in these books still often fall into distinct gender roles. You are more likely to see boys playing outside and dads off to work, leaving behind the housewife mums whose daughters help out with the washing up, for example.

Finally, there are still big differences in the subjects males and females choose to study. Whilst it is up to the individual student what subjects they choose, most are still influenced by their parents, teachers and peers. Girls are more likely to be found studying the social sciences, languages, health and social care, textiles and home economics. Boys, on the other hand, are more likely to choose PE, sciences, ICT, resistant materials and electronics. It is clear that schools are a major force when it comes to gender role socialisation. It is worth remembering, however, that this may not be the case in single-sex schools, where pressure to choose gender-specific subjects may be lessened.

ACTIVITY 40

Try to get hold of statistics for the option choices made by boys and girls in your school. Count up the number of students of each gender studying each subject and then turn these into percentages so you can compare males and females across different subject areas. After discussion with the rest of your class, present your findings as a report for your teacher. Try to comment on why you think boys and girls are still making different option choices (if they are in your school) and how this may affect them later on in life.

Peers

You will know better than anyone how important peer groups are in your day-to-day life. To fit in it is crucial that you accept and conform to group norms, and many of these are to do with gender. In male peer groups it is normal to take part in activities such as football, computers, games consoles, bikes and music. If you are a girl, though, interests are very different. This time it is expected that make-up, fashion, shopping and dance will be top priorities. Peer pressure can be very strong and it can be hard to be a shopping-loving boy in a male peer group or a female rugby fanatic in a female peer group. By not conforming to peer-group gender norms, children run the risk of being laughed at, bullied or excluded from the group.

As children get older, peer group pressure can get even stronger, particularly when relationships and members of the opposite sex become an issue. Research by Sue Lees (1993) found evidence of double standards in operation when it came to sex. Boys were proud of and praised for their sexual conquests, whereas girls were judged negatively as 'slags' and 'slappers' if they had sex outside a long-term relationship. Interestingly, these insults aimed at females were just as likely to be given by other girls as they were by boys.

ACTIVITY 41

Think of your own experiences as a male or female member of a peer group. Do you think that Sue Lees' findings are still true or are things changing? Why do you think that girls get involved in negatively labelling other girls for their sexual behaviour? Should there be double standards based on gender when it comes to sexual behaviour?

Workplace

The workplace typically takes over our gender role socialisation when education has finished. Obviously the exact ways that this socialisation takes place will depend on the type of work being done. However, there are still some clear trends and patterns. Typically, men still occupy those positions that attract better pay and a higher status. They are also found in quite different jobs to women, which often reflect gender stereotypes and assumptions; female nurses and male mechanics, for example. Males frequently have power over women in the workplace, which feminists claim is evidence of the **patriarchal** society we live in. Workplace inequalities are, therefore, likely to reinforce and maintain the gender expectations that have been built up by other agents of socialisation.

ACTIVITY 42

1. Working with a partner, conduct a survey on at least 20 adults – equal numbers of males and females – to find out what job they do. Analyse your findings to see if there are any trends relating to gender.

2. Now make a list of the jobs that you think males and females are most likely to be found in. Use your research findings to help you. Once you have done this, try to list the qualities that you think are required and valued in these jobs. What conclusions can you draw from your findings?

The role of social control in maintaining and reinforcing gender identities

With every agent of socialisation teaching us acceptable patterns of behaviour, there will be social control in place to try to ensure that we conform to expected norms and values. In terms of gender, these operate via a series of negative or positive sanctions which strive to make sure that we stick to what is expected from a male or a female. If we deviate from these expected paths, then we are likely to be stopped – by ridicule, anger, rules or, in the most extreme cases, force. The film and stage show *Billy Elliott* tells the story of a young working-class boy who loves to ballet dance. So worried is he about the reaction of his family and peers that he keeps his talent and passion a secret. In terms of gender identity this clearly shows that doing something considered feminine – in this case dancing – is quite simply not acceptable for males. It takes a strong character to resist the negative sanctions likely to be applied here, so most of us do not ever try; we just go along with what is seen to be acceptable for our gender.

Another example combines issues of **sexuality** and gender identity. A woman with a shaven head, no make-up and wearing baggy, masculine clothes walks down her street. She is not conforming to the gender norms of her society that demand her

KEY CONCEPTS

Patriarchy – a society dominated by males, where they have more power than women.

Sexuality – our sexual behaviour and choice of sexual partners.

to dress and act in a feminine manner. So what happens? The likelihood is that even in these supposedly tolerant and liberal times, she will get looked at, comments will be made behind her back and, in the worst case scenario, she will suffer verbal or physical abuse. In the workplace she may have to hide this look and dress in a way that is thought to be acceptable for women at work; a more feminine appearance will be required. She is clearly being controlled by the agents of socialisation around her.

Stereotypical assumptions about the nature of men and women

Most of the assumptions which society makes about males and females are based on simple **stereotypes**. So parents are referring to stereotypes of what it means to be a boy or a girl when they socialise their children into their gender roles. It is a similar story for peer groups, education and the workplace, and the media is riddled with gender stereotypes; they are at the core of most media output. Of course, no stereotypes are fixed; they can shift and alter as society changes and moves forward. Male interest in grooming and beauty products is a good example here, as seen in the increasing numbers of adverts for male moisturisers, hair products and fashion accessories today. This was not the norm ten years ago. However, changing stereotypes tends to be a gradual process, and stereotypes are often around for a very long time. Just look at the female-housewife stereotype. We can refer to this as old fashioned and traditional if we like, but the reality is that it is still in evidence in all agents of socialisation, from the perfect wife in a television advert, to the gentle push to do work experience in a nursery by schools, to the buying of a toy vacuum cleaner as a Christmas present. Gender stereotypes are at the heart of gender socialisation and are thus a very important part of the learning process.

Femininities and masculinities

What is seen as feminine or masculine in one society or period of time will not necessarily be seen as feminine or masculine in another. Think back to the Tchambuli tribe you read about on pages 38–39; being feminine there was about being aggressive and strong. These are not qualities that you would think of as 'feminine' in contemporary British society. More likely are ideas such as pretty, caring and passive. The other important point to remember is that definitions of **femininity** and **masculinity** are not fixed; they move with the times and there does not have to be just one definition. To be masculine means that you act in a way that your society considers to be typical of a male, and the same for being feminine. In postmodern society there are so many choices to be made that there is no longer just one accepted version of either femininity or masculinity. So, yes, being a housewife is an example of feminine behaviour, but then so is having a career or dressing

---

ACTIVITY 43

1. Consider the following scenarios, and discuss what methods of social control are likely to be used in order to ensure that gender-appropriate behaviour, norms and values are maintained. Try to include a wide range of agents of socialisation in your answers.

   a. A new boy joins your school; he wears make-up and nail varnish.

   b. A 40-year-old woman becomes managing director of a major finance company. She is unmarried and has no children.

   c. A married man gives up his job to look after his newborn child. His wife returns to work full-time.

   d. A young girl hates playing with dolls and pretend kitchens and instead prefers climbing and playing outside with her brother and his friends.

   e. A Year 10 boy wants to take Textiles and Health and Social Care as two of his GCSE option choices.

   f. A man is employed as a solicitor in a big firm but comes to work wearing women's clothing, as he is a transvestite.

2. Divide your class up into teams. Each team will be given an agent of socialisation from the following:

   a. family

   b. mass media

   c. workplace

   d. peer group

   e. education.

   Your job will be to prepare a three-minute argument to try to convince the rest of your class that the agent you have been assigned is the most influential in terms of controlling a person's gender identity. Think carefully about the language, examples and evidence that you use. After each team has presented their argument you will be able to ask questions to try to convince others that you are right.

in a sexy way. It is a similar situation when you consider masculinity. Being strong and muscly is clearly masculine behaviour. But then so is being a loving family man or an image-obsessed 'pretty boy'. These multiple versions of masculinity and femininity typically co-exist in modern societies, although it is probably true to say that some remain more dominant and acceptable than others.

ACTIVITY 44

Examine the following descriptions carefully. What examples of masculinity and femininity can you find?

- a mother nurturing a small child, pretty and with make-up, wearing a skirt and blouse
- a group of homosexual men in a bar or club
- a female bodybuilder
- a middle-aged man waving a Union Jack, tattooed, with a child on his shoulders, with a shaven head, crying at a football match
- a group of twenty-something women, walking down the high street and entering a bar or a café, smiling and laughing, carrying briefcases and laptops
- a young male Goth.

Can males be feminine and females be masculine? Discuss.

KEY CONCEPTS

Stereotype – a generalised and simplistic view of a group of people which ignores individual differences. They are often negative – women are bad drivers and blondes are bimbos are two examples of gender stereotypes that you may have come across.

Femininity – the quality of acting in a way that a society deems is typically female behaviour.

Masculinity – the quality of acting in a way that society deems is typically male behaviour.

KNOW YOUR STUFF?

Check your understanding by completing these questions:

1. What is the difference between ascribed and achieved status?
2. Name and describe three agents of socialisation.
3. Define the following concepts: **hidden curriculum; peer pressure; canalisation; role models**.
4. Identify and describe three subcultures in the contemporary UK.
5. Show how a person's norms and values are relative to their gender, religion and age.
6. Identify and explain three ways in which our gender identities are socially controlled.
7. What methods of social control can be used to make people conform in the education system?

Revision

With your examinations so close, it is time now to revisit some of the key topics and areas that you learned about in Part B of Sociology Basics. It is important that you feel fully prepared both in terms of the content you will be asked about, and the way that you will be assessed in the exam room. This is the aim of the Exam Café so get comfy, get ready and get revising.

Revision checklist

We start by checking exactly what areas of sociology you could be questioned about in the examination. See what you remember and then make sure that you fill any gaps in your knowledge by looking back through the textbook and your class notes. Once you have done this, test yourself again. Keep repeating this process until you are happy that you know all the key content.

Copy and complete the revision charts below.

Culture

Key concept	Tick off if you know it	What does it mean?	Give an example of it	Page references
norms				
values				
identities				
status				
ascribed status				
achieved status				
roles				
multiple roles				
role conflict				
culture				
subculture				

Socialisation

Key concept	Tick off if you know it	What does it mean?	Give an example of it	Page references
primary socialisation				
secondary socialisation				
formal social control				
informal social control				
rewards and sanctions				
family				
media				
peers				
education				
workplace				

Identity

Key concept	Tick off if you know it	What does it mean?	Give an example of it	Page references
gender identities – construction, maintenance and reinforcement				
stereotypical assumptions about men				
stereotypical assumptions about women				
femininity				
masculinity				

Revision tips

As you know, successful preparation is the key to your revision. Being organised and knowing what to expect cannot be underestimated. But the same techniques do not always work for all of us. So what kind of revision should you be doing? Well, that all depends on the kind of learner that you are. Read on and see if you can spot yourself in the following descriptions. Once you have recognised what kind of learner you are you will then be able to see which revision techniques are likely to work best for you.

Matt does not enjoy discussions and debates in class and he does not like to listen for too long either. He remembers concepts and studies by what they look like on the page. His learning is most successful when there are images and diagrams involved and he loves tasks that require him to use his imagination.

Raj likes to listen to the teacher telling him new things; he finds it easy to remember what he hears. He also likes to say what he thinks and talk ideas through with a partner. He really enjoyed a lesson where he made a podcast and he could also listen to all the others his classmates had done on different topics.

Li-Ying's favourite school subject is drama. She loves it when her sociology teacher includes role-play activities in lessons and is always first to put her hand up to volunteer for a part. She enjoyed learning about research methods in sociology because she got to actually try out the different ways of investigating. This really helped her to understand the topic. She enjoys doing research on the computer and doing mix and match style activities too. The more involved she is, the better she learns.

So how should Matt revise?

Matt is what is known as a **visual learner.** He needs to make sure that he does not try to revise from pages of notes or by reading textbooks. His learning style means that he will be most successful if he can produce spider diagrams, mind maps and flow charts of all the key content. His brain will only process the information if he can see it. Another idea he could try is to create silly stories to help link different ideas and words in his mind. All these techniques will help him to visualise the material and so should make his revision more effective.

So how should Raj revise?

Raj is an **auditory learner**. He learns best by listening and talking, so he needs to ensure that these two factors are included in his revision program. The best advice is for him to find a group to revise with so they can talk topics and concepts through and test each other. He could also record his notes as podcasts and listen to them via his computer or MP4 player. This way he will be hearing them rather than reading them and this will really suit his style of learning.

So how should Li-Ying revise?

Li-Ying's preferred learning style is known as **kinaesthetic** or **tactile** and means that she needs to make her revision as active as possible if she is to be successful. Quizzes and interactive computer programs will work well, as will word association games and activities done with her peers. She learns best when she figures things out for herself, so simply reading information is not recommended.

ExamCafé

Exam preparation

Sample student answers

Let's have a look now at some 'do's' and 'don'ts' when it comes to answering exam questions. GCSE students Jack and Rosie-Ann are going to have a go at answering an exam question

> Identify and explain two stereotypes of males found in the mass media. [4]

and then we'll see what can be said about their answers.

Jack

A stereotype of the male is the wage earner such as a businessman. You see this a lot in the media. And you also see the big, strong guys with all their muscles like in action films but in magazines too.

Comments
Jack has identified two different stereotypes of males here and has linked them both to the media. However, there is no explanation of either stereotype – he neither explains why these stereotypes exist nor what they and their implications actually are.

Rosie-Ann

The first stereotype of a male that I shall identify is the unemotional one. It is a norm in society for men not to show their emotions and the media typically reflects this role. So in films men may kill without shedding a tear and in television soaps will be unlikely to discuss problems and show their emotions. This is our cultural expectation for a man. The second stereotype is that the man is dominant and has the most power. This is shown in the media in many ways. For example, through all the male action heroes in the movies with their strength and love of violence and through the male breadwinners shown in many television dramas that make all the financial decisions. Feminists criticise this patriarchy but in the media these stereotypes are still the norm, perhaps because the media is still so male dominated when it comes to ownership.

Comments
Look at how long and detailed Rosie-Ann's answer is compared to Jack's. This is not necessarily a good thing, as when writing under exam conditions Rosie-Ann may not have time to write all this. However, it is clear that she fully understands the issues that the question is raising. Whilst she does not need to write as much as this, she has done very well. Firstly, there are two different and accurate male stereotypes identified. Secondly, she has provided examples of both of these. She clearly explains all the points she makes and integrates sociological concepts and theory into her response. This is excellent.

Practice questions

Now that you are fully prepared for the exam it is time to put your knowledge and skills to the test. There are three practice questions included for you here to have a go at. See how you do!

> Using your wider sociological knowledge, identify and describe **one** subculture. [2]
>
> Identify and explain **two** ways the mass media might socialise a person into their gender identity. [4]
>
> 'The peer group is the most effective agent of socialisation.'
> Evaluate the arguments **for** and **against** this claim. [12]

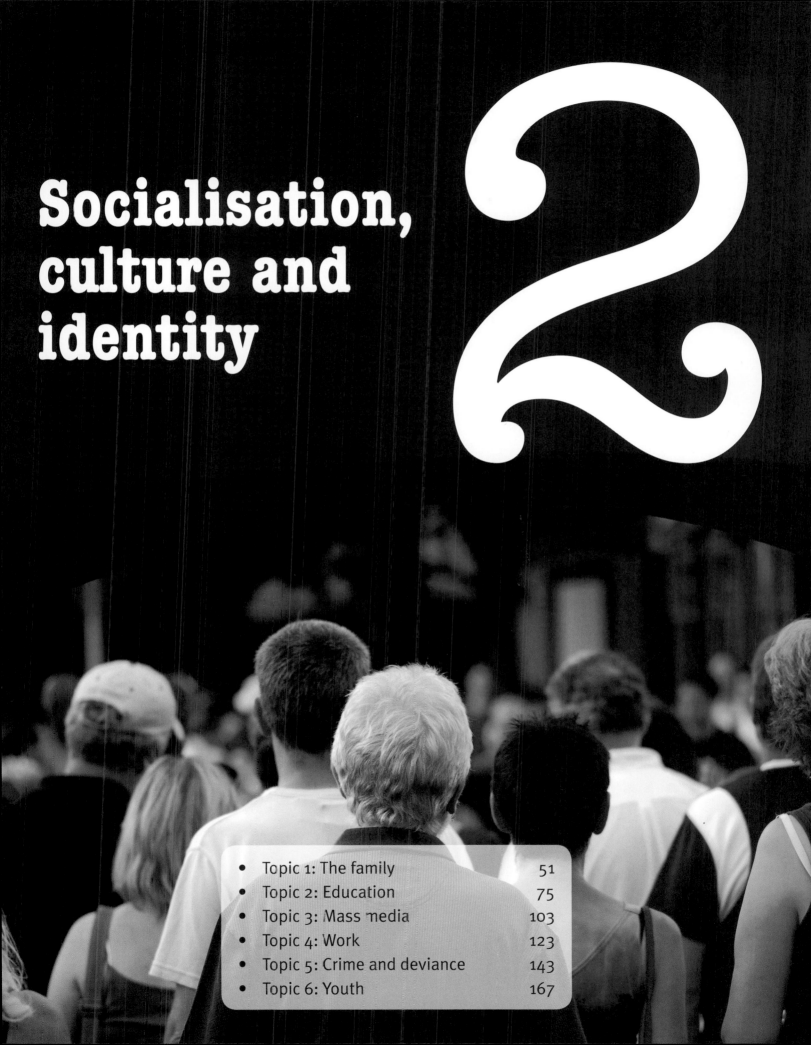

Socialisation, culture and identity

Unit 2
Topic 1: The family

The key areas you will study in this topic are:

- The link between family and identity
- The importance of the family to its members and to society
- Traditional definitions of the family
- Structural changes in the family
- Changing family relationships

PAUSE FOR THOUGHT

1 What would life be like without families?

2 Were families 'better' or 'worse' in our grandparents' days?

3 Is there a typical 'British family' today?

4 Can we choose the type of family we'd like today or does society limit our choices?

5 Is family life the most important part of life?

6 Are there winners and losers in family life?

Topic 1: The family

The family and identity

Spend five minutes on this: draw yourself in the middle of a piece of paper and then add the people you consider to be your family. Why have you included each person? Compare your answer with your partner:

- Are your families the same? Why/why not?
- Why did you include certain people? Why did you leave others out?
- Does the word 'family' have more than one meaning to you? For example, do you have a 'close family' as well as an 'extended family'?

The development of individual identity and the learning of social roles

Our **identity** is shaped by our experiences in society and the people with whom we come into contact. The way others see us influences how we see ourselves.

This can be seen most dramatically in the case of Kamala, whom we study on page 54. Kamala is thought to have spent her early life with a she-wolf. Kamala could, therefore, only really see herself through the eyes of this wolf. Not surprisingly, she acted like a wolf and, we assume, thought she was a wolf.

Most of us are involved in, and are influenced by, many different groups in society. These groups (family, school, religion, peers, the mass media and workplace) are agents of socialisation (teaching us society's culture) and agents of social control (controlling our behaviour).

In each group to which we belong, we learn to play different **social roles**. Some are roles we can choose (such as being a parent), whilst others (such as daughter or son) are simply given to us. It is these achieved roles and ascribed roles which become an important part of our identity.

In this chapter we will focus particularly on the influence of **families** on our lives and our identity. However, it is important to remember that family is only one influence on us. Take ethnic identity: many of us are from ethnically mixed backgrounds. In 2008, society celebrated the successes of Barack Obama in the American presidential election and Lewis Hamilton in the Formula One Championship. Although both have or had white mothers and are from ethnically mixed backgrounds, the mass media frequently referred to both as 'black'. How important might the media, as opposed to the family, be in shaping ideas about issues such as our ethnic identity?

The role of the family in socialisation and identity

The families we belong to can have a big effect on our identity.

1. Why are so many people keen to research their ancestors today?
2. Should everyone have the right to know about their early family life? (HINT: consider adoption, lone-parent families, surrogate mothers, sperm donors.)
3. Is the way children see themselves affected by: being an only child; being the eldest child; being a celebrity's child?
4. Are people judged by the family they belong to?
5. Research task: Some children have the role of 'family carer' from an early age; this usually happens if there is only one parent, who is ill or disabled.

   How might being a 'family carer' affect a child's identity?

   Go to *www.heinemann.co.uk/hotlinks* and enter express code 7573P. Click on the *Joseph Rowntree Foundation website* and read the article on young carers.

How important are family roles for our adult identity?

For many people their family roles are an important part of their adult identity. Are the Beckhams usually photographed alone, as a couple or as a family?

It might be harder today for young people to choose an adult identity within the family.

- Family roles are changing, so the role models provided by our parents, or grandparents, generations might seem out of date.

- We might have more choice of family identities today. When Sue Sharpe questioned Year 10 working-class girls in the 1970s, their main aim was to fall in love, get married and have children. Is this still the case today?

ACTIVITY 47

- 'I intend to stay single.'/'I intend to have a partner.'
- 'I might cohabit, but I wouldn't marry.'/'I might marry but I wouldn't cohabit.'
- 'I couldn't stay with the same partner all my life.'/'I'd want a partner for life.'
- 'I don't want children.'/'I want children.'
- 'I wouldn't have children before 35.'/'I'd have my children while I'm young.'
- 'I'd want a partner of the same sex.'/'I'd want a partner of the opposite sex.'
- 'I'd like to stay at home: my partner can earn the money.'/'I want to have a career.'

1. Discuss each pair of statements: are the two choices equally acceptable in Britain today? Why/why not? Does your gender, ethnic group and/or social class influence your answers?
2. Would your parents or grandparents agree with your answers?

Socialisation

The family is a child's first social group, so this is where the earliest learning, or primary **socialisation**, takes place. It is also the 'gatekeeper', introducing children to other agents of socialisation: the mass media (how much television?), the peer group (which friends?), formal education (which nursery?) and religious organisations.

Families introduce children to language, which is vital for future learning and shaping how they see the world. If parents use language to explain things ('Don't touch the cooker, it's still hot from making lunch, you'll burn yourself.'), the child sees the world in an ordered way, where cause ('hot cooker') leads to effect ('sore finger').

Families give children essential skills and knowledge (e.g. how to hold a spoon, the names of things). They also teach social **norms** (e.g. saying 'thank you', taking turns) and society's **values** (e.g. the value of human life or of property). Families also pass on their beliefs (e.g. by introducing the child to religion).

The family influences the child's personality. Whether a child is kind, aggressive, cheerful, hardworking, secretive or honest is affected by the way it is treated in its early years.

Socialisation continues throughout life: teenagers still learn from their families, and adults rely on their children and grandchildren to keep them up to date.

Families use different methods of socialisation (see the activity below).

KEY CONCEPTS

Identity – how we see ourselves and how others see us.

Social roles – parts we play in society; each role has its own social norms which tell us how we should act in that role.

Family – consists of people we are related to by ties of blood, marriage, adoption, civil partnership or cohabitation. There are many different types of family.

Socialisation – the process of learning to become a member of society.

Norms – the rules within a culture (e.g. no killing).

Values – ideas about what is worthwhile and important in a culture (e.g. human life).

ACTIVITY 48

Copy out and match the main methods of socialisation with the definitions in the table:

METHOD OF SOCIALISATION	DEFINITION
1 Deliberate instruction	A The child copies what it sees other family members doing (e.g. they are gentle with the baby, so the child is also gentle).
2 Role models	B The child is punished for breaking the family's rules (e.g. told off for being rude), so is less likely to repeat the behaviour in future.
3 Positive sanctions	C The family tells the child what, how and why to do something (e.g. 'I want you to put all your toys in the box').
4 Negative sanctions	D The child is given a reward for behaving correctly (e.g. praised for tidying up the toys), so is likely to repeat the behaviour in future.
5 Play	E The child is given toys or games which develop skills (e.g. holding, throwing) or social norms (e.g. taking turns).

How well do families socialise children?

ACTIVITY 49

Research and debate this issue:

'Are families failing in the socialisation of children?'

HINTS: What problems have been identified, e.g. child obesity, gang membership?

Are these 'real problems' or a media 'moral panic'?

Is the family doing anything wrong?

Does the problem lie somewhere else, e.g. the media, advertising?

GradeStudio

You will have your own ideas about family life, but do not just give your own personal experiences and opinions in the exam. You should be using concepts, examples and evidence from research. Which of these is a better paragraph about socialisation in the family, and why?

'In my family I learned a lot and I'm glad my parents were strict with me.'

'The family is important for primary socialisation. Parents often use rewards (positive sanctions) and punishments (negative sanctions) to teach children the rules such as how to behave at mealtimes.'

During socialisation we learn about society's **culture**. But do children really need socialisation?

It would be unethical (morally unacceptable) to set up an experiment to deprive a child of socialisation.

We can, though, study cases of 'feral' or unsocialised children. These children have either been brought up by animals or locked away from other people. Therefore, they have not been socialised by a 'normal' family or by other members of society.

Examples of non-socialised children

Kamala and Amala

In 1920 two girls were discovered by Reverend Singh, who ran an orphanage in northern India. The girls were 'rescued' from a wolf's den and the she-wolf, who had presumably adopted them, was killed. Kamala was about eight years old; Amala was younger. They looked wild, with matted hair

and dirty bodies. They behaved very differently from normal children. They crawled on all fours, snarled, bared their teeth, were most alert at night and howled at the moon. When they slept they lay curled on top of each other. They tore off clothes that were put on them, and refused food until they saw the raw meat and bones put out for the dogs. Their hearing, eyesight and sense of smell seemed well developed: they could smell raw meat from a great distance.

Reverend Singh kept detailed diaries of his attempts to socialise Kamala and Amala (see www.feralchildren.com). Sadly, Amala died one year later, but Kamala lived at the orphanage for nine years until she, too, became ill and died. In her time with the Reverend Singh's family, Kamala learned a number of skills and social norms: she learned to walk, to become friendly and trust people, eat cooked meat, wear clothes and sleep at night. Kamala also learned to speak, but it took her nine years to learn about 40 words; an average five-year-old has a vocabulary of 2000 words.

ACTIVITY 50

1. In what ways did Kamala and Amala learn from the she-wolf?

2. If normal socialisation starts late (as in Kamala's case), how successful does it seem to be?

Isabelle

Isabelle spent the first six years of her life in a dark room with her mother, who was deaf and unable to speak. Isabelle was frightened and aggressive, especially towards men, when she was found. She could not talk or walk properly, but she was given expert help. Isabelle made a remarkably quick recovery and, by the age of eight and a half, had caught up with other children: she could talk, read, count, respond to other people and continue normally with her schooling.

KEY CONCEPTS

Culture – the way of life of a group of people; it is learned and shared. The main parts of culture include knowledge, skills, social norms, values and beliefs.

Functionalist sociologists – sociologists who believe that each part of society has roles to fulfill in order that society can survive as a whole.

1. What important activities and experiences would Isabelle have missed during her isolation?
2. Many feral children make little recovery. Why did Isabelle recover so quickly?
3. Look at www.feralchildren.com. Research another child who lived with animals and another isolated child (e.g. Anna or Genie). Note the child's name, early experience, age and condition when found and recovery.

Conclusions about non-socialised children

- Children need good physical care.
- Children have the ability to learn: Kamala and Amala learned from the she-wolf.
- Socialisation is essential in order to become full members of society. The genes we inherit from our parents only give us the *potential* to become members of society.
- *Some* children recover if their early socialisation is disrupted: Isabelle did.
- If language learning starts too late, a 'critical time' might have passed and language might never develop fully.

Contemporary functions of the family

Functionalist sociologists argue that each part of society has functions (or jobs) to perform. What are the family's functions?

The regulation of sex

The family has traditionally controlled sexual behaviour. Families give people the opportunity to have a sexual relationship with a partner. They also limit sexual behaviour: for example, laws against incest forbid sex between close relatives, and in the UK couples are not allowed to marry before the age of 16.

Social norms about sexual behaviour are changing. Sex before marriage, cohabitation and same-sex relationships are now more socially accepted, but concern about sexual abuse of children has grown.

Reproduction

Most children are born within families, and most women have children. However, women are having fewer children and having them later in life. Women now have an average of 1.8 children; the average age for women to have their first child is 27 (30 if they are married). More women are remaining childless. Two reasons for these changes are:

- the high cost of having children and the effect on the parents' lifestyle
- the changing role of women; women now have more control over their lives (including their fertility) and more choices (including better career and leisure opportunities).

Since 2001 the number of births has increased each year; one reason for this could be births to mothers who were born in countries where larger families are common.

Physical care

Human babies and young children are very dependent on others for care. It is not only young children who need physical care: older children need care when they are unwell. Illness or disability can also affect adults. Britain's ageing population means that more elderly people need physical care. Families give much of this care: one million women and 0.75 million men provide 20 hours or more unpaid care each week to a sick, disabled or elderly relative. The importance of family care is shown by the poorer health and shorter life expectancy of men who live alone.

Socialisation and social control

In addition to socialisation (see page 53), the family is an important agent of social control. The shame they would feel if their family found out stops many people breaking the law.

Parents are legally responsible for their children: if children regularly miss school their parents might be taken to court. Children who are neglected or abused by their parents might be taken into care.

Emotional support

People need emotional support: they need to feel that someone cares about them, will listen to their problems and share their successes. A secure and loving family background can give people the confidence to cope with the challenges they face outside the home.

Economic support

In the past, family members often worked together as a unit. This is less common today, but economic support remains a key family function. Longer education makes children financially dependent for longer: a recent survey estimated the cost of bringing up a child to be £165,000.

Families earn money, provide a home and make decisions about saving and spending. Advertisers encourage families to spend money, so budgeting and avoiding debt are important family responsibilities. The family's economic function can be seriously threatened by events such as unemployment or illness.

A place in society

The family gives its members a place in society: a name, a home, relatives, neighbours, a locality, an ethnic group, a social status and a religion. Some of these, of course, might change later through:

- geographical mobility (moving away, e.g. to university)
- social mobility (achieving a higher social class, e.g. through career success or winning the lottery, or a lower social class, e.g. through imprisonment or illness).

ACTIVITY 52

How many family functions can you identify in this extract?

'Got up at 7.00; mum made us some breakfast; asked for some money for the school trip; my brother's been grounded because he got back late last night. Said I'd call in at my nan's on the way home, see if I can cheer her up – she's feeling really low after her fall; she might want a bit of shopping. Looking forward to my cousin's wedding at the weekend: all the family will be there. Then I'll see if I can get a Saturday job: dad can't get much overtime at the moment, so things are a bit tight.'

How many functions?

Some sociologists believe the family has fewer functions today, because other organisations (e.g. schools, hospitals) are taking over. Others argue that, because family members are now healthier, better off and better educated, they have more functions and perform them better than in the past.

ACTIVITY 53

'The NHS looks after our health, and schools look after our education.' In what ways do families influence:

- our health
- our success in education?

Criticisms of family functions

1. Feminist sociologists think family functions largely benefit men. For example, physical care and emotional support are largely provided by women, even if they are also in paid employment. Men benefit more from family life in terms of improved health and life expectancy than women. These inequalities are passed on to the next generation through gender role socialisation.

2. Marxist sociologists think that family functions really only benefit the social class that owns businesses (the bourgeoisie): for example, the family provides, free of charge, new workers (through reproduction) who are well behaved (through socialisation). Family responsibilities keep the workers working hard (providing economic support), and if their jobs are damaging or frustrating the family helps them recover (providing physical and emotional support).

3. Some critics claim that the family does not perform its functions very well today. More women are remaining childless (choosing not to reproduce); there were 12,500 children on the child protection register in 2007 at risk of neglect (receiving insufficient physical care) and the 2004 Mental Health Survey estimated that 10 per cent of 5–16-year-olds had a mental disorder (suggesting inadequate emotional support).

Traditional definitions of the family

What is a household?

The term **household** refers to the people you live with. But are all households families? Is your household the same as your family or does your family extend beyond your front door?

Consider the following examples. Are they households? Are they families? Look at the key concepts on pages 52 and 57 first.

1. a person living alone
2. four students sharing a flat
3. a lone parent with their son
4. grandparents, parents and children living together
5. parents and children, with grandparents in the next street.

(All are households, except 5. All are families except 1 and 2.)

1. Conduct a class survey: find out how many people live in each of your households and then calculate the average household size for your class.

2. Average household size in Britain has fallen to 2.4 people. Why is your class average bigger than this? (HINT: consider the age, ethnic group and social class of your sample.)

The traditional nuclear family

In Britain in the 1950s, functionalist sociologists, the government and most people thought the 'normal family' was the traditional **nuclear family**.

KEY CONCEPTS

A household – one person living alone or a group of people who have the same address and share either one meal a day or their living accommodation.

Nuclear family – a two-generation family, consisting of parents and their dependent children (i.e. children until 16, or under 18, if in full-time education).

Marriage – a legally recognised tie between a husband and wife.

What was the traditional nuclear family like?

- Parents were married.
- They did not cohabit (live together) before marriage: the bride's white wedding dress symbolised her virginity.
- In the **marriage** ceremony they agreed to stay together until death.

'Monogamy', where a person may have only one marriage partner (unless a previous marriage has ended in death or divorce), was the only permitted form of marriage. Anyone marrying more than one partner committed the crime of 'bigamy'.

- Husbands and wives had different roles.
- The husband was the leader: the family was 'patriarchal' or male dominated. His main responsibility was outside the home, as the 'breadwinner'. In the marriage ceremony he vowed to 'love, comfort, honour and keep' his wife.
- The wife's 'mother/housewife role' involved household chores, childcare and providing emotional support to other family members. In the marriage ceremony she vowed to 'obey, serve, love and honour' her husband.

Which features of the traditional nuclear family are suggested in this image?

Of course, not all nuclear families in the 1950s matched this image: for example, the couple often decided to marry because of pregnancy.

Feminist sociologists criticised the traditional nuclear family. They thought that:

- men dominated their wives
- the mother/housewife role was unsatisfying
- the 'happy family' image hid a 'dark side' of domestic violence
- women had few choices: other options (staying single, being a single parent, having a same-sex partner) were considered deviant.

However, some New Right sociologists and politicians saw the 1950s traditional nuclear family, with its low divorce rate and division of roles, as a 'Golden Age' of family life. Despite the powerful nuclear family 'image' in the 1950s, not everyone lived in nuclear families.

ACTIVITY 55

RESEARCH TASK
Speak to two older people about the type of family they were brought up in.

The traditional extended family

In the 1950s, Young and Willmott (1957) studied Bethnal Green, then a white working-class community in East London. They found that most people belonged to **extended families**, which usually included three generations: grandparents, parents and children. Family members saw each other frequently. Families were **matrilocal**: that is the mother/daughter tie was very close; so when a daughter married she wanted to live near her mother. A local saying was:

'A son's a son until he gets a wife.
A daughter's a daughter all her life.'

The **traditional extended family** gave more than friendship. Young wives wanted help and advice from their mothers about pregnancy, childcare and the problems of married life. Men also benefited: for example, a 'good worker' might get a relative a job by speaking to his boss.

Other studies of working-class communities in the 1950s showed that many people (especially women) relied on support from their extended families.

The disappearance of traditional families?

In *The Symmetrical Family* (1973), Young and Willmott argued that family life was changing.

Firstly, traditional extended families started to break up. There were many reasons for this: for example, when local councils demolished old 'Coronation Street'-style terraced houses, parents with young children were often rehoused on new estates away from the grandparents and other relatives. The manual jobs which men relied on (e.g. unloading ships in the London docks) disappeared, so families moved away for employment. Some young people moved away due to 'upward social mobility': they did well at grammar school and obtained a professional job.

Secondly, Young and Willmott suggested a new type of family was developing: the 'privatised symmetrical nuclear family' (see pages 66–67).

ACTIVITY 56

Discuss the following questions.

- What are the advantages/disadvantages for different family members of living as part of an extended family?
- Are extended families important today?
- Are nuclear families changing and, if so, in what ways?

Cross-cultural evidence

Culture influences family life. This can be seen by looking at evidence from different societies. This evidence is known as 'cross-cultural evidence'.

Murdock's view

Murdock (1949) compared 250 different societies and found the nuclear family in each one. He therefore claimed nuclear families were 'universal', that they are found in every culture. However, in some societies the nuclear family was 'hidden' inside much larger extended families, showing that culture did in fact influence family life.

One example would be enough to disprove Murdock's claim, and an anthropologist called Kathleen Gough (1968) found one:

The Nayar

The Nayar, in India in the 1800s, had no nuclear families.

A woman married a 'ritual husband' before puberty, but, apart from attending his funeral in due course, she had no relationship with him.

She also had up to 12 'visiting husbands' who could spend the night with her: the husband who arrived first in the evening would leave his weapons outside so that no other visiting husband would disturb them. Visiting husbands gave gifts but did not support their wives or children at all. One husband was required to state that the child was his (though he did not have to be the father).

Mother and children were looked after by the female relatives and brothers they lived with. This arrangement had advantages: the visiting husbands were soldiers and therefore lived uncertain lives.

Adapted from 'Is the Family Universal – The Nayar Case', E.K. Gough (1968)

The family in Tibet

Families vary between societies because of different marriage rules:

- polyandry – a rare form of marriage in which a wife may have more than one husband
- polygyny – a form of marriage in which a husband may have more than one wife – this is common, especially in Islamic societies
- polygamy – this term includes polygyny and polyandry.

In rural Tibet polyandry was the form of marriage. When a woman married a man she also married his brothers. This system seems to have worked well because of the strong bond between brothers. Women felt secure: if one brother was away trading or herding animals, the others looked after the farm and cared for her. The wife had a sexual relationship with each brother and treated them equally. The brothers helped with household tasks and took equal responsibility for any children. Children called the oldest brother 'father' and other brothers 'uncle' regardless of who the biological father was. In the harsh environment of Tibet, polyandry limited the number of children born and meant that the family farm did not have to be split into small, uneconomic pieces when sons married.

A Tibetan wife with her two husbands and their children

The family in multicultural Britain

Minority ethnic groups who have come to live in Britain bring their own cultures and distinctive family patterns.

In many Asian communities patrilocal extended families are traditional. Dench, Gavron and Young (2006) studied family life in Bethnal Green. Extended families had almost disappeared from the white community, but were very common among Bangladeshis; over a quarter of Bangladeshis lived in extended family households, usually consisting of the married couple, their children and the husband's parents.

The mother-headed (matriarchal) household, often supported by other female relatives, has been recognised as one important family type in the West Indies. This type of family is still much more important among the Afro-Caribbean community in Britain than, for example, among Asian groups.

Structural changes in the family

Different types of family

Is the nuclear family dying?

Table 2.1.1: Percentages of nuclear families in Great Britain

	1971	1991	2007
% of households that are nuclear families	35	25	21
% of people who live in nuclear families	52	41	36

Adapted from: Social Trends No. 38, Office for National Statistics, Palgrave Macmillan, 2008

The statistics in Table 2.1.1 could suggest the nuclear family is dying: they show a fall in the percentage of nuclear family households, and of people living in nuclear families. However, they do show that more than a third of people (36 per cent) still live in nuclear families. Also, because the table only gives three 'snapshots' of the nuclear family, it does not include anyone who *will* live in a nuclear family in the future or *has* lived in a nuclear family at other times in the past. Many people live in nuclear families at some stage of their family life course. The nuclear family is not dead yet, but it might be changing.

How is the nuclear family changing?

Cohabitation

In the traditional nuclear family, marriage was the norm; **cohabitation** was deviant and rare.

However, the number of first marriages per year has fallen from nearly 400,000 in 1971 to about 170,000 today. Couples are also marrying later: the average age of first marriage is now 29 for women and 31 for men. Traditionally, women married an older partner, but now 25 per cent of women marry a younger man.

Sue Sharpe (2001) questioned 11–16-year-olds. Most saw marriage as 'a choice rather than a necessity'; they liked the idea of living with someone first with the possibility of marriage later. Gender affected their views: boys were keener on marriage than girls. Some girls from the poorest neighbourhoods did not think boys would make reliable partners, so social class also affected views on marriage.

ACTIVITY 57

Explain fully why two of the following points could make marriage 'a choice rather than a necessity' today.

- Sex before marriage, cohabitation and civil partnerships are more socially acceptable.
- There is less social pressure to marry (though forced marriages do occur: see page 70).
- There is less financial pressure on women to marry.
- There is more awareness of the 'dark side' of marriage.
- People are less willing to commit long term to someone and feel more able to act as individuals.
- Women's priorities have changed.
- In a secular (less religious) society, fewer people see marriage as a religious duty.
- Getting married is expensive.

It is important to remember that most people do marry: many people feel it is the best environment for raising children and like the commitment and security which marriage offers. There are ethnic variations: Indians, Pakistanis and Bangladeshis have high rates of marriage, low rates of cohabitation and, on average, marry younger than the UK average.

Cohabitation has increased rapidly. Twenty-five per cent of unmarried adults are cohabiting. For some, cohabitation is a first step towards marriage, but for others, it is not. The New Right expressed concern about the effects of cohabitation on children because cohabiting couples have a higher risk than married couples of splitting up.

ACTIVITY 58

1. Why do you think that:
   * marriage is still popular
   * people are marrying later
   * Sue Sharpe found that boys are keener on marriage than girls
   * ethnic group affects marriage rates?
2. Can you draw up a balance sheet for marriage versus cohabitation: what are the main advantages and disadvantages of each?
3. Does the mass media influence people's views about marriage? How?

Divorce

In 1900 **divorce** was rare (500 per year) and generally seen as deviant. So, were marriages more successful then? Perhaps people expected less from marriage than we do today. Perhaps couples who were unhappy felt they had to stay together in an 'empty shell marriage'. (This is a marriage which survives, although one or both partners consider it a failure.)

Since the 1960s divorce in the UK has increased rapidly, reaching a peak of 180,000 divorces in 1993. Today it is estimated that about 45 per cent of marriages will end in divorce. Most divorce petitions (applications) are made by women. So, why has divorce increased?

Legal change has made it easier and cheaper to apply for divorce. The 1969 Divorce Reform Act allowed couples to divorce if they could show that their marriage had broken down beyond repair ('irretrievable breakdown'). The 1984 Family Law Act allowed couples to apply for divorce after one year of marriage instead of three years.

Changing attitudes: divorce is more acceptable since it has become more common, and many people see no point in preserving a damaging relationship. In a more **secular society**, fewer people see marriage as a religious commitment.

Changing expectations: people expect more from marriage today, so disappointment is more likely. People approach marriage in a more calculating way. Instead of a lifetime commitment they are more likely to ask 'is this marriage still working for me?' This approach is called 'confluent love'.

Changing role of women: combining work and employment now gives women a 'dual burden'. Wives are less dependent on their husbands: family resources are divided on divorce and women's employment opportunities have improved.

Isolation: some couples are isolated from their relatives today, so there is less to keep them together if their marriage has problems.

Lack of children: having fewer or no children might also mean there is less to keep the couple together.

Longer life expectancy might also affect how couples look at their relationship.

KEY CONCEPTS

Cohabitation – living together as partners without being married.

Divorce – the legal termination (ending) of marriage, leaving the couple free to remarry.

Secular society – a society that is not ruled by religious beliefs.

The effects of divorce on children

Many children are now affected by their parents' decisions about divorce (or separation). Rodgers and Pryor (1998) looked at 200 previous studies and concluded that:

* short-term distress is common
* there is a risk of longer-term problems (e.g. poorer health, educational achievement, behaviour, income), but most children do not experience them
* the child's age and gender do not affect the outcome of divorce
* parents' ability to cope, the amount of family conflict and the quality of contact with the absent parent do affect the outcome.

Sue Sharpe's study (2001) suggests that awareness of divorce is one reason why young people see marriage more as a choice than a necessity.

Serial monogamy

Nearly 40 per cent of marriages today are remarriages for one or both partners. Some people see this as evidence that marriage remains popular: people might be unhappy with their first *partner*, but they still like the idea of *marriage*. However, the remarriage rate is falling, suggesting more divorced people now live alone or cohabit. **Serial monogamy** gives people a second opportunity to find a satisfying relationship. However, second marriages are more likely to fail than first marriages. Why do you think this might be?

Boomerang families

Nuclear families normally contain *dependent* children. Recently, more adult children are returning (or staying at) home to live with their parents, creating **boomerang families**. Parents might prefer this to being 'empty nesters', and children can benefit, especially financially. However, Parentline Plus (2008) said that, in some cases, 'boomerang' children in their 20s and 30s turn their parents' home into a battleground, causing money problems and verbal or physical abuse.

Family diversity

There is a wide range of family types in Britain today.

Couple families

There are now more couple families. Firstly, some couples are delaying having children; secondly, more couples today remain childless through their lives. Finally, because people live longer, they have more years together as a couple after their children have left home. In 2007, 25 per cent of people lived in couple family households.

Lone-parent families

About a quarter of families with children are now **lone-parent families**. Most lone-parent families result from divorce, separation or single motherhood; few today are caused by the death of a partner. Most lone-parent families are headed by a mother, so greater economic independence of women (as well as changing social attitudes) helps explain their growth. Lone parents vary in age, ethnicity and economic circumstances, so it is hard to generalise about them; for some, lone parenthood is a temporary phase.

Feminists see lone parenthood as a positive choice, particularly if women are exploited in a two-parent family. However, they recognise that some lone parents experience problems such as low income,

lack of childcare support and social disapproval. The New Right has generally been more critical; in particular, they say that boys need positive male role models in the family to copy during socialisation.

Reconstituted (or blended) families

If a relationship ends, children usually stay with their mother, so in most **reconstituted families** children live with their biological mother and their step-father. Ten per cent of families with dependent children are reconstituted families. A positive view of reconstituted families sees them as giving people a new opportunity to form a successful family. A negative view points out a higher than average failure rate and a risk of conflict (e.g. between step-parent and step-child).

Beanpole extended families

The shape of extended families is changing. People have fewer children, so extended families are 'narrower', with fewer siblings or aunts and uncles. At the same time, people are living longer, so extended families are becoming 'taller'.

Grandparents play a vital role in the **beanpole family**. More 'dual-earner households', single-parent families and divorces mean that grandparents are often called upon for childcare and for financial support. They might also be looking after their own (often very elderly) parents. No wonder Julia Brannen (2003) called grandparents the 'pivot generation': the success of the family hinges on what they do.

Grandparents might get great satisfaction from their (unpaid) family role. Evidence suggests that some find it a burden and a worry: having raised one family, they feel they deserve their retirement.

Gay and lesbian families

With changing social attitudes and laws, there has been a significant increase in same-sex partnerships and same-sex families. The Civil Partnership Act (2004) gave same-sex couples an officially recognised ceremony and similar legal rights to married couples (e.g. pension and inheritance rights). About 17,000 civil partnerships were formed in the first year of the act, about 60 per cent of them between men.

A small, but growing number of children are brought up in same-sex families for all or part of their childhood. This has led to a debate about the advantages and disadvantages for children of living in this type of family.

Statistics and family life today

The graph in Figure 2.1.1 shows changes in marriage and divorce, two factors which have changed families in Britain.

Marriages and divorces[1]

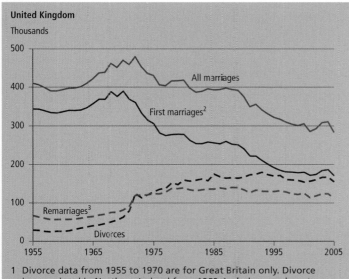

United Kingdom
Thousands

1 Divorce data from 1955 to 1970 are for Great Britain only. Divorce became legal in Northern Ireland from 1969. Includes annulments.
2 For both partners.
3 For one or both partners.

Source: Office for National Statistics; General Register Office for Scotland; Northern Ireland Statistics and Research Agency

Figure 2.1.1: Graph showing changes in marriage and divorce rates since 1955

ACTIVITY 59

1. What are the main trends (changes) shown in marriage and divorce in Figure 2.1.1?
2. How can you explain these changes?
3. What types of family have become more common as a result of the change in divorce rates?

KEY CONCEPTS

Serial monogamy – a person has more than one marriage partner in their lifetime. The main reason for increased serial monogamy is increased divorce rate.

Boomerang family – a family in which non-dependent children return home to live with their parents.

Lone-parent family – a mother or father living without a partner, and their dependent child(ren).

Reconstituted family – a family in which one or both partners has been married or cohabited before, and has a child or children, creating step-relationships.

Beanpole family – a tall, narrow extended family often containing four (or five) generations.

Table 2.1.2 shows the changes taking place in the type of households people live in.

Table 2.1.2: Percentage of people in different types of household in the UK in 1971 and 2007

	1971	2007
One person alone	6	12
A couple	19	25
Parents and their dependent child(ren)	52	36
Parents and non-dependent child(ren)	10	6
Lone parent and child(ren)	4	12

Source: Adapted from Census, Labour Force Survey, Office for National Statistics, Social Trends 38, 2008, Palgrave Macmillan

ACTIVITY 60

1. Use Table 2.1.2 to identify which three types of household have increased since 1971.
2. Why has each of these types increased?
3. Boomerang families have increased recently. Does Table 2.1.2 show this?
4. Which type of household has been missed off this table?

Table 2.1.3 shows how ethnic group influences the type of household people live in.

Table 2.1.3: Household types (as a percentage) of different ethnic groups, Great Britain, 1999

	White	Black	Indian	Pakistani and Bangladeshi
One person	29	30	14	7
A couple	29	10	18	9
Nuclear family	30	24	50	63
Lone parent and children	9	29	9	8
Extended family	0	0	7	10
Other	3	7	2	3
Total	100%	100%	100%	100%

Source: Adapted from Labour Force Survey, Office for National Statistics

Social class, ethnicity and family diversity

Social class and family life

Social class, as measured by occupation or income, still influences family life.

Income affects the area in which people live, the quality of their housing and whether they own or rent it. Income also affects the family's life chances and lifestyle: a child from a better-off family is more likely to do well at school, be healthier and travel in a safer, more modern family car.

Those who are better off and better educated are more likely to marry, to delay marriage, to have children later or remain childless, and to stay married. Teenage mothers are more likely to come from poorer neighbourhoods, the areas in which Sue Sharpe found that girls were least attracted to the idea of marriage.

Working-class families tend to live closer to their relatives (as seen in the traditional extended families in Bethnal Green, page 58), whilst middle-class families might live further apart. However, it is easier for family members from all social classes to keep in contact today, with the help of modern technology (e.g. cars, email and mobile phones).

Research generally shows that conjugal roles are more shared in middle-class families, though a recent study suggests that some middle-class fathers feel they would suffer 'career death' if they became too involved in childcare.

Ethnicity and family life

Table 2.1.3 showed the link between ethnic group and households. For example, it was quite rare for Pakistanis, Bangladeshis or Indians to live alone, yet quite common for the white and black groups to do so. Nuclear family households and extended family households were found most often in the Asian groups and lone-parent families were most common in the black community.

The family life of minority ethnic groups is influenced by their cultural traditions: these might explain, for example, early marriage (often arranged and within an ethnic group and religion), patrilocal residence, early parenthood, larger families and lower rates of cohabitation, divorce and employment of wives amongst Pakistanis and Bangladeshis.

Family life is changing in all ethnic groups, including the white majority, and family life varies *within* each ethnic group. In some communities, however, there can be considerable pressure on young people to follow traditional norms of family relationships.

The effects of family diversity

The family life course

In the 1950s the family life course was mapped out clearly for most people: grow up in a family, find a partner, marry and live together, have children, children leave home, live with partner until death. Family diversity gives most of us much more choice about family relationships.

But family diversity creates uncertainty, too. We might experience several different 'families' during our lives. Decisions made by adults (e.g. to separate) can affect children and grandparents (who might see less of grandchildren and receive less informal care from family members).

Diversity and society

Family life is changing rapidly in Britain, but people (including politicians and sociologists) still disagree about the effects on society of increased family diversity. It clearly does have effects, for example the longer life expectancy of married men compared with single and (especially) divorced men.

For New Right sociologists, who saw the traditional nuclear family as the 'best' family to carry out family functions such as socialisation, diversity is a problem. For some sociologists such as feminists who saw the 'dark side' of the traditional family, family diversity can reduce problems such as domestic violence.

Postmodernist sociologists do not make judgements about whether one type of family is 'better' than another; they just say they are 'different'. Most sociologists, however, prefer to research the positive and negative effects of social change.

Might some forms of family diversity be more desirable than others? For example, the government treats teenage pregnancy as a 'problem'. Are 'new reproductive technologies' which enable people to become parents very late in life a benefit or a problem for society?

Alternatives to the family

'Cared for children'

Some children who are unable to live with their natural parents are raised by foster parents or in children's homes. There has been concern about the care young people receive in children's homes and their 'life chances' (e.g. in terms of health and employment opportunities) after they leave.

Communal living

Communal living gives people the advantages (and disadvantages) of living with a group that is much larger than the typical household. However, communal living is rare in Britain.

In Israel, kibbutz members worked together on the land. Property was shared and members were given food and other necessities. Couples shared a room but their children were brought up separately in children's houses. Although parents had a close relationship with their children, they did not have the daily childcare tasks. The effects of socialising children in this way interested researchers.

After a period of decline, the kibbutzim are responding to changing social norms and attracting new members. They now offer a 'greener' and more 'individualistic' lifestyle; rules about sharing have been relaxed; members earn their own income and can own their own cars (see Gazzar, 2008).

In a secular society such as Britain, communal living can attract people seeking a religious life. For example, since 1929 there has been a community of Cistercian monks on Caldey Island, near Tenby. The monks live a strict life, taking vows of chastity, poverty and obedience, observing silence between 7 p.m. and 7 a.m. and getting up at 3.15 a.m. each day for their first act of worship.

Redfield is a small community in Buckinghamshire. Members join individually or as families (e.g. single parents or married couples) and live in a large house as one large household, sharing tasks, meals, leisure activities and decision making. Members work in the community (e.g. looking after livestock, vegetables and buildings), though some have part-time jobs outside. Redfield takes care when selecting new members; members also have many opportunities to express their views; this might help to explain why the community has been successful since 1978. Go to *www.heinemann.co.uk/hotlinks* and enter express code 7573P. Click on the *Redfield Community website* for more information.

ACTIVITY 63

Do some internet and/or book research to prepare a discussion on communal living, considering the following questions.

- What would you see as the advantages of communal living?
- What types of people would it be most suitable for?
- What are the possible disadvantages?
- Can they be solved?
- Why do you think there are so few communes in Britain?
- Could you design a commune?
- What would its values be?
- How would it be organised?
- How would you select members?
- What rules would you have?
- How would it pay its way?

Friends

Are friends the 'new family' for some people today? Is the boundary between friends, sexual partners and family members blurring? Friends might perform some family functions (which ones?) and might be very important at certain times (when?). Friendship, however, does not give the same legal rights and responsibilities as marriage or parenthood.

Living alone

12 per cent of people now live on their own; in 1971 it was only 6 per cent. Why is this?

- Some are elderly, mainly women who have outlived their partner. On average, women live longer than men and have an older partner.

- Some are middle aged, especially men who have experienced divorce or the failure of cohabitation, because the children are more likely to stay with their mother.

- Some are young: it is more socially acceptable and affordable for young people to live on their own today.

Some people see **singlehood** as an attractive option; it leaves people free to live their own lives and make their own choices. In the past, being single or childless were seen as 'unfortunate'; now being independent and 'child-free' has a more positive image (perhaps mainly for those with good incomes and good health). This could also be evidence of growing individualism. People living alone might, of course, have a supportive family living elsewhere.

Changing family relationships

Family members might play many different roles in the family: for example, wife, mother, grandmother and sister. This section looks at the main changes over time in family relationships, as well as the dark side of family relationships.

ACTIVITY 64

RESEARCH TASK

Have family relationships changed? Interview a relative or friend who is a grandparent or parent. Your interview can be unstructured, so you just need to plan some headings to guide the conversation. Make brief notes and report your findings to the class, either on a poster or as a PowerPoint presentation.

Areas to ask about might include:

- what changes they have seen in family relationships
- differences in being a child in the family then and now
- differences in being a husband or wife then and now
- differences in being a father or mother then and now.

Report back on the main changes they mentioned and any views they have about why the change has occurred and whether they see it as good or bad for family life.

Remember that the class might also want to know about the type of person you interviewed including age, gender and ethnic group.

The domestic division of labour and decision making in the home

Most research into family relationships looks at **conjugal roles**. In the Industrial Revolution it was normal for husbands, wives and children to work in factories. However, by the late 1800s children and married women were removed from the workplace: children went to school and married women were expected to stay at home. Conjugal roles, therefore, became very different, or segregated. Husbands were the 'breadwinners' whilst married women had the 'mother-**housewife**' role.

Sociologists have studied six main issues to see whether conjugal roles have become more equal today:

1. Who earns the money?
2. Who does the household tasks?
3. Who looks after the children?
4. Who makes the decisions?
5. Who controls the money?
6. How much domestic violence is there?

The symmetrical family

Young and Willmott suggested in 1973 that conjugal roles were becoming symmetrical. The **symmetrical family** was different from the traditional extended family and from the traditional nuclear family:

- It was nuclear – just parents and dependent children.
- It was privatised – cut off from relatives and neighbours.
- It was symmetrical – husband and wife had similar roles.

Young and Willmott thought that this new family type developed first among middle-class families and was gradually spreading to working-class families. They called this the 'principle of stratified diffusion'.

They interviewed 2000 adults in London, and 400 adults between the ages of 30 and 49 filled in 'time budget diaries'.

They found that the symmetrical family had *similar* roles, not *identical* roles. More wives had paid work and husbands were spending more time at home, helping with housework and childcare; decisions were also more likely to be shared. However, husbands were still the main breadwinner and wives did not expect their husbands to take an equal role at home, just give a bit of help. Middle-class men generally helped more than working-class men.

Table 2.1.4: Average weekly hours spent on paid work and household tasks by married 30–49-year-olds

	Husbands	Wife: full-time work	Wife: part-time work	Wife: no paid work
Paid work and travel to work	49	40	26	0
Household tasks	10	23	35	46
TOTAL	59	63	61	46

Adapted from 'The Symmetrical Family' by M Young & P Willmott, 1973, Routledge and Kegan Paul

KEY CONCEPTS

Singlehood – remaining single; the term 'creative singlehood' refers to remaining single as a positive lifestyle choice.

Conjugal roles – the roles of husbands and wives or couples who are living together as partners.

Housewife – an unpaid role which made wives financially dependent on their husbands.

Symmetrical family – a family in which conjugal roles are similar but not identical. (Some sociologists use the words 'shared', 'joint' or 'integrated' conjugal roles instead.)

Ann Oakley felt that Young and Willmott exaggerated the amount of 'symmetry' in conjugal roles. Oakley (1974), a feminist sociologist, conducted in-depth interviews with 40 London mothers who had young children. The mothers still felt housework and the children were their responsibility and were grateful for any 'help' their partners gave. This study, too, found that middle-class men were more likely to help at home, especially with childcare.

In fact, both these studies showed unequal conjugal roles (look at Table 2.1.4). Oakley highlighted the inequality. Young and Willmott highlighted the fact that roles were changing.

Why have conjugal roles become more similar?

Many reasons have been put forward for more symmetrical roles, including:

- privatised families: no extended family available to help
- changing attitudes: marriage seen more as a partnership
- changing laws: women's legal rights make them more equal partners
- comfortable homes: men have become more home-centred
- fewer children: women's lives are no longer dominated by childbearing and childcare
- the feminisation of the workforce: more women have paid employment.

Earning money

In the nineteenth century, married women and mothers left the workforce. In the late twentieth century, they started going back. There are many reasons for this:

- the growth of service sector jobs and of part-time jobs
- laws giving women equal rights at work
- high levels of educational achievement and changing priorities of girls
- dissatisfaction with the mother-housewife role
- reliable contraception to limit family size
- the growth of consumerism
- longer life expectancy.

Although 20 per cent of women now earn more than their male partners, women do not yet have an equal role in the work force: many women, for example, work part-time. Increased female employment is seen by some as the main reason for more equal conjugal roles, giving women more control, choice and independence. However, others say it simply puts extra strain on women in particular, and family life in general.

The part-time trap

Many women work part-time. The 'part-time trap' is a situation in which the part-time worker is still expected to do the domestic tasks because she is 'only working part-time'.

The dual burden

This is a situation in which women's employment is simply added to their existing responsibility for the 'mother-housewife role', because men are unwilling to do a fair share of domestic work.

ACTIVITY 65

Look at Table 2.1.4 above, showing Young and Willmott's findings.

1. Was there evidence of a 'dual burden' or a 'part-time trap'?
2. Do men have a 'dual burden'?

The triple shift

Duncombe and Marsden (1995) argued that women had 'a triple shift': this involved paid work, housework and childcare, plus 'emotion work'. They interviewed 40 white couples who had been married for 15 years. The wives felt that men were unwilling to carry out the 'emotion work' needed to keep their relationship special (e.g. showing love and affection, remembering anniversaries); the husbands did not seem to see the problem.

There have been many studies of housework and childcare since the 1970s, using different research methods and samples and reaching different conclusions. Some stress that women still generally have the main responsibility for these activities; others suggest a move towards more equality.

Lagged adaptation

Gershuny (1992) gave an optimistic view, showing that men are gradually taking on a greater share of household tasks; he used the term 'lagged adaptation' to show that there seems to be a time lag between women taking up paid work and men getting more involved at home.

Househusbands

In some cases the woman is the breadwinner and the man stays at home as a **househusband**. Why might this happen? This 'role reversal' is still quite rare. Why is it rare? Is it likely to increase in the future?

The Time Use Surveys (2000, 2005) show:

- At all ages women spend longer on household tasks than men.

- Gender affects which tasks are carried out: men are still more likely to do household repairs and women are more likely to do shopping, cooking and cleaning.

- When hours spent on paid work and household tasks are added together, on average men and women do similar amounts of work; men spend about an hour a day more in paid work and women spend about an hour a day more on household tasks.

- The time men and women spent on household tasks fell between 2001 and 2005.

The commercialisation of housework

Is time spent on housework really falling? Is there less to do? Are we getting others to do it? Until the First World War (1914–18) many middle- and higher-class families employed cooks, housekeepers, gardeners or maids. Today, once again, people who can afford it are paying others to deliver shopping or clean the house, as well as using convenience foods and labour-saving devices.

Childcare

Studies generally show that men are more involved with their children today: for example, it has become expected that men will attend the birth. However, feminists suggest that men are more likely to help than take responsibility, and more likely to do the enjoyable tasks than the unpleasant ones. The picture is complicated: for example, many fathers lose contact with their children after divorce or separation, yet Fathers 4 Justice campaigns for fathers who feel they are denied access to their children by ex-partners and the courts.

Decision making

Making decisions is one way in which people exert power in a relationship. Edgell (1980) studied decision making in a small sample of middle-class families and found that the decisions the couple felt were most important (e.g. moving home) were usually made by the man.

Recent studies show that men do not always dominate family decisions. Even in communities where the man's status as family head is important, women, at the centre of the family, often seem to have a great deal of influence. Economic power affects family power, so higher female earnings or male unemployment can give women more say in family decisions.

Money management

As men have traditionally earned more than their partners, they have tended to control the money. One study showed that women were most likely to control the money in families which did not have enough money to go round (and as a result they would be the ones to make most sacrifices). Recent studies show a move towards greater equality in money management.

Variations in conjugal roles

Age, health, ethnic group, social class, occupation and stage of the life course can all influence how couples organise their conjugal roles; for example, a couple's shared roles might become more segregated once their first child is born.

Couples also make choices about how they organise their lives together, though strict community norms or a lack of money can limit choice. Others have more freedom: same-sex couples, for example, can create their 'own' relationship because there is no traditional 'gender script' for same-sex couples to follow.

In the growing number of lone-parent families, of course, it is generally women who have sole responsibility for decision making, childcare and household tasks.

The main conclusions from research into conjugal roles are:

- they are more equal today
- but inequalities remain
- these vary a lot between families.

One of the most disturbing inequalities, domestic violence, is studied on page 70.

Changing relationships between family members

We have already looked at changing conjugal roles and the increasing involvement of grandparents in family life.

Parent/child relationships

What changes have taken place? Children are now more likely:

- to survive childhood: infant mortality and child mortality rates are low
- to be cared for by a non-parent in their early years (often a grandparent)
- to have better living conditions, their own room and more money spent on their education, toys, clothes and other consumer goods
- to have more parental supervision because of concerns about their safety
- to have a say in family decision making
- in two-parent families, to have fathers who are involved in childcare and household tasks and to be in a dual-earner family; these are sometimes said to be 'cash rich but time poor'
- to experience the breakdown of their parents' relationship (but less likely to experience the death of a parent)
- to spend all or part of their childhood in a reconstituted, single-parent or same-sex family
- to depend on their parents financially for longer and to live in a boomerang family when adult.

Social class differences remain: for example, middle-class children are more likely to be better off and better housed, to have parents who are older, to be healthier and to attend independent (and sometimes boarding) schools.

Ethnic differences are also evident: for example, children in Asian communities are more likely to be part of extended families, to have more siblings, and to have parents who are married and remain married.

Gender differences remain, for example in the amount of domestic tasks children are expected to do and the amount of supervision they have from parents.

The picture is complicated, firstly, by the fact that the three variables of class, ethnicity and gender overlap. Secondly, all families are different: your family is not exactly the same as anybody else's because family members can create (within limits) their own family life.

The dark side of the family

Functionalist sociologists gave a very positive view of the family, and many people do seem to share that view.

ACTIVITY 66

1. Why might many adults feel happiest around their families?
2. Might happiness with family life vary with the respondent's gender? Why?
3. Might the answers be different if young people were asked and, if so, in what ways?
4. Why might some people be very unhappy with their family life? List the main reasons.

On the other hand, some researchers present a negative view of the family. For example, Leach (1967) criticised the nuclear family. He thought it was too small to give people everything they expected, such as love, sexual satisfaction, happiness and financial security. Conflict and disappointment made the nuclear family 'the source of all our discontents'.

Some people are harmed by family life and this situation is called 'the dark side of the family'. Of particular concern are situations where force is used to control family members. With **domestic violence**, child abuse and elder abuse, home becomes a place of fear rather than somewhere that people feel safe and loved.

KEY CONCEPTS

Househusband – a man with the main responsibility for domestic tasks and childcare, whose partner is the main breadwinner.

Dark side of the family – a situation in which family life damages its members.

Domestic violence – threatening behaviour, violence or abuse (psychological, emotional, physical, sexual or financial) committed by a family member against another.

Domestic violence

Domestic violence is not new: Henry VIII's wives did not all survive to a happy old age. However, only since the 1970s has it been seen as a social problem: a situation in society which is harmful and needs action to solve it.

Measuring domestic violence

It is not easy to obtain valid statistics for domestic violence. The Official Crime Statistics are not very helpful because:

- there is no crime called 'domestic violence'
- they only show the 'tip of the iceberg', because many victims do not report domestic violence.

The British Crime Survey gives a more accurate picture. The BCS is a victim survey with a large sample of 16- to 59-year-olds in England and Wales. It asks victims to record any 'frightening threats and/or physical assaults'.

Table 2.1.5: Experience of domestic violence in England and Wales in 1999

Experience of domestic violence	Women	Men
Yes: in my lifetime	26%	17%
Yes: in the last year	4.2%	4.2%
Yes: 3 or more times in the last year	2.0%	1.5%
I have been injured by it in the last year	2.2%	1.1%

Source: Adapted from Catriona Mirrlees-Black and Carole Byron: Domestic Violence: Findings from the BCS Self-Completion Questionnaire, Home Office Research, Development and Statistics Directorate, Research findings No 86, 1999

Only 10 per cent of victims in the last year had told the police about the violent incident; less than 50 per cent had told anyone, usually a friend.

ACTIVITY 67

What does the BCS tell us about:

1. the amount of domestic violence?
2. whether domestic violence is a social problem?
3. the relationship between gender and domestic violence?
4. the usefulness of the official crime statistics for measuring domestic violence?

Violent men

'The vast majority of serious and repeated domestic violence is committed by men against women, with an average of two women killed each week by their partner or ex-partner.' *(Source: 6th report of the Home Affairs Select Committee, 2008)*

Rather than blaming individual men, feminists blame a patriarchal (male-dominated) society which allows men to:

- have unrealistic expectations of their partners and of themselves
- think they can use violence to control the family and deal with their partner's 'failings'.

Blaming a patriarchal society for domestic violence helps explain why many women experience domestic violence. It does not explain why many men never use violence or why some women use violence. Other explanations are needed to explain why certain men are willing to use violence.

New concerns

Male victims (and violent women): Luckhurst (2003) argued that male victims are largely invisible, yet one helpline for men, 'It Does Happen', received over 100,000 calls after being mentioned on GMTV. Male victims, like female victims, often stay with their partner, risking 'repeat victimisation'. Men also worry that the police will not take them seriously or might think they started the violence.

Violence in same sex relationships: Catherine Donovan (2007) found that 40 per cent of women and 35 per cent of men in same-sex relationships had experienced abuse, with emotional abuse most common. Typical victims were under 35, in their first relationship and had low incomes.

'Honour'-based violence: this occurs in communities where families can be shamed if a member disobeys their parents or becomes too 'westernised'. This violence might be carried out by several family members. A related issue is 'forced marriage': a marriage without the agreement of both partners. The government's Forced Marriage Unit deals with about 300 cases each year; the true figure is unknown.

Is domestic violence increasing?

One BCS finding is that young respondents (especially women aged 20–24) were most likely to say they had 'experienced domestic violence in their lifetime'; surprisingly, the lowest figures came from people in the survey who had lived longest (those in their 40s and 50s).

1. How would you explain the above finding?
   a. Older respondents might forget about violence earlier in their life.
   b. Young people today talk more openly about personal events.
   c. Violence affecting young people is probably increasing today.
   d. Older people might not want to put personal information on a computer.
2. Why might domestic violence be increasing today? Why might it be falling?

Child abuse

Although most public concern is about 'stranger danger' and 'paedophiles', some children are abused by their own families. The Child Protection Register for England lists all children thought to be suffering from (or likely to suffer from) significant harm. The four main types of **child abuse**, with figures from the 2007 Register, are:

1. neglect   12,500
2. physical abuse   3500
3. sexual abuse   2000
4. emotional abuse   7100

(Source: the NSPCC website)

Child abuse – harm caused to a child or young person under 18 by an adult. (NSPCC definition)

1. What is the most common form of abuse, according to the Child Protection Register?
2. **Research task:**

The Children's Act 2004 changed the law on smacking. Parents were allowed to give a 'mild smack', but could be charged with assault if, for example, the smack caused bruising. Investigate the smacking debate (e.g. using online newspapers).

On average, one child under ten is killed each week, usually by a parent, the parent's partner or another relative. Even when children are known to be at risk, they are not always protected from abuse: for example, the cases of Victoria Climbié in 2000 and 'Baby P', in 2008. Social change (such as the increased breakdown of relationships) might put more children at risk of abuse. Parents' rights are also a concern. Some parents have found it very difficult to get their children back after 'experts' have wrongly accused them of harming their children.

1. Approximately how many hours have you spent in secondary school studying the following?
   (a) maths   (b) sociology   (c) parenting
2. How well prepared are you for parenthood? Think about your family. For instance, do you have any experience of younger siblings and new babies?

Do children ever abuse their parents?

Help the Aged's 2006 report on Elder Abuse suggested that 46 per cent of abusers were the victim's relatives and 25 per cent were the victim's sons or daughters. So far there has been little research on elder abuse, but it is another 'dark side' of family life.

In this chapter we defined the family and studied the family's functions, focusing especially on socialisation. We looked at traditional nuclear and extended families before investigating changes such as increased cohabitation and divorce. We examined newer types of family, as well as alternatives to family life. Roles in the family (especially conjugal roles) and the 'dark side' of family life (e.g. domestic violence and child abuse) were studied in the final section of the chapter.

1. What are the functions of the family?
2. What were traditional nuclear and extended families like?
3. Is the nuclear family still important?
4. What is happening to marriage, cohabitation and divorce?
5. Which types of family are becoming more common? Why?
6. Are the roles of husbands and wives equal today?

ExamCafé

Revision

Common mistakes

You need to learn all the key terms for this topic, so find the method that suits you best and start early. You could put them on revision cards, stick them round your room or classroom, test each other whenever you get a chance, for example before your lesson starts.

Make sure you explain your points fully in the 8-mark and 24-mark questions; examples are always useful, so when you make your revision notes make sure you add some. Up-to-date examples are good, so keep your eye on the news in the weeks leading up to the exam and add anything interesting to your revision notes.

Summarising content

The 24-mark question always asks you to look at both sides of an issue. Make a list of possible issues, and prepare some points for both sides of the debate. Topics could include:

- whether socialisation is the main function of the family
- whether we really need families
- whether family life has changed
- whether the nuclear family is the best type of family
- whether marriage is disappearing
- whether roles in the family are equal
- whether there is a dark side to family life.

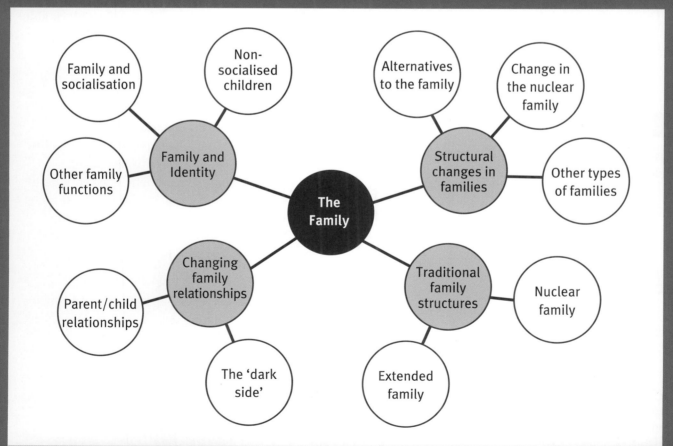

Exam preparation

Sample student answers

> 'Marriage is no longer important.'
> Evaluate the arguments for and against this claim. **[24 marks]**

Consider two student responses to this question.

Emily

Marriage is no longer important because people don't have to get married any more. They can just live together if they want to. People do this because they don't want to stay with the same person for ever so they can just leave if they want to.

Marriage is too expensive for people so they decide to save the money and spend it on other things like their home.

Many people get divorced these days. It is much easier to get divorced now. People see celebrities getting divorced so they get used to the idea that divorce is OK.

Many gay people live together today, but they can't get married, so this shows marriage is not so important.

People do still get married but it is mainly older people who think marriage is the thing to do; young people aren't so bothered.

In conclusion, marriage is no longer important because lots of people just live together instead of getting married.

Comments
The first sentence makes a clear link with the question. The concept 'cohabitation' could be named though, and Emily could explain the growth of cohabitation in more detail.

Comments
Emily mentions one valid point in this paragraph. The point could be linked more clearly to the title: 'Marriage might not be so important because…' The comment is a bit too assertive: it would be more accurate to say 'Marriage might be too expensive for some people', because it certainly is not too expensive for everyone.

Comments
This paragraph makes another valid point and suggests two reasons for the increase in divorce. Emily could use more concepts in the answer, for example, she says that people 'see celebrities' but does not actually refer to the mass media's influence on social attitudes.

Comments
Another valid point, and a clear link is made to the title of the question. Again the answer would be improved with more detail and concepts (e.g. civil partnerships).

Comments
Emily has remembered that there must be evidence for and against the question, so has improved her mark by including a point here which disagrees with the question. Age is an important variable, but others could also be added: ethnic group would be an obvious one for this question.

Comments
Emily knows that a conclusion is needed. This is a rather brief one. In a debate like this a good conclusion will usually need to show awareness of both sides of the argument and/or variations between different groups in society.

Comments
Overall this is a sound answer, but would be improved by more detailed explanations, more concepts, clearer links to the question and a more balanced conclusion.

Exam**Café**

An impressive first paragraph. It shows a clear link to the question, some concepts, awareness of change (the fall in first marriages) and several reasons are given.

Comments

Another good paragraph. It is clearly focused on the question and draws on concepts and a piece of research to discuss the increase in cohabitation. Marriage might not be so important because there is more divorce. Laws such as the Divorce Reform Act mean people can get divorced if their marriage suffers 'irretrievable breakdown'.

Comments

The issue of divorce is linked clearly to the question and it is clear that Thomas can give some sociological reasons for the increase in divorce.

Comments

Although there is only one paragraph to challenge the statement in the question, it includes three valid points.

Comments

A sound conclusion: it shows awareness of change, introduces a new idea (living alone) and points out that the importance of marriage varies.

Marriage is a legal tie between a husband and wife; in Britain it is monogamy. Marriage might not be so important any longer because the number of first marriages has halved since 1970. There are lots of reasons for this: there is less pressure on people to get married. Girls used to need a husband to support them but today they are more independent and have better job opportunities. People aren't so religious, so they don't get married for religious reasons. Some people just think it's too expensive to get married.

Marriage might be less important because more people cohabit today; they live together without being married. This is not deviant any more. Sue Sharpe said young people see marriage as a choice today, not something they have to do. More same-sex couples live together today and they can have a Civil Partnership instead of marriage.

Women might get dissatisfied with marriage because of the 'double burden' or 'triple shift'.

However, marriage might still be important. Many people still get married, even if they cohabit first. Many people get remarried after a divorce and form a reconstituted family. Some people think marriage is very important for children, because couples who cohabit are more likely to split up.

In conclusion, marriage isn't as important as it was because of cohabitation and divorce; also more people just live alone today. Marriage seems more important to some groups than others: Asian ethnic groups are more likely to get married and stay married.

Comments

Overall this is a very good answer because it focuses clearly on the question, looks at both sides of the debate, uses concepts and knowledge to explain its points, and gives a balanced conclusion.

Unit 2
Topic 2: Education

Consider these facts about the current situation regarding education:

- The Government believes that education is so important that the official school leaving age is being raised to 18
- Increasing numbers of students are being enrolled onto Higher Education courses
- Toddlers are participating in pre-school classes
- Adults are returning to education as mature students.

The message is clear – education is important. Yet during this topic you will be questioning whether education really does matter that much and whether things are really as positive as they may appear.

PAUSE FOR THOUGHT

1 What is the point of going to school? Would society really be such a dreadful place if we were not so educated?

2 Do girls do better than boys in your school or college? If so, why do you think this is?

3 What do we learn in the education system?

4 Should parents be allowed to 'buy' their children a place in a private school?

5 Why do you think that Afro-Caribbean students are the ethnic group most likely to be excluded from school?

Topic 2: Education

Education and identity

Development of individual identity and the learning of social roles

Think back to the chapter called 'Sociology Basics' where you learned a wide range of sociological key concepts and started to explore links between the individual and society. One of the key concepts that was introduced to you there is that of 'agents of socialisation', with education being a crucial one. We will start this chapter by considering how education helps individuals to develop their identities and learn social roles.

Our identity begins to form from a very early age and is basically the way that we see ourselves and also the way that others see us. With education being such a big part of our lives today, it has a big impact on our identity. It is not just what we learn in the classroom that is important here; it is all the other kind of learning that goes on in education too. This is the informal, non-academic learning that takes place every day as part of school life, often without us realising that it is going on. This may include the learning of rules, routines, relationships, discipline, gender roles and expectations. So, for example, a boy learns very quickly that crying when he is upset is not part of a masculine identity. Similarly, the girl who loves sport, getting dirty outside and hates washing her hair also learns through education and other agents of socialisation that this part of her identity needs to be changed or hidden.

ACTIVITY 71

Discuss your ideas with a partner about how schools can help children to learn their gender identities.

This is all part of us learning about our culture, our whole way of life. Education develops our knowledge of this and reinforces what we have been taught by our families. So, very quickly we become fluent in a new set of norms and values. For example, would you ever put your hand up at home to ask to go to the toilet? Or sit down in silence at

a pop concert. Or what about sitting on the floor (probably with your legs crossed) when you go to the cinema? Anywhere other than in education this would be very odd behaviour indeed! Yet in school we do these types of things without question. School has taught us these norms and we have learned that if we do not follow them, then there will be consequences.

It is a similar situation when it comes to values. Certificates, stickers and assemblies are all used to remind us what is considered important at school. We are rewarded for working hard, for sharing and for being a good citizen. And, finally, education makes sure that we all know our roles and the behaviour expected of us when in them. At school the key roles played are obviously those of student and teacher. Teachers can tell you off, they stand at the front and you listen to them (or at least pretend to!). Students do what other people tell them to, whether they want to or not. They are all gradually learning their place in society. Imagine the chaos if one day we did not follow the norms and did not slot into our familiar roles and behaviour . . .

Now try the activity opposite.

RESEARCH LINK

For more information on observation as a research method look at pages 10–12 in Unit 1, Sociology Basics.

Hopefully the activity will show you just how many norms, values and role expectations there are in the education system and how they have become a part of our everyday, taken-for-granted routines. Would school and society be able to function without them? That is debateable. Some sociologists, such as functionalist sociologists, believe they are crucial if we are to live in an orderly and harmonious society. Others, Marxists for instance, see this informal learning as just another example of those with power controlling the thoughts and actions of those with less power. They believe that this increases and maintains inequalities in society, and so see education as a tool used to keep the masses in their place.

1. Working on your own, make a list of all the norms, values and roles that you can think of that are taught in schools. These can be from your current experiences as a GCSE student or from earlier stages in your education.

2. Now think about how all of these are actually taught to you; after all there is no exam to sit in 'being quiet when the teacher is talking'! Discuss your ideas in a small group and then feed back to your teacher.

3. Next, working in four small groups, you are going to come up with two very different classroom scenarios.

   • Group one will outline the behaviour and expectations of students in a typical, orderly classroom where all the usual norms and roles apply.

   • Group two will develop a scenario where all the rules that we take for granted are turned upside down, where students do not act as they should or as they are expected to.

   • Group three will look at things from a teacher's perspective and jot down what typically goes on in terms of norms and behaviour.

   • Group four will outline teacher actions that go against the norm.

When all the small groups are ready, try out a couple of the scenarios. Choose one student from group three to play the role of the teacher in the 'typical' classroom, and one from group four to play the teacher role in the 'untypical' lesson. Send them outside the classroom. Group one should then act as students for the teacher from group three and group two will be students for the teacher from group four. When you are not involved with the role play you should observe and make notes on what happens. When finished, discuss your findings with your class and your teacher.

The role of education in socialisation and identity

Education is clearly a major agent of socialisation and one of the institutions that teaches us how we should behave and think in order to fit into society. It continues the process of primary socialisation that was started by the family and is also central in terms of secondary socialisation. Imagine if you had never been socialised, how would you be able to function and survive in society? Think back to the feral children you looked at in 'Sociology Basics' (see page 35) and in 'The Family' pages 54–55 and

all the problems they had. Education is one way that society can make sure that we know what is expected of us in our specific culture and that we are socialised adequately. The diagram below illustrates some important factors in terms of how education can be seen as an agent of socialisation.

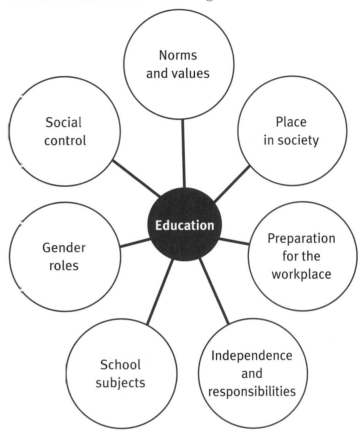

Examples of how education can be seen as an agent of socialisation.

1. Using an A4 piece of paper create your own spidergram like the one above. Label this 'Education and Socialisation'.

2. Add any other ways that education socialises us to the diagram.

3. Make a bulleted list to identify what education teaches you in relation to each title on your diagram and how it does this.

GradeStudio

Make sure you are clear what is meant by command words such as 'what', 'give . . . examples', 'how', 'identify' and 'explain', as these could all feature in any exam questions on education. Check with your teacher if you are unsure of any of these.

The role of education

Functions of education

What role does education actually play in society? As you can probably imagine, sociologists have very different views on this. Read on to see what you think.

Functionalist sociologists believe that education is crucial in order to have a smooth-running and efficient society, as it socialises people into commonly accepted norms and values in society. Functionalists see society as a human body with all the agents acting like human organs. If one organ or agent is not working, then the whole body or society will stop working properly. So, without an effective education system, they think society would not work. For functionalists, then, education has a very positive role to play.

Marxists take the opposite view to functionalists, in that they believe that society is not based on agreement and harmony, but instead is split by divisions of inequalities in terms of power, money and status. This means society is effectively a series of conflicts, the most important of which for a Marxist is based on social class. So, for example, the ruling class have the power; they are the bosses who exploit the working class 'wage slaves'. For Marxists, education is a tool of oppression used by the ruling class to keep the masses in their place. So, education is good for the powerful people in society who can use it to force the rest of us to accept their norms and values as the right ones. For the less powerful, though, education does not have many benefits at all; it is just a way of controlling us.

Keep these two very different perspectives in mind as we start to explore what education is actually for. You will need to apply these ideas to the information presented to you in this section.

The economic role

Schools teach the skills and knowledge that will allow people to develop into good workers who can contribute positively to society. These include such things as literacy, ICT skills, numeracy and communication. However, not everybody will learn these skills to the same level; some people will choose vocational (work-based) rather than academic courses, some will move onto further or higher education and, of course, the levels and grades achieved in a subject will be different for each student. Therefore, it could be argued that students are not all being taught the same skills set, meaning that different students are being prepared

for different jobs later in life. In a nutshell, middle- and upper-class children tend to learn the skills needed for high-status, professional jobs, whilst working-class children learn what is needed for the lower-status jobs in society.

ACTIVITY 74

1. Write down all the subjects that you are currently studying. Go through each one and think about what skills and knowledge they are teaching you to help you later in the work force.

2. Based on what you have done in task 1, how well do you think that your education is preparing you for the future?

The socialisation role

Schools are agents of secondary socialisation and thus teach children the norms and values central to our culture. By doing so, people come to feel that they belong to the culture and that they, by and large, agree on the important things in life. This is known as social integration (that is, making people feel that they belong by emphasising all the things they have in common, such as norms and values) and is crucial if people are to be good citizens who follow the rules and do what is expected of them. Not everyone takes such a positive view of the socialisation that schools do, though, and instead see it more as a means of controlling and even brainwashing people to accept the inequalities in our society.

RESEARCH LINK

For more information on agents of secondary socialisation look at pages 35–37 in Unit 1, Sociology Basics.

The selective role

School has a very important role to play in terms of sorting out which people should be doing which jobs in society. Not everyone has the same ability level and so schools can help to grade students so that the most able go on to university, enabling them to eventually reach the high-status, influential and demanding jobs in society. This benefits everybody, as we have the best people doing the most important jobs. Again, though, this point of view has its critics. Not everybody thinks that all students get equal opportunities in schools, and believes that right from the beginning some are going to do better than others, regardless of their abilities. Social class, gender and ethnicity all seem to play a part in how well students do at school – this seems to contradict the idea that the grades you get are just down to your ability.

ACTIVITY 75

What do you think of the ideas presented above? Discuss with your classmates whether the people with the best qualifications do actually get the best jobs in terms of pay and status.

The social control role

The teaching of discipline, respect and punctuality is at the heart of every school's daily life. Students learn the rules and most choose to accept them. Those that do not will get punished until they do as they are told and **comply**. From one point of view, this is a good thing, as it ensures that children leave school knowing that if they are to succeed in life they have to **conform** and be compliant. As a result of this, society runs pretty smoothly. From a different perspective, however, this is not such a good thing, as it teaches children to accept what others tell them without question. The end result is a society that rarely stands up to authority and so allows the powerful people to continue making the rules that they benefit from.

ACTIVITY 76

1. Do schools successfully control students? Give examples.
2. If not, what tactics and strategies do students adopt to resist their school's attempts to control them?
3. Using a website such as 'YouTube', have a look at Pink Floyd's video 'Another Brick In The Wall'. What does this say about social control in education?

KEY CONCEPTS

Compliance – to do what is wanted and expected of you, to follow orders and rules.

Conform – to accept what you are told and so behave and think in the way that is expected of you.

ACTIVITY 77

1. Reread all the information that has been presented to you above. Your task is to decide which bits of information support the functionalist view and which support the Marxist way of thinking.
2. Divide your page into two columns; call one 'Functionalism' and the other 'Marxism'. Then write statements in each column, in your own words, to show what each perspective would say about the role of education. Do this individually to see what you know. Once everyone has finished check your answers with your teacher.
3. You are now going to **evaluate** these two perspectives and see which of the two, if either, you agree with. Your teacher will split you into groups, where you will need to produce a presentation that supports either the functionalist or the Marxist view. You might want to do this as a PowerPoint presentation, making sure that you clearly explain your perspective and why that is better than the other point of view. You will then debate against each other and see who has the strongest argument. Make sure you are ready to argue and defend your position!

GradeStudio

Evaluate – remember that this is a skill that is tested in the examinations. It means to look at things from more than one point of view, to weigh up the pros and cons of an argument and to make a judgement based on the available evidence. Doing mini debates, such as the one above, in class will help you to develop your evaluation skills.

Socialisation: learning and the curriculum

As we have already seen earlier in this chapter, education is an important agent of socialisation in the UK. Education in its broadest sense happens all the time. We learn from being with our friends and family, from religion and, increasingly, from the media. These very general developments in our skills and knowledge base are known as **informal education** and, in some societies, are the only ways in which people are educated. In modern, industrial societies, however, we also have specific institutions designed to educate us, namely schools, colleges and universities. These provide us with what is known as the **formal curriculum**, where there are courses to follow and examinations to be sat. The formal curriculum is the subjects that we study in lesson time, the official curriculum. Sitting alongside the official curriculum in schools, we also have something known as the **hidden curriculum** which includes all the learning that goes on in a school that is not directly taught in the classroom and is not subject based. As we considered in topic 1, the hidden curriculum ensures that we learn the importance of following the rules, being in a routine and doing as other people tell us to. Most of the time we do not even realise this is happening; it becomes part of our common sense experiences, and is what is referred to as **informal learning**.

KEY CONCEPTS

Formal curriculum – subjects that are studied and examined in schools and colleges; sociology, media studies and history, for example.

Hidden curriculum – what schools teach students through day-to-day school life, i.e. this is not part of the formal timetable. This will reflect society's attitudes and values and prepare students for their future role and place in that society.

Informal education/learning – non-directed learning that occurs outside the classroom and does not have a curriculum to follow.

Segregation – separating students, often males and females, and so giving them different experiences and opportunities in school. This could be through single-sex schooling or through keeping them apart within a mixed gender environment.

The hidden curriculum

We know that schools informally teach students norms and values through the hidden curriculum. Some people think this is a good thing, others disagree. You will be starting to develop your own ideas on this too by now.

GradeStudio

To reach the top grades in the exam it is important that you are able to use sociological concepts and theories accurately to help you evaluate and explain a point of view. Earlier in this chapter we considered the role of education as an agent of socialisation and you learned what two different sociological theories had to say on this. Can you remember what the theories were and what they said? If not, check back now.

However, what is clear is that the hidden curriculum effectively passes on a wide range or norms and values to students which, most of the time, they do not question. So we are 'taught' about such varied issues as rules, gender roles and equality and these become reality for most of us. But how does this actually happen?

Gender roles

Students still opt for very different subjects in schools – more girls study textiles, for example, while boys are more likely to take design and technology. This effectively **segregates** males and females, something that is also seen in many PE lessons. Boys are likely to do the more physical activities such as rugby and football, whereas girls may be offered dance or aerobics. This can be even more obvious in single-sex schools where girls and boys are completely segregated. Teachers may also have quite different expectations of girls than boys, which could potentially affect job opportunities. So if teachers expect girls not to be good at science they are unlikely to push them towards a science-based career. Finally, teachers may ask boys to do different things to girls, such as asking girls to help tidy up and getting boys to help lift things. This says a lot about the perceived future roles of girls and boys.

Hierarchy

Schools are a good example of a hierarchy, where those at the top (management and teachers) have more power and influence than those at the bottom (the students). Students see this every day and so accept it as normal. Many sociologists would argue that this prepares them for the world of work, where they are likely to have a boss to tell them what to do.

Social control

Students quickly learn that they need to obey rules and that, if they do not, a punishment will follow – the dreaded detention, for example. This effectively prepares students to follow and accept the rules in wider society, such as the importance of being on time.

Learning to accept boredom

'This is so boring' – how many times have you heard that in a typical school day? Many people would argue that schools purposely bore you – they train you in how to deal with being bored so that you will be used to it when you start work and have to complete the repetitive and routine tasks typical of many office and factory jobs.

Inequalities

We still have a relatively 'white' curriculum in our education system. A lot of topics chosen for study, many of the authors and a lot of the illustrations do still tend to focus on the white experience – white culture and white history, for example. We also learn that the more intelligent you are, the more likely you are to gain the teacher's praise, to win awards and to be seen as a 'good' student. Many would argue that this teaches us to accept that we will not all be treated the same in society and that this is normal and acceptable.

Competition

Schools are typically very competitive institutions. You might compete to see who can get the best grades, you compete on the sports field and you compete for roles in the school play. This is similar to society as a whole. As the UK is a capitalist society, competition is at the heart of everything we do. We compete for material goods, jobs, the best car, status and so on. Again, schools are training you for this competition, making you better at it and teaching you that it is normal.

Lack of power

In schools today you may be prefects or leaders, sit on a school council and discuss and debate in the classroom. However, your actual powers are very limited. You will be very unlikely to have any say in financial or curricular decisions which, most of the time, will be made by the leadership group and the governing body. So by the time you leave school you will be used to being powerless; as they say, you don't miss what you don't know!

ACTIVITY 78

Have a look at your school's prospectus. You will find it contains information on the different subjects on offer – in other words, the formal curriculum. Your task is to rewrite a few pages, only you're going to focus on the hidden curriculum offered by your school. In small groups, discuss and write down some ideas about what to include.

When your group is happy with the content and style, turn your ideas into an official-looking document such as a leaflet or even a web page. Make sure you add a few relevant photographs to illustrate some of the different aspects of your school's hidden curriculum, as well as additional features such as student or teacher quotes.

Alternatives to schooling

Despite what you might think or have been told, it is not actually compulsory in the UK to go to school. What is compulsory, though, is to receive an education.

Home schooling

An education can be delivered at home by either tutors or parents. According to research conducted by Glasgow University in 2008, approximately 50,000 children are now thought to be home-schooled and this figure is still increasing. The main reason for this seems to be parental dissatisfaction with the stresses children are put under by the constant testing and target setting that characterises our education system. English pupils now typically start formal learning at four years old, among the youngest in the world, and go on to be the most tested throughout their education.

'Deschooling'

Another alternative to schooling is a movement known as 'deschooling' which began in the 1970s. The main idea here was that children were put off learning by schools and that they would learn more if they could learn what they wanted in their own community, without being forced to do anything. You basically learned what was relevant to you.

Alternative schools

If parents choose not to educate their child(ren) at home, they still have alternatives within the education system. Steiner schools, for example, can be found all over the UK – and they have approximately 1000 schools worldwide – these offer parents an alternative to more traditional schooling. Here classes are mixed ability, mixed gender and multi-faith and the schools are open to all ability levels. The curriculum is very flexible and offers students the chance to learn in a relaxed and creative learning environment at their own pace. Artistic and practical skills are given equal time and status to academic ones.

Probably the most famous and radical example of a free school is Summerhill in Suffolk, established in 1921. This offers the 80 or so students enrolled there a progressive and democratic education, based on the idea that students should not be forced to do anything – including attending lessons! At Summerhill students can decide which, if any, lessons they attend and can basically do as they please, as long as they do not harm anyone else. School meetings decide on the day-to-day running of the school. These are held three times a week, attended by staff and students and a simple vote decides school policy.

So, as you can see, there is a much wider choice out there when it comes to education than you perhaps at first realised, and there are certainly plenty of alternatives to schooling.

ACTIVITY 79

RESEARCH TASK

Check out more details on alternatives to schools on the internet. Have a look at Summerhill, Steiner schools, deschooling, home schooling and anything else that looks relevant. Make notes on any interesting things you find out. Using the information you have gathered discuss the following questions with your classmates.

1. If you could choose, would you still come to school? Why or why not?

2. If you were a parent, would you send your child(ren) to a traditional school or would you prefer an alternative to schooling? Why?

3. What do you think about Summerhill and Steiner schools? What are their good and bad points? Do you think there should be more schools like them?

ACTIVITY 80

With the person next to you, think about what is taught to children in the pre-school stage. Make a note of your thoughts, then discuss them with the rest of the class.

1. Why do you think the government decided to give free pre-school education to all three- and four-year-olds in the UK?

2. Would you have done this if you were prime minister?

Educational changes and their effects

The structure of the current education system

Most education in the contemporary UK is provided by the government and is paid for through the tax system. There is a clear structure and a progression route for us all to follow. However, there is still a great deal of variety in terms of how the system is organised.

Pre-school education

Education today starts before you have even started school. Typically, children in pre-school education are between three and five years of age and might attend for just a couple of mornings or on a more full-time basis. You might well have experienced pre-school education yourself by going to nursery or to playgroup. The Labour government thought this stage of the education system was so important that it introduced a scheme in which all three- and four-year-olds in the UK would receive free nursery school education.

Primary education

This stage in the education system refers to infant and junior schools. These schools usually take any child from a particular area and are for both boys and girls (co-educational). The majority of primary education is provided by the state through the LEA (local educational authority). Some primary schools, though, are private, meaning that fees must be paid in order to attend.

Secondary education

Secondary schools provide education for pupils aged between 11 and 16, although many secondary schools also have a sixth form for students up to the age of 18. As with primary schools, most students attend state secondary schools but some are educated privately where fees are paid.

You might be thinking that all secondary schools are the same, but this is not quite the case:

- **Comprehensives:** these schools take pupils of all different abilities and backgrounds, and are intended to provide 'education for all'. They were introduced into the UK in 1965. Most secondary school students attend this type of secondary school which, because it is open to everyone, is said to provide inclusive education.

- **Specialist Comprehensive Schools:** these schools receive extra funding to specialise in a certain area of the curriculum, for example foreign languages.

- **City Technology Colleges (CTCs):** these began in 1993 and specialised in science and technology to try to make education more suitable for developing the skills needed in industry and the economy. They receive money both from the government and from the private sector. CTCs tend to offer their students a wide range of vocational courses and often have a longer school day than usual.

- **Academies:** these are a recent development in the secondary school sector. They are state-funded but also sponsored by such sources as business, the community or an educational provider. Many of the lowest-performing state schools are expected to become Academies in an attempt to raise and improve standards. These may well replace CTCs.

- **Grant-maintained Schools:** this type of school is allowed to select some pupils through entry exams and receives its funding from government grants rather than LEA budgets. This gives schools much more control of the management and day-to-day running of the institution. These schools are often described as 'opting out' of local authority control.

- **State Grammar Schools:** a small number of educational authorities in the UK still have the grammar school system of the past. Grammar schools can select those children that do best in an examination that they sit at age 11. Counties such as Kent, Lincolnshire and Buckinghamshire still operate the grammar school system.

Further education

This is education for students aged 16–18, sometimes in a school sixth form and sometimes in a further education or sixth form college. Students may study for a range of courses such as A Levels, Diplomas, BTECs and GNVQs. The Labour government introduced the educational maintenance allowance (EMA) scheme in 2004 to encourage more young people to stay in further education. This means that students whose parents or carers earn below a certain amount are paid to continue with their studies.

GradeStudio

Remember that in the exam it is really important to know all these different stages in the education system. If you give a response such as, 'education you do after you've left school', you will not score very highly. A better explanation would be 'further education is completed mainly by 16–18-year-olds at school sixth forms or colleges. Students study for a range of different qualifications such as A Levels and Diplomas.' It is now clear that it is **further education** that is being explained and that the candidate understands what this is all about.

Higher education

Students are typically admitted to universities to complete this stage of their education at age 18. Today, however, universities are finding that more and more adults are also choosing to return to education to improve their qualifications or to retrain. The range of courses on offer is vast and students tend to complete degree courses or HNDs. If they want and can afford to, some may choose to continue further to obtain a masters degree or even a PhD. Higher education can be a costly process, though, and students typically have large loans to repay when they finish.

ACTIVITY 81

Read the following extract from an article criticising some of the newer degree courses on offer:

£40m waste of the 'Mickey Mouse' degrees

By STEVE DOUGHTY - 20 August 2007 – www.dailymail.co.uk

'Mickey Mouse' university degrees are costing taxpayers more than £40 million a year, a report said yesterday. Researchers found more than 400 lightweight courses on offer at 91 different educational institutions. In each case, the subject matter was judged intellectually threadbare and inferior to on-the-job training. Ministers had promised that soft courses would be driven out of universities. But the report from the Taxpayers' Alliance suggests they are becoming even more common. The pressure group singled out as especially useless a course called 'outdoor adventure with philosophy'. Offered by Marjon College in Plymouth, it features 'journeys, environmental management, creative outdoor study and spirituality'. The alliance criticised the University of Glamorgan for a degree course examining 'complementary strands of science, science fiction and culture' while the Welsh College of Horticulture was lambasted for offering a BSc in 'equestrian psychology'.

Researchers said the courses failed to give students a proper education or training.

Discuss the questions on page 84 about this article with a partner.

ACTIVITY 82

1. Do you agree with the authors that the government is wasting money and young people's time by encouraging so many students to go on to university?

2. Do you think the degree subjects outlined in the article are useful or not?

3. Some people argue that a degree should lead to a possible career, while others argue that it is a unique chance to learn something for its own sake. What do you think and why?

4. Produce a flow chart to show all the different stages a person can go through in the education system in the UK. This will help you when it comes to remembering details of the education system in the examination.

RESEARCH LINK

This is an example of how media materials can be used by sociologists. For more information look at pages 21–22 in Unit 1, Sociology Basics.

State schools and independent schools

Schools are either funded by the state (your parents do not pay for you to attend) or privately (parents pay fees to the school to send their child(ren) there). Schools that are paid for privately are known as 'independent schools'. These can be either **private** or **public**. Sometimes pupils will 'board' at these schools, meaning they will live in and just go home in the holidays. Around 8 per cent of pupils in the UK are educated in the independent sector.

Faith schools

There are approximately 7000 state-funded faith schools in the UK today and, apart from a tiny minority, these are Church of England and Roman Catholic in denomination. The **National Curriculum** is still taught to students attending these schools, but in religious education lessons and assemblies there may be more focus on the religion of the school than in other schools.

Evaluation of different types of schools

As you can see, there are many different forms and types of education in the UK today. Sociologists have different views and opinions on them, which will lead you to some interesting debates in class.

GradeStudio

Evaluation is a skill you will need to develop for the examinations, so discussing the advantages and disadvantages of different types of education is great practice for this.

Why were comprehensive schools introduced?

The main reason for introducing these schools was to try to create a fairer educational system in the UK. Before their introduction, children had to sit an exam that decided which kind of school they would attend. People were critical of this **selection**, as it tended to be the more privileged middle-class children who passed the exam. The idea behind the comprehensives was that all children from a local area would go to the same school, whatever their ability or background, and an inclusive education would be provided. Educating children from different classes and ethnicities together was also thought to be a way of breaking down barriers and making a more tolerant and equal society. All abilities would be catered for in a comprehensive school, from students with special educational needs, to the gifted and talented. Everyone, they said, would be treated equally and be given the same chances to succeed in education and in life.

Were they successful?

Comprehensives soon became the type of school that most children in the UK attended so, in this sense, yes, they were clearly successful. However, many were critical – read on and see what you think.

- Some educationalists argued that **mixed ability** teaching in comprehensive schools was not working. The most able students were not being stretched and the less academically able students could not keep up. This, they argued, led to a lowering of standards.

- To counter this, most comprehensive schools began to **set** and **stream** their pupils. This tended to result in the middle-class students ending up in the higher sets and streams and so doing better than the working-class students. Some sociologists would say that this did not make the system any fairer than before.

- Sociologists also commented that comprehensives never really got a mixture of social classes anyway, as the community the school served typically reflected a particular social class. So, an inner-city comprehensive, for example, would be dominated by working-class students.

KEY CONCEPTS

Private school – any school that charges a fee for pupils to attend.

Public school – higher-status private schools with very high fees. Members of the Royal family and the very wealthy are educated in these schools.

National Curriculum – subjects and tests that the government has decided must be done in all state schools.

Selection – choosing students to attend a school because of their ability.

Mixed ability – students of various abilities are taught together in the same class.

Setting – students are put into different classes in different subjects depending on their ability.

Streaming – students are taught with the same class for all their subjects based on their general ability.

SATs – standard assessment tests taken at the end of Key Stage 2. (The government have stopped the SATs at KS3 in 2008.)

GCSE – The General Certificate of Secondary Education is the name of an academic qualification awarded in a specified subject to students typically aged 14–16.

Why do some parents choose to pay for their child's education?

Some parents believe that their child will get a better education if they pay for it rather than sending them to the local comprehensive. Due to the high fees charged for sending a child to private school, these schools tend to be dominated by the middle and upper classes. So why do parents choose to do this?

- Classes tend to be smaller than in state schools so the children get more one-to-one attention and are thus thought to do better academically.

- There tends to be a highly academic focus in the independent sector which encourages and expects the students to do well. This means that examination results are normally good.

- There is also likely to be an extensive range of extra-curricular activities on offer to the students which they would be unlikely to be able to access in most comprehensive schools.

- With more money coming into the schools, the independent sector is more likely to have better and more up-to-date resources and facilities for the students to use.

Why are some people against the independent sector?

Some people believe that the independent sector is an unfair system of education. The following reasons may be given to support this point of view:

- Independent schools typically recruit from the higher classes in society. This may make them elitist and so reduce tolerance and acceptance in society.

- As parents have to pay to send their children to private school, clearly not all students get the same chance to go there. This does not seem fair.

- Why should some students get a better education than others just because they are from better-off families? Many would say that this is morally wrong.

- On a more practical level, private schools may be a long way from where the students live, meaning they have to travel long distances to attend. With many private schools also requiring attendance on a Saturday morning, this reduces the time that families can spend together.

Changes since 1988

The Education Reform Act of 1988, introduced by the Conservative government, brought many changes to the education system that most of you will have experienced first-hand yourselves. These changes did not, however, apply to the independent sector.

The National Curriculum

This was a huge change in educational policy, meaning that for the first time all state secondary school pupils would study the same subjects and be tested against government set targets in **SATS** and **GCSE** examinations.

RESEARCH TASK

Have a look at some private and public schools on the internet. Begin with any you have heard of already or any that are in your local area. If you are stuck for ideas, go to *www.heinemann.co.uk/hotlinks*, enter express code 7573P, and click on the following websites:

- Eton College
- Hymers College
- Manchester Grammar School
- Harrow School

Read the following statements and discuss whether you agree with them. Be prepared to share your views with the rest of the class and debate the issues.

- It's up to parents whether they want to pay for their child to be educated in the independent sector – it's their money so it's their choice what they do with it.
- Setting and streaming give students a better education than mixed ability teaching.
- Comprehensive schools give all children the chance to succeed.
- Public and private schools are a disgrace; the government should shut them all down immediately.
- Faith schools have no place in the contemporary UK.
- Comprehensive schools make society fairer and more equal.

KEY CONCEPTS

Ofsted – The Office for Standards in Education, Children's Services and Skills inspects and reports on educational institutions to monitor performance, care and standards.

Compulsory schooling was split into four key stages:

- Key Stage 1: reception and years 1 and 2 (ages 5–7)
- Key Stage 2: years 3–6 (ages 8–11)
- Key Stage 3: years 7–9 (ages 12–14)
- Key Stage 4: years 10–11 (ages 15–16).

This new curriculum aimed to ensure that all students studied what the government believed to be the most important 'core' subjects – English, maths and science. In the past when subjects such as these were not always compulsory, it was found that a lot more males than females chose science, for example. This affected the jobs that both sexes were able to do afterwards and resulted in a lack of equality in society.

What was to be taught within subjects was also set by the government, meaning that all students studied roughly the same topics and there was little teacher choice. Many are critical of this, as they feel that the curriculum is too narrow and that teachers are no longer able to use their own judgement in deciding what is best for their classes and students.

Testing has also increased dramatically under the National Curriculum – you are now some of the most tested young people in the world! At the end of most key stages a student's progress is tested in order to measure their performance against other students in the country. Monitoring of students falling below their expected targets can then take place by a Government inspection team such as **Ofsted**. Schools that are under-performing can also be identified and action taken as necessary.

New types of schools

We have seen in the earlier section that many new types of schools have emerged since the 1988 Education Act. Academies, City Technology Colleges and grant-maintained schools are all good examples of these.

Competition and choice

With all the increased testing that was a part of the National Curriculum, there was more public labelling of schools as 'good' and 'bad'. League tables of SATs and GCSE results began to be published and reported on by the media, both locally and nationally. This, and increased knowledge of and access to Ofsted inspection reports, gave parents more information on how a particular school was performing and allowed them to compare schools against each other. The aim was to create more competition between schools and so drive up standards. If schools knew they might lose students if their results were not very good then the government believed they would perform better. Not everyone agrees with this point of view, though, as league tables do not take into account the background and circumstances of the pupils and may even put schools off accepting more difficult or less able students.

To further increase competition between schools, the government also directed that all schools should publish prospectuses – this was also to increase parental choice. In addition it was decided to inspect schools regularly (Ofsted) and to publish these reports. Again, they justified this by saying it helped parents make better, more informed choices, but it also pitched schools into even more competition with one another.

ACTIVITY 84

1. Look at your own school's prospectus. How accurate a picture of your school do you think that it gives?

2. See if you can find out when your school was last inspected and what was said about it. Do you think the judgements made were fair?

3. Find the league tables for secondary schools in your local area. Where does your school appear? How accurate do you think league tables are in measuring the success of a school? What do you think are the main problems with them?

Local management of schools

The 1988 Education Reform Act also increased the amount of power and responsibility schools had over their own budgets and staff. This reduced the role of the LEAs, which had previously been very influential in determining how schools were run.

Issues in contemporary education

Vocational education

This can also be referred to as 'vocationalism' (work-related qualifications and training) and refers to several attempts by the government and educationalists to increase students' opportunities to take part in work-related learning. The move to bring more work-based skills into education reflects the view held by a lot of people working in industry that our current educational system is not preparing pupils adequately for the world of work. So we now have a range of new qualifications on offer such as GNVQs, BTECs and the work-based NVQs.

The new Diplomas take this one stage further by bringing employers directly on board with the development of the curriculum and the experiences of learning. Schools will be working in close partnership with further education colleges to provide appropriate courses of study for all pupils. Government provision of apprenticeships and training programmes for those leaving school at 16 is also an indication of how important this new development in educational policy is thought to be, in terms of helping young people to find work and providing employers with appropriately skilled young people.

This approach has not been without its critics, though. There is a lot of disagreement about whether vocational education really has the same worth and value as the more traditional, academic route. For example, many believe that it is just a newer version of the unfair, divisive system that was around before comprehensives, where the less able are pushed into doing these lower-status subjects. Employers are also sometimes sceptical about how useful these courses actually are in preparing young people for the world of work.

Developments in higher education

At the same time as this move towards vocationalism, there has also been a move by the government to get more students to stay on into

ACTIVITY 85

Copy out and match the following key terms with the correct definition:

KEY TERM	DEFINITION
1 Greater parental choice	a) English, maths and science
2 League tables	b) They used to decide how schools ran their budgets and their staff.
3 Core subjects	c) Introduced in 1988
4 Education Reform Act	d) It meant that all children had to study the same subjects and be assessed at the end of most key stages
5 National Curriculum	e) Giving parents more information on schools would allow them to make the right decision for their children
6 LEA	f) Published statistics of how schools have done in SATs and GCSEs

further and higher education. They want this to become the norm rather than the exception. Financial grants and loans have been introduced to try to encourage more young people to lengthen the time they spend within the educational system. This, it is hoped, will lower unemployment levels and produce a well-educated nation which is able to compete on a global level in the fields of industry and the economy.

Other developments

Current educational thinking seems to be adopting a more flexible approach to learning and it would seem that many of the rigid requirements of the 1988 Education Reform Act are now starting to change. Some schools, for example, are having just a two-year Key Stage 3, while others are experimenting with entering students early for GCSEs and A Levels. Testing and attainment, though, remain at the heart of any changes, with schools under increasing pressure to secure a good position in the league tables and obtain a good Ofsted report if they are to remain competitive and attract parents and students.

Big changes are also underway with the new KS3 curriculum, which aims to try to redress the balance between what all students have to do and what individual students would be best suited to studying. Again, greater flexibility seems to be central to this, as demonstrated by the government's abandonment of KS3 SATs testing. What the impact of this on the education system and the students within it will be, however, remains to be seen.

ACTIVITY 86

RESEARCH TASK
Ask your parents and teachers how they think education in schools has changed since they were pupils. Do they think these changes are for the better or the worse? Record their answers and share them with your class to make a class report.

Patterns and trends in educational achievement

Educational inequality

In the **meritocratic** society that we allegedly live in, who could blame a person for believing that how well you do in education is down to how hard you work and how intelligent you are. Unfortunately, this is not quite true, and much sociological research has been conducted over the years to indicate that success in the educational system

seems to be linked to membership of a particular social group. So girls are more successful than boys, white and Chinese students do better than Afro-Caribbean and Bangladeshi students, and wealthier students do better than poorer ones. There is no evidence that this **inequality** has anything to do with intelligence and, therefore, sociologists believe that other factors must be preventing certain groups from doing well. This is what we shall be looking at in the next few sections of the chapter: what the trends for educational achievement are and what explanations exist to explain these trends.

KEY CONCEPTS

Meritocracy – a society where a person's ability determines how well they do in life in terms of their social status and wealth.

Inequality – not everybody in society has the same chances of success.

Class and educational achievement

A person's social class seems to play a big part in how well they do in the education system; the higher your social class the more successful you will be. Figure 2.2.1 on the opposite page is taken from official government statistics and provides some evidence for this trend.

RESEARCH LINK

For more information on using official statistics as a form of secondary evidence look at pages 20–21 in Unit 1, Sociology Basics.

 GradeStudio

Data analysis questions like the one on the opposite page are great practice for the education exam, as this is a skill that you will be tested on. It is easy to make silly mistakes when doing them, so read all the information and charts/tables carefully to pull out the required answers.

The trend here is clear to see – working-class pupils do not do as well as middle- or upper-class students in education. They get fewer qualifications, at lower grades and are less likely to continue with further or higher education. All of this is likely to affect their employment and life chances. So what are the reasons for this?

Look at the chart below carefully and then answer the questions that follow.

Figure 2.2.1: Exam results differ by social class – percentage of students, by parental social/economic class, gaining five or more GCSE grades A* to C in England and Wales in 2002

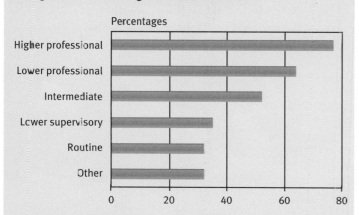

1. According to the chart in Figure 2.2.1, what kind of jobs did the parents of children who were least likely to achieve five or more GCSEs graded A*–C have?

2. What percentage of children whose parents had higher professional jobs achieved five or more GCSEs graded A*–C?

3. What do your answers to the two questions above suggest about the link between educational achievement and social class?

4. According to the report below, children with parents in what profession were least likely to go into further or higher education?

'Like attainment at school, participation in further or higher education is strongly influenced by people's social and economic background. In 2002, 87 per cent of 16 year olds with parents in higher professional occupations were in full-time education. This compares with 60 per cent of those with parents in routine occupations, and 58 per cent with parents in lower supervisory occupations.'

Source: the UK National Statistics website.

5. What reasons can you think of to explain these links between social class and educational achievement? Discuss as a class.

Explaining the relationship between social class and educational achievement

Material explanations

For most children school is free. However, it is still true to say that material factors such as poor diet, low wages and poverty can have an effect on educational achievement. Let us start by thinking of the home circumstances for many poorer students. They are more likely to live in overcrowded, poor housing where there may be a lack of a quiet space to complete homework. As their parents have a low income or are unemployed, they are also unlikely to have access to computers and educational books. Money for school trips, revision courses and sports equipment may also not be available, all of which could reduce the chances of working-class students being as successful as middle-class students of similar ability.

When it comes to the end of compulsory education, parents on lower incomes may find it difficult to financially support their child in continuing their education. This may mean that the young person needs to get a part-time job to support themselves, which could then cause problems with the competing demands of school and work. The Labour government's introduction of the Educational Maintenance Allowance (EMA) has helped to reduce these issues, but it is still true to say that a lack of money probably has a negative effect on a young person's chances of being successful in the education system. Sociologists refer to these barriers to success as **material deprivation**.

KEY CONCEPTS

Material deprivation – not having the money needed to buy items that can help children succeed in education.

Cultural explanations

Cultural explanations for why working-class children do less well in education than middle- and upper-class children focus around the idea that working-class culture is the main barrier to success. By 'culture' sociologists are referring to the working-class way of life, including such factors as language, attitudes, environment and values. It is, therefore, the way that these children are socialised that is seen to cause their educational underachievement.

Middle-class parents typically place more value on education than do working-class parents, as they are probably well educated themselves and so are likely to understand the school system better. This means they feel confident in advising and helping their children with school issues and are happy to come into schools, meet teachers and ask for help if needed. They attend more parents' evenings than working-class parents do and are not afraid to push for what they want. These very different attitudes to education are thought to be important factors in determining how well a pupil does at school.

When not at school, middle-class families are more likely to participate in cultural visits to galleries, libraries and concerts, and so from an early age the middle-class child is being socialised in a number of elements that will be both useful and valued in schools. Even the way that parents and children speak may be a relevant factor to consider. Language is crucial for success at school, both spoken and written. 'Correct' English is expected and praised and, as middle-class children are more likely to have been brought up using and seeing this as the norm, they will probably find settling into school and doing what is required easier. They are more likely to have parents who read broadsheet newspapers and appreciate and discuss the arts, for example. School life may well seem little different to that experienced at home.

Schools are often referred to as 'middle-class institutions', implying that they are based on middle-class principles and values. The obvious implication of this is that the children most familiar with these middle-class ideas will be most successful – namely the middle-class students. The sociological term to describe the idea that working-class children do not have the culture needed to achieve well in education is **cultural deprivation**.

The way that children are socialised has an effect on their success in education.

U2

SOCIALISATION, CULTURE AND IDENTITY

ACTIVITY 88

Explain how the points listed below might affect how well a pupil does at school:

- parents do not see the point in staying in education any longer than you have to
- lack of money for a new school uniform
- parents always attend parents' evenings
- poor diet
- damp housing leading to high levels of student illness
- family reads broadsheet newspapers, listens to Radio 4 and regularly visits national art galleries
- lack of a quiet space to work at home.

Schools

Finally, we should also consider the role that schools may play in determining who the 'winners' and 'losers' are when it comes to the relationship between educational achievement and social class. Teachers themselves are probably very influential in determining how well a student does. Teachers may hold certain stereotypes of pupils from different social classes and this could affect the way they treat them. Students who behave in a way deemed 'unacceptable' or 'bad' are negatively **labelled** and, as schools and teachers themselves are middle class, it is likely that the working-class students are most likely to be given these labels.

KEY CONCEPTS

Cultural deprivation – having insufficient knowledge of the culture, norms, values and customs that help children to do well in education.

If the students come to believe the labels they have been given, a **self-fulfilling prophecy** occurs. The results can be disastrous as the student becomes demotivated and sees little point in working hard at school.

Their bad behaviour could also see them placed in the lower sets and streams which will mean that not only is less expected from them academically, but they might also lose confidence in their own abilities. Evidence shows that working-class students are more likely to find themselves in the lower sets and streams and this could be an important factor in explaining why working-class students do less well at school than middle-class students.

ACTIVITY 89

Think about your own experiences at school and then discuss them with your class. Do you think you or your friends have ever been labelled, positively or negatively, by teachers? If so, how did this make you feel? Did it change your behaviour at all? Could it have affected your educational achievement?

1. Identify three reasons why a working-class student may receive a negative label more often than a middle-class student.
2. Do you think setting and streaming students in schools is a good idea, or is mixed ability teaching better?
3. Are pupils set or streamed based on their ability or do you think other factors also play a part? If so, what kind of things and why?

GradeStudio

Remember that 'identify' is a command word that you will often see in the exam. To do this well you should number each of your points, make sure they are all relevant to the question set and that they are all different.

It is not just teachers in schools who can affect educational achievement. The other students also have an important influence. By using setting and streaming to separate children into different ability groups, schools effectively create a divide between the 'achievers' and the 'failures'. In response to this, students in the lower sets and streams – and remember these are more likely to be working-class students – may develop an **anti-school subculture**. This means that they do not value or

see the point of education and do everything they can to demonstrate this. This may take the form of truancy, messing about, cheeking the teachers or breaking school rules. All this is just a way of rebelling against the system that has told them they are not going to achieve. This attitude more or less guarantees that they are not going to do well in education and so could be another important reason to help explain the trends in social class and achievement that we have seen earlier.

ACTIVITY 90

Do anti-school subcultures exist in your school? How can you identify an anti-school subculture? (Consider values, attitudes, appearance and behaviour here.) Are they associated with one class more than any other?

KEY CONCEPTS

Labelling – thinking of a person or group of people in a particular way which then determines how you behave towards them.

Self-fulfilling prophecy – often a reaction to being labelled, where a person acts in the way that other people expect them to act.

Anti-school subculture – a small group of pupils who do not value education and behave and think in a way that is completely opposite to the aims of a school.

Gender and educational achievement

On the whole girls continue to outperform boys at all levels of education in the UK from Key Stage 1 to higher education. The difference in achievement between the sexes starts at an early age.

- In England, for Key Stage 1 (five to seven years old) to Key Stage 3 (11 to 14 years old), girls scored consistently higher than boys in the summer of 2007.
- At A Level, in England, Wales and Northern Ireland, young women continued to outperform young men in virtually all subject groups in 2005–2006.
- Figures from the Universities and Colleges Admissions Service (UCAS) show that there are more women than men entering full-time undergraduate courses: in autumn 2006, a total of 390,000 applicants gained a place, of whom 210,000 (54 per cent) were women.

ACTIVITY 91

Study Figure 2.2.2 and the information below carefully and answer the questions that follow.

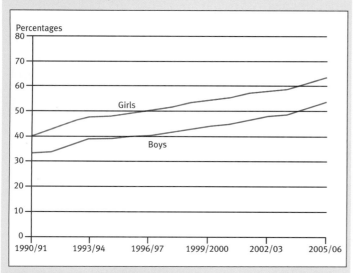

Figure 2.2.2: Girls continue to outperform boys – percentage of students, by gender, gaining five or more GCSE grades A* to C in England and Wales

1. What is the general trend seen in the performance of girls and boys at GCSE level in the chart?

2. What was the percentage of GCSE grades A*–C achieved by (i) boys and (ii) girls in 2005/06?

3. What reasons can you think of to explain the trend in the chart?

   'The subjects selected for vocational qualifications differ between men and women. Men are more likely to study vocational qualifications for construction, planning and the built environment (with almost 100 per cent of these awards going to men), or engineering and manufacturing technologies (89 per cent of all awards), whereas women are more likely to study health, public services and care-related vocational qualifications (around 86 per cent of all awards).'

Source: the UK National Statistics website.

4. Are you surprised by the information in the quotation above? Why or why not?

5. How will the vocational subjects studied by girls and boys affect the types of jobs they go into? Try to consider such factors as pay, status and career/promotion opportunities here.

6. Why do girls and boys still choose different types of subjects to study? Does it matter? Discuss with your class.

So, as you can see, a person's gender seems to play a big part in how well they do in the educational system. We now need to examine the reasons for this.

Explaining the relationship between gender and educational achievement

Feminism, home and culture

Feminism has changed expectations of females as well as giving them greater opportunities to be successful, both in terms of education and the wider society. Girls no longer see marriage and children as their only goal in life and, instead, are often ambitious and determined to be successful. This was seen in Sue Sharpe's study in 1994 – the girls she researched were assertive, confident and saw no need to depend on a man. In order to achieve their goals, girls need to do well at school and this is backed by the law, namely the Sex Discrimination Act (1975), which makes **sex discrimination** in education illegal. This has led to the introduction of a number of equal opportunities policies in schools and colleges, all of which have helped girls to achieve. Boys, meanwhile, have seen traditionally male jobs such as mining and agriculture gradually disappear, whilst 'feminine' jobs such as office work have increased massively. Males are far more likely to be unemployed than females. This uncertainty about future work may demotivate boys and lead to them seeing little point in working hard at school.

ACTIVITY 92

RESEARCH TASK
You are going to do some research to see whether Sue Sharpe's findings from 1994 are still true today. Working in small groups, design a questionnaire or an interview to investigate female attitudes and aspirations. Make sure you include some questions specifically about education too. Carry out your research on a sample of five to ten girls and then analyse your findings. Report back to your class and compare what you have all found out.

RESEARCH LINK

For more information on designing a good questionnaire and interview look at pages 4–9 in Unit 1, Sociology Basics.

An interesting idea that has been suggested to explain why boys are less likely to be successful in education than girls involves male values and masculinity. To be masculine boys are expected to look and act tough, be interested in sport and girls, be up for a laugh and to have no interest in education. Now when it comes to doing well at school this could cause boys a number of problems. Even though they know how important qualifications are in order to do well in life, their 'laddish' school **subculture** is likely to look down on male students who work hard. It will be difficult to resist the **peer pressure** and so many boys will do the bare minimum when it comes to school in order to look 'cool' with their friends.

RESEARCH LINK

For more information on masculinity, femininity and the associated stereotypes look at pages 38–43 in Unit 1, Sociology Basics.

Schools

Schools themselves also have a big part to play in determining gender differences in educational achievement. We should start by examining the role of the teacher. Teacher expectations of girls and boys are often very different, with teachers expecting boys to be more disruptive and less likely to complete their work, for example. This may mean that teachers are not as strict with boys as they are with girls and that boys are not pushed to achieve as much as girls. Alongside this is the fact that more teachers are female than male, meaning that education may be perceived as 'feminine' and 'girly' and thus not something that boys are particularly interested in.

When it comes to behaviour and attitude in the classroom, there are lots of differences between boys and girls. It is a well-known fact that girls mature faster than boys, meaning that when it comes to that crucial exam time they are far more likely to take revision and preparation seriously and so achieve better grades. Evidence shows that girls put more effort into their work and how they present it, are better organised in terms of bringing equipment and meeting deadlines, concentrate more in class and spend longer doing their homework than do boys. Coupled with this is the fact that boys are more likely to misbehave in class, be sent out for poor behaviour and are more likely to be excluded. The end result is that boys miss out on a lot of valuable teaching time and so underachieve.

A final point worth mentioning is that the subjects studied by boys and girls in schools are still very different, despite the introduction of the National Curriculum which ensures that they follow a set of compulsory core subjects. Subject choice tends to reflect wider societal gender stereotypes, so you will probably not be surprised to hear that girls are more likely to study languages, social sciences and textiles, whilst boys tend to opt for sciences, design and PE. This may be because certain subjects are still thought of as feminine or masculine, but it is also thought to be linked to the careers that males and females typically go into. Female employment rates in teaching, social work and childcare are very high and so the subjects they choose at school can be said to prepare them for later work in these 'caring' professions. Gender role socialisation could also be a factor here, with parental behaviour and expectations influencing the subject choices made by boys and girls at school.

ACTIVITY 93

Subject choices still seem to be very stereotyped. Do you think schools should ban options and instead make all students, male and female, study exactly the same subjects to make sure they all have equal opportunities when they leave school?

Ethnicity and educational achievement

When it comes to educational achievement and ethnicity, things become rather more complicated than when we are looking at, say, gender or social class. What is very evident, however, is that ethnicity does affect a pupil's educational achievement and that the ethnic group you belong to is likely to have a bearing on how successful you are. The chart in Figure 2.2.3 gives you more information about this. Study it carefully and then have a go at the questions that follow.

GradeStudio

Ethnic groups do not all have the same experiences of education. To reach the top bands in the examination you need to make sure that you are able to distinguish between different groups (say, Indians and Pakistanis) and avoid inaccurate generalisations, such as 'ethnic minorities do not do very well at school'.

ACTIVITY 94

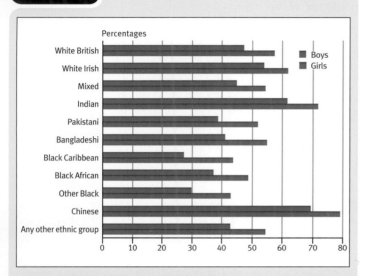

Percentages

Figure 2.2.3: Chinese pupils have best exam results – percentage of students, by sex and ethnic group, gaining five or more GCSE grades A* to C in England in 2004

Source: the UK National Statistics website.

1. According to the chart, which ethnic groups are most likely to achieve five or more GCSEs grades A*–C?

2. Which ethnic groups do least well at GCSE level?

3. What reasons can you think of to explain the trends you have identified?

4. How does gender affect how well a pupil from a particular ethnic group does at GCSE level?

All available evidence points very clearly to the conclusion that when it comes to ethnicity there are clear 'winners' and 'losers' in terms of educational success. Indians, Chinese and whites tend to do well; Afro-Caribbeans, Pakistanis and Bangladeshis less so. A person's ethnic group is likely to affect how many GCSEs they get and at what grades, whether a person continues into further and higher education and even their chances of being permanently excluded. It is clearly a very important factor that needs to be explained carefully in order for us to have a better understanding of inequalities in terms of educational achievement.

Explaining the relationship between ethnicity and educational achievement

Home and culture

Here we will be looking at how a person's home life and cultural background can affect their success in education. Firstly, let's consider cultural differences. For some ethnic minorities the language spoken at home may not be English or, if they have only recently arrived in the UK, English may be their second language. This can cause difficulties at school in terms of accessing the curriculum and communicating with teachers and other students. It also means that parents may be unable to help with homework and coursework tasks. This could obviously disadvantage a student.

Other factors to consider are parental attitudes and expectations. Indian families, for example, typically place a high value on education and working hard and are very keen for their children to do well at school. This may lead to them putting pressure on their children to succeed, which could be a reason for Indian pupils being one of the 'winners' when it comes to education.

In stark contrast to this, research from 2004 showed that 33 per cent of Muslims of working age in the UK had no qualifications – the highest proportion for any religious group. This could have a big impact on Muslim children (often Pakistani and Bangladeshi) as, if their parents have not had a positive experience of education, then this could easily be passed on to them.

A final important factor to consider links closely with social class, as it is typically those ethnic groups disproportionately located within the lower classes that do least well in the education system. Bangladeshis, for example, are far more likely to be working class than Chinese or Indians. Therefore, a lot of the reasons we considered in the section on social class and educational achievement are also relevant when it comes to ethnicity.

Schools

It is not just home and cultural factors that have an influence on how successful a person or social group is in education. Schools themselves are also very important. We should start by considering again the role that social class may play here. Some schools in working-class inner city areas have a lot of ethnic minority students enrolled. These may not do as well as schools in more middle-class locations that may attract better-quality teachers, have better resources and higher levels of parental support. So it may be the case that it is social class rather than ethnicity that is the crucial factor here.

Returning to ethnicity, however, several things in a school could have a bearing on how well a student does in education.

1. Firstly, there is a real shortage of teachers from ethnic minority backgrounds, which may give the impression to pupils that school is a 'white' experience, so limiting their chances of success.

2. Secondly, teachers may have particular ideas and expectations of ethnic minority students. A number of studies have found that white teachers subconsciously label some ethnic groups negatively and expect less of them than they would of a white student. This can be very influential when teacher opinions begin to affect the sets and streams that a pupil is put into. For some pupils this label may seriously hamper their chances of success and may even develop into a self-fulfilling prophecy, whereby the student begins to act in the way that the teacher thinks of them. This seems to be particularly true of Afro-Caribbean students, and may go some way to explaining their relatively poor performance at school.

The curriculum

Linked to this is the school curriculum, which many argue is ethnocentric. This means looking at other cultures from the point of view of your own culture and ignoring other possible ways of seeing the world. The idea here is that what is taught in schools may be seen as irrelevant by some ethnic minorities. Think about it for a moment; history lessons are often very focused on Britain and Europe and may forget the history and contributions of other cultures. Some researchers have even gone so far as to say that UK schools are institutionally racist, in that expectations and the curriculum are based on white European ideas.

With the introduction of multiculturalism (a society in which different cultures co-exist and are all accepted and valued) things have definitely got better, but it may still be the case that images of ethnic minorities in books are either largely non-existent or stereotyped. The end result of this may be that some ethnic groups feel switched off from education and so do not achieve well.

A final point to consider concerns exclusion rates for some minority groups, notably Afro-Caribbean boys. It seems that ethnicity also affects your chances of exclusion from school and, if you are an Afro-Caribbean male, you are approximately six times more likely than students from other ethnic groups to be permanently excluded from school. Obviously exclusion has a negative effect on a student's likelihood of being successful in the education system.

There is no simple answer as to why this is. Some sociologists say that it is because Afro-Caribbean students behave worse, which could be for many different reasons – a 'white' curriculum, differing norms and values, status frustration, perceived lack of jobs in 'white' society. Alternatively, it could be due to institutional racism in schools and teacher labelling.

ACTIVITY 95

What do you think is more influential when it comes to educational success, gender or ethnicity? Explain your answer.

 GradeStudio

A question in the exam asking you about differences in educational achievement according to social class, gender or ethnicity is likely to expect you to know the following:

(i) general statistical patterns of success (at, say GCSE, A Level and degree level)

(ii) factors from both inside school (e.g. teacher labelling) and outside school (e.g. parental attitudes) that can affect chances of success

(iii) the effects of both material (linked to money) and cultural (linked to a pupil's way of life) factors on how well a person achieves in education.

KNOW YOUR STUFF?

As you can see there are no easy answers here. The explanations for inequalities in educational achievement are complex and varied. What is clear, though, is that these inequalities do exist and that perhaps the UK is not as meritocratic as we would like to think. Any explanation, whether it be to do with social class, gender or ethnicity, needs to take a number of different factors into account if it is to be successful.

Check your understanding by discussing these questions:

1. Summarise the key differences between Marxist and functionalist views of education.

2. Identify and describe two alternatives to schooling.

3. Outline the main patterns of educational achievement according to social class, gender and ethnicity.

4. Can you define the following sociological terms? Material deprivation; self-fulfilling prophecy; cultural deprivation; stereotyping; labelling; anti-school subculture.

5. Evaluate whether it is school or home that has more influence over how well a child does in education.

ExamCafé

Revision

Revision checklist

Copy and complete the table below to remind yourself of the key concepts you could be tested on in this section of the exam. A good way of checking the depth of your knowledge is to write a short explanation of each one to someone, as if they were totally new to sociology. Can you explain each concept clearly, including a few well-placed examples? If you can, then you've got it.

1. Education and identity	Explanation
Identity	
Norms	
Roles	
Values	
Culture	
Socialisation	
Questions to consider:	
How do individuals learn social roles and develop an identity?	
What role does education play in this?	
2. The role of education	
Education	
Socialisation	
Segregation	
Social Control	
Formal curriculum	
Hidden curriculum	
Questions to consider:	
What are the functions of education?	
How does education socialise us?	
What are the alternatives to schooling?	

3. Changes and their effects	
Comprehensive education	
Setting	
Streaming	
Selection	
Ofsted	
Inclusive education	
National Curriculum	
SATs	
Questions to consider:	
What is the structure of today's education system?	
What have been the main changes in education since 1988?	
What are the key issues in contemporary education?	
4. Patterns and trends in educational achievement	
Inequality	
Opportunity	
Material deprivation	
Cultural deprivation	
Labelling	

Common mistakes

There is a lot to learn when it comes to the education topic, so make sure that you really do know the material that has been covered. The tips below should help you.

- First of all, remember that there are a lot of different types of schools and stages in the education system which you will be expected to know. If you get these mixed up you will lose marks. A lot of students get confused with the term 'public school' – check this carefully if you are not sure, but basically these are very expensive and very high-status independent schools, not for the general public at all!

- Next, make sure you are confident in your use of sociological key concepts – too many students think that once they have done their Sociology Basics exam they will not need these anymore. However, you will be expected to know about and use these terms throughout the education exam too. So you might be asked about the ways that education socialises children or how schools can be seen as agents of social control, for example.

- Don't get confused about the different kinds of curriculum found in education; the formal/ official curriculum is very different to the hidden one and examiners will expect you to know the differences between them.

- Learning the trends in educational achievement with regard to gender, social class and ethnicity is relatively easy to do. What is much harder is remembering all of the explanations for why there are such differences in educational achievement. You need to know your labelling theory from your cultural deprivation from your self-fulfilling prophecy! There are a lot of theory and concepts to learn here and you won't be able to get away with just throwing anything in to an answer; you need to select the best explanations for the specific question. My advice is to include concepts in your revision notes – so when you are producing your revision cards for gender and educational achievement make sure you include reference to labelling, stereotyping, gender role socialisation, segregation, subculture, social control and so on, and clearly show how they apply to the topic.

Exam preparation

Understanding exam language

Get this right and the exam will go so much better! You would not try to unlock a door without a key and the same principle applies here – make sure you know exactly what the question wants you to do and then you are far more likely to produce a high quality answer. Your 'key' is to understand the exam language that is going to be used. Your teacher will probably have already gone through this with you, but this is so important that it really is worth going over again. So what command words can you expect in the education exam?

- **From the source** – here you will need to refer directly to the source that you have been presented with. Make sure you read it carefully and pull out the exact information required of you.

- **Give an/another example** – this time you are expected to use your wider sociological knowledge to answer the question. The source might help you with this, but it won't give you the required response.

- **Identify** – use your sociological knowledge to select and name a reason/way/example (as directed by the question).

- **Explain** – as well as describing whatever you have identified, you should try to make it understandable by going into more detail and trying to offer reasons and evidence to support your points.

- **Evaluate the arguments for and against** – an instruction such as this should be a signal that you need to be writing an extended answer, in other words a 'mini essay'. To do this well you need to think about the structure of your writing – introduction, main body and a conclusion. But you need to make sure that you are evaluating as well – looking at the statement or claim from more than one point of view and weighing up all of the available evidence. It does not really matter whether you personally agree or disagree; the crucial thing is that you do address the arguments both for and against.

ExamCafé

Sample student answer

Have a look at the sample question on education and the answer that GCSE student Jess has written. The comments should show you what is good practice in the exam and what you should avoid.

> Identify and explain two reasons why children from the working class do not achieve as well at school as children from the middle class. [8]

Jess

Working-class children do not do as well at school as children from the middle or upper classes. There are many different reasons for this and I will now explain two of them.

Firstly, working-class children's parents will not be as well off as children from the middle class.

This will mean that they will be unable to afford many of the things that the middle-class children will get to help with their studies. So they might not be able to have their own laptop or study guides or a private tutor to help them. Because the middle classes can afford these things they have an advantage and this is one reason why they will achieve better.

My second point is about the teachers.

Teachers are meant to treat all their students equally, but it may be the case that they actually have different expectations of middle- and working-class students. They may stereotype working-class students as not being as bright or as well behaved as middle-class children and so they could treat them differently. Because the teacher has negatively labelled the working-class students they might pick up on this and start to act like the teacher expects them to. This is known as a self-fulfilling prophecy and is another reason why working-class children don't do as well at school as the middle class do.

Comments
By including the signal word 'firstly', Jess is showing good exam technique. This clearly separates her two points.

Comments
This second point is a really good one and is full of sociological concepts such as labelling and stereotyping that would make it a top band answer. It is quite long, though, and Jess would have to be careful in the exam that she did not run out of time. Regular exam practice in timed conditions would help her with this.

Comments
As good as this introduction is, there is no point doing one in an 'identify and explain' question like this. Top tip – get straight into answering the question.

Comments
This first point is a good one and clearly explains one reason why middle-class children may do better academically than working-class children. It does not include any sociological concepts, though, and could have easily been improved by reference to, say, material deprivation.

Comments
Overall this is a very good response. Jess has focused well on what the question is asking and has clearly identified two different reasons. She has then gone on to explain these clearly and fully. Her second point is very conceptual; her first point is less so and could have been improved.

Practice questions

Use the example questions below to test both your subject knowledge and your exam skills. Revise first then give them a go. Try to limit yourself to the 30 minutes that you would get in the exam. Once you have finished check how well you have done using your notes to help you and then write yourself the 'perfect' exam answers. Alternatively, find a 'study buddy' and do the practice questions together in exam conditions, then mark one another's answers, discussing what you have done well and what you could improve, and how.

Gender and subject choice:

The percentage of boys and girls who chose the subjects below at GCSE

	Food Technology	Design and Technology
Girls	98%	2%
Boys	4%	96%

1. (a) **From the source**, identify which subject more girls chose.   [1]
    (b) Give another example of a subject in schools that is popular with girls at GCSE.   [1]
    (c) **From the source**, identify which subject more boys chose.   [1]
    (d) Give another example of a subject in schools that is popular with boys at GCSE.   [1]

2. Concepts:
    (a) Gender role socialisation
    (b) Gender role models
    (c) Gender segregation
    (d) Gender labelling

    Which of the above concepts matches the following statements?
    (i)   All girls are labelled as quiet.   [1]
    (ii) The process of learning gender norms and values.   [1]
    (iii) The separation of boys and girls in PE.   [1]
    (iv) Girls wanting to be mothers to copy their mothers.   [1]

3. Identify and explain **two** reasons why schools are important.   [8]

4. 'Schools are the greatest influence on whether a student achieves.' Evaluate the arguments for and against this claim.   [24]

Unit 2:
Topic 3: Mass media

The key areas you will study in this topic are:

* Exploring media and identity
* Types of mass media
* Content of mass media
* The relationship between audience and media.

PAUSE FOR THOUGHT

1 Look at the following list. Which ones are examples of mass media:

Internet blog   Television   Radio   Leaflets   Satellite channels

Computer games   Newspapers   Magazines   Cinema   Telephone

Internet   DVD   Mobile phones   Theatrical plays

2 Brainstorm the different uses of the media.

Topic 3: Mass media

Mass media is any form of communication that can be transmitted to many people. But why would a sociologist study it? Sociologists are interested in society, how it operates and how institutions within it affect people's lives. Mass media can be seen as important in understanding the changing nature of society – especially in terms of the balance of power (who has it) and the effect this has on equality.

The activities you completed on page 103 ought to have helped you to see that the mass media has very few limits. All of the examples in question 1 were forms of mass media.

The uses of the media are many, but broadly speaking you should be able to fit your ideas from question 2 into these categories:

- to advertise
- to entertain
- to give information/educate
- to communicate
- to socialise.

ACTIVITY 96

Match each of the following media with at least one of the above uses:

Soap operas	The news	*Big Brother*
The internet	Party political broadcasts	
Adverts	Travel programmes	Internet blogs
Heat magazine	DIY programmes	

GradeStudio

Many students do not use key concepts enough in their work and fail to use the term 'socialise' correctly. This term means to pass on norms and values. When using 'socialise' in sociology, its meaning should not be confused with the more general usage: 'to mix in social settings for fun'.

Media and identity

ACTIVITY 97

Naomi Campbell　　*Beth Ditto*

Discuss with a partner which of these women is more beautiful and why.

Discuss what features make one of the images more attractive to you?

Which woman do you think most of the British public would choose and why?

Who and what we see as beautiful is highly influenced by the **media**. This in turn affects how we view ourselves. We are faced with many media images every day, telling us either directly or indirectly how to look and behave. Gauntlett (2002) wrote that the media provides advice about how to be attractive to others. It does so through role models and different **stereotypes**. Certain celebrities become the model for different **roles** in society. For example, some may feel that still being glamorous when you are a mother is important when they look at Angelina Jolie or Posh Spice.

ACTIVITY 98

Make a list of *how* the media can affect your behaviour.

GradeStudio

Students always struggle with the command word 'how'. When used in an exam question it is asking for actual ways and processes. So when asked how the media can control your behaviour, students often just list lots of examples of control without being able to focus on the practical ways in which the media gains control. For example, a weak answer may say, 'The media controls my behaviour by telling me what clothes to buy.' A stronger answer would say, 'The media controls behaviour both directly and indirectly. One example of direct control is through advertising. This is when the media is used to tell me what I should buy, such as what clothes are "cool".'

Development of individual identity and the learning of social roles

Ways the media affects our behaviour

The media controls our behaviour, even though control is not its sole reason for existence. Due to this, the media is said to be an informal agent of social control (see page 37 in Unit 1). It indirectly supports society's social control by:

- showing underlying values of what is good
- demonising the undesirable
- showing consequences for actions, e.g. the good guy always wins (reward/punishment)
- socialising through showing desirable norms and values
- showing role models.

In addition it controls our behaviour more directly through advertising.

All these issues will be discussed in depth later in the chapter. However, they are also important when considering the affect of the media on our own identity.

ACTIVITY 99

Make a note of each of the above ways the media acts as an informal agent of social control and give examples of each one.

GradeStudio

Be careful of using examples that others may not have heard of unless you explain them sociologically. Not everyone is familiar with every soap opera plot and character! A weak answer may say, 'The media shows that bad dies always lose like Shaun Slater', whereas a good answer might say, 'The media support society's social control through hidden messages. For example, there are always negative consequences shown for bad characters in soap operas. In EastEnders one character, Shaun Slater, has been punished for all his bad deeds by ...' Keep any examples short and ensure that you highlight the sociological point: the bad guys getting punished, a message to all.

ACTIVITY 100

Look at the following famous people, bands and types of music:

Madonna: Dance music	*Slipknot*: Thrash metal
Kylie Minogue: Disco	*Beyoncé*: R&B
Guns N' Roses: Rock	*Bob Marley*: Reggae
Marilyn Manson: Heavy Metal	

1. Divide these into two lists: dislike and like.
2. Now consider why you like them. Make a list of three reasons.
3. Now consider the style of the band or singer and compare them to yourself. Would you dress the way they do? Can you identify with their image?

Our **identity** is how we see and define ourselves. Often our identity is modelled on people in the media. If we are asked to name a person in the media we think we are most like or most wish to be like, we often can.

The role of the media in socialisation and identity

Sociologists have written that, in multicultural Britain today, the media has a place in creating new identities. One study of Punjabis in London by Gillespie (1995) found that ethnic minorities often used the media to look outside their primary **socialisation** to discover new **norms** and **values.** One girl being researched discussed the difference in gender roles in the Australian soap opera *Neighbours* compared with her own upbringing. This secondary socialisation offered by the media has helped second-generation Indian families to create their own set of norms and values, their own identity. Ali (2003) called this new identity 'Brasian' (British Asian).

ACTIVITY 101

Watch a soap opera and make a content analysis of norms and values within the episode. Before you begin, decide on the areas you wish to observe. Ideas could include norms associated with: gender, age, class, ethnicity and/or with a given public place, for example the pub or a café. Consider whether the norms presented agree with your own primary socialisation, or differ in any way.

RESEARCH LINK

Content analysis is used in many studies of the media. For more information on them look at pages 12–14 in Unit 1.

It is easy to see that if the media socialises society, it actually helps create **culture** (a group set of norms and values). In fact Gerbner and Gross in 1976 wrote of the American media that 'its chief function is to spread and stabilize social patterns'. It does so by presenting messages of what society sees as important. In British contemporary society, materialism is valued (the belief that buying and owning goods is a sign of importance). This is reflected in the portrayal of successful television characters as rich; those who own big houses and cars.

ACTIVITY 102

Which of the following do you feel British people value?

> materialism   education   religion   privacy
> modesty   celebrity   monarchy
> politicians and parliament   the traditional family
> rituals and traditions

How do you see those presented in the media?

Types of mass media

Mass media, as already defined, is any form of **communication**, whether written or technological that is invented to allow transmission to many people. Whilst every teenager is interested in many types of mass media, a sociologist's interest is not in researching iPods and mobile phones, but in understanding the changing nature of mass media with a view to understanding the *effects* of those changes. Sociologists consider how the media changes the nature and values of a society, and then whether such changes empower people, or actually divide or stratify people.

As written by Blundell (2001), important changes in media can be subdivided into:

- convergence of technology
- globalisation
- intertextuality
- interactivity.

Convergence

To **converge** means 'to come together'. One important change to media is that technology has brought different forms of media into one. For example, from a telephone you can now access the internet. This can be called the convergence of technology. Another way media has converged is through ownership which will be discussed later in this chapter.

ACTIVITY 103

With a partner look at the following mass media:

> Internet blog   Television   Radio   Leaflets
> Satellite channels   Computer games
> Newspapers   Magazines   Cinema
> Telephone internet   DVD   Mobile phones
> Theatrical plays

1. Make a list of as many examples of **convergence** of technology as you can.
2. Which form of media seems central to all convergence of technology?

In a world where digital technology (particularly the internet) features so highly, what are the possible consequences and problems? Information on the internet is very different to the previous content of the media because it is:

- largely written by its audience
- largely **self-censored**
- can be anonymous.

Use the internet to research some information on a famous person. Compare the first three sites you find through a search engine. Make a report which answers the following questions:

- Who is the site written by?
- When was it written?
- What pieces of information did you find that agreed with each other?
- What pieces of information did you find that disagreed with each other?
- Did you find one set of information more valid than another, and if so why?

KEY CONCEPTS

Socialisation – the process by which we learn norms and values.

Norms – a set of unwritten social rules.

Values – beliefs of right and wrong and what is important.

Culture – a group set of norms and values.

Mass media – any form of communication, either written or technological, that is invented to allow transmission to many people.

Communication – any form of dialogue, either written or verbal, between people.

Convergence – the coming together of different forms of media.

Self-censorship – when the audience is expected to police and monitor all necessary restrictions on the freedom of speech.

Interactivity – audience participation in the creation of media.

Was this activity easy to do? In general, finding out the source of information available on the internet can be difficult, yet obviously sources are of fundamental importance. With the growth of all types convergence, one possible effect is the repetition of information. For example, if anyone can post information on encyclopaedia sites such as Wikipedia, then others quote those definitions without cross-checking them, so the whole world could be repeating inaccurate (or certainly very biased) ideas. (This has been a popular concern of much science fiction, such as Ben Elton's *Blind Faith*.) This seems to be a good example of what Trowler in 1996 called *digibabble*; that is digital junk created by people with limited skills and knowledge.

Below is an extract from an editorial by John Seigenthaler in *USA Today*, 29 November 2005, entitled 'A false Wikipedia biography'.

John Seigenthaler's complaint is not an unusual one about Wikipedia, a reference site for many people. This example shows how 'digibabble' can have an effect on people's lives.

Interactivity

Traditionally, the media was presented to its audience. It was seen as the 'authority' or certainly above 'normal people'. Looking at the presentation of the news on the BBC in the 1950s and comparing it to the news on Five today you will see a very different image. Previously, audience participation in the media was limited. Famous exceptions included Mary Whitehouse, a 'British campaigner for morality and decency' (Wikipedia), who was known for complaining about the content of the media. Now the media is reliant on audience participation and is more **interactive**.

'"John Seigenthaler Sr. was the assistant to Attorney General Robert Kennedy in the early 1960s. For a brief time, he was thought to have been directly involved in the Kennedy assassinations of both John, and his brother, Bobby. Nothing was ever proven."'

'This is a highly personal story about internet character assassination. It could be your story.'

'I have no idea whose sick mind conceived the false, malicious 'biography' that appeared under my name for 132 days on Wikipedia, the popular online free encyclopedia whose authors are unknown and virtually untraceable.'

'When I was a child, my mother lectured me on the evils of "gossip." She held a feather pillow and said, "If I tear this open, the feathers will fly to the four winds, and I could never get them back in the pillow. That's how it is when you spread mean things about people."'

'For me, that pillow is a metaphor for Wikipedia.'

Adapted from: *USA Today*, 29 November 2005

U2
T3
MASS MEDIA

Copy out and complete the table below.

	Form of media				
	Television	Radio	Publishing	Internet	Other examples
Example of audience participation	Reality programmes such as *Big Brother*				*Add as many examples as possible*
Possible advantage	Everyone gets their '15 minutes of fame'				
Possible disadvantage	Cheap and unskilled labour				

Intertexuality

Another change in media is **intertextuality**. This refers to media that is about other media. Examples include: programmes that review films, such as Jonathan Ross' *Film 2009*; computer game review programmes; magazines that discuss soap operas; and programmes, such as *The Simpsons*, which delight in references to other shows. What other examples can you think of?

All of this makes media self-perpetuating. It heightens the interest and importance of media. In the past it was thought that new media would take over from old media; that the video (now replaced by the DVD) would stop people going to the cinema. However, that did not happen. Intertextuality only serves to popularise media further in an already media-saturated society.

Globalisation

The world is now interconnected globally, and changes in mass media both reflect and maintain that. Examples of **globalisation** of the media are:

- through cable and satellite you can watch programmes from countries other than your own
- through digital technology such as the internet you can instantly contact people from all over the globe
- international news is available at all times, both in print and online.

What other examples can you think of?

Effects of media being global

There are clear advantages and disadvantages to media being global.

Advantages

- Freedom of information should be a good thing. Countries should no longer be able to hide political crimes such as torture or imprisonment without trial. International communities should, with knowledge of such crimes, try to prevent them from happening.

- Having programmes and news from international communities allows a culture of understanding, and offers migrant workers a link to home.

- There are personal advantages, such as communication with loved ones or enjoyment.

- It supports online communities.

Disadvantages

- The globalisation of media is largely based on digital technology. However, this costs money, and globalisation could be said to divide those who have and those who do not. If some individuals do not have the money, their access will be greatly limited.

- If a government wishes to prevent freedom of information they can do so by not allowing digital technology to enter the nation or limiting what people have access to. An example of this is the Chinese media coverage of the Olympic Torch route in 2008. Only footage of countries that were pro-China and happy to host the Olympic Torch route, such as North Korea, was shown in China.

SOCIALISATION, CULTURE AND IDENTITY

U2
T3

A study by the Open Net Initiative looked at thousands of websites across 120 internet service providers and found that:

- different countries and states are filtering their citizens' access to the internet
- 25 out of 41 countries studied were filtering content
- websites and services such as Skype and Google Maps were blocked in some countries
- countries for which evidence of filtering was found included: Azerbaijan, Bahrain, Burma/Myanmar, China, Ethiopia, India, Iran, Jordan, Libya, Morocco, Oman, Pakistan, Saudi Arabia, Singapore, South Korea, Sudan, Syria, Tajikistan, Thailand, Tunisia, Turkmenistan, UAE, Uzbekistan, Vietnam and Yemen.

Other possible problems with the globalisation of media include a move from national culture to a global culture, ignoring any celebration of difference. It has been argued that there is an MTV culture, where young people around the world all follow an Americanised ideal culture rather than their own national culture. This argument seems to blame the global images directed towards young people for the erosion of national identity.

ACTIVITY 106

Do a search on the internet for images of young people from different countries and create a collage. Are there similarities between the young people in the images or are there clear national differences?

Finally, there are individual problems with the wrongful use of technology, for example where chat rooms are being used to groom victims of paedophiles.

KEY CONCEPTS

Intertextuality – media that is about other media.

Globalisation – the opening up of the world economically through production and consumption.

ACTIVITY 107

Make a table for and against the claim 'Globalisation of media is good for all'.

Use the above ideas and any others you have. To improve your evaluative skills, try to think of a reason for and then one against each idea before moving on to the next.

GradeStudio

In the exam you will be expected to be able to write an essay evaluating an idea. A possible claim could be: 'Globalisation of media is good for all'. To gain maximum marks you would need to argue for and against the claim. The best responses contain examples and use a brief introduction and conclusion. Practise writing them. A good introduction will outline what the claim is stating, defining any concepts. A good conclusion will offer an overall judgement where possible, for example: 'So it would appear that for some, globalisation of the media has benefited their lives. However, it has also enlarged the gap between the rich and the poor.'

Ownership and control

Perhaps the most influential effect of globalisation is not in the use of media, but in its ownership. An important discussion in the sociology of media is over its control and ownership. Sociologists such as Moore have categorised the trends in ownership in three ways:

1. Concentration – a small number of large media corporations own all the media.
2. Globalisation – the few large media corporations are now transnational and thus have media all over the world.
3. Diversification – as shown by convergence, the large media corporations own all the different types of media.

However, media ownership can also be divided into either:

- media barons such as Rupert Murdoch and News International

or

- public corporations such as the BBC (which is supposed to be unbiased and non-profit making). Often these are funded by a licence, which in effect means they are owned by the audience.

Table 2.3.1: Titles, channels, etc. owned by News International

Publication, channel, etc.	Base	Sector
20th Century Fox	US	movies
The Advertiser	AU	news
ALPHA	AU	magazines
AmericanIdol.com	US	online
AskMen.com	US	online
The Australian	AU	news
Big League	AU	magazines
Blue Sky Studios	US	movies
Broadsystem	US	other
BSkyB	UK	broadcast
DOW Jones financials	US	online
Far Eastern Economic Review	HK	magazines
Fiji Times	FJ	news
Fox Sports Enterprises	US	other
FX	US	broadcast
Gemstar - TV Guide International Inc.	US	other
HarperCollins	US	Books (and AU; CA)
London - thelondonpaper	UK	regional
MarketWatch from Dow Jones	US	online
myspace.com	US	online
National Geographic Channel United States	US	broadcast
National Geographic Channel Worldwide	US	broadcast
National Rugby League	UK	other
New England Business Bulletin	US	magazines
New York Post	US	news
News Digital Media	AU	online
News of the World	UK	news
News Outdoor billboards	BG	other (and CZ; IL; IN/PL; RO; RU; TK; UA)
News.com.au	AU	online
Rotten Tomatoes	US	online
Scout.com	US	online
Sky	UK	broadcast
The Spectator	US	regional
Sun	UK	news
Sunday Times	UK	news
Times	UK	news
Times Literary Supplement	UK	magazines
Wall Street Journal	US	news
Wall Street Journal Radio Network	US	broadcast

Source: the *London Freelance website*.

1. The above table outlines all the TV channels, publications and websites owned by News International. Use it to find:

   a. two examples of concentration

   b. two examples of globalisation

   c. two examples of diversification

   d. two possible examples of intertextuality.

2. Research another example of global media ownership and make a presentation for the class showing examples of concentration, globalisation, diversification and intertextuality.

SOCIALISATION, CULTURE AND IDENTITY

U2
T3

Marxists

Marxists focus on the ownership of the media as being very important in understanding how the capitalist owners control the public. Ownership of so many different types of media allows the ruling class to promote their norms and values to the public.

Pluralists

Pluralists believe that the Marxists are wrong and that it is the audience who has ultimate control of contemporary media. They argue that this is due to increased interactivity as well as the importance of ratings. What the public wants, the public gets!

 Grade Studio

Whilst theory is not a requirement at GCSE, any candidate who uses theory accurately will be credited. When looking at ownership and the media it is easy to use Marxism and pluralism to aid a discussion over who has ultimate control.

ACTIVITY 109

Trowler (1996) debated the effects of ownership and the digital age. Below are his arguments. Draw up a table with two columns, headed 'Positive effects of the digital age' and 'Negative effects' and sort the arguments accordingly.

- Daily tasks such as shopping and working will be done from home, reducing pollution and saving time.
- Copyright will no longer exist, as in the digital age it will be impossible to enforce the law.
- Censorship will become a thing of the past, as there is too much information and controlling it will not be possible.
- Gaining information will be easy.
- Race, gender and disability will not be important; only creation of interesting information. So everyone will be equal in the virtual digital age.
- The large media companies will take over smaller internet providers, which will simply continue the patterns of concentration.
- Whilst everyone will be able to access the internet, the specialist services and efficient software will only be available at an extra cost, thus further dividing the rich and poor.

Grade Studio

The changes in the media can be seen to benefit some, whilst further disadvantaging others. It is important when discussing change to remember the sociological themes of equality and power. Practical changes are not as relevant to sociology. So a candidate who discusses changes such as 'faster internet connections' will not score highly, as this practical advantage is of little sociological consequence. However, candidates who discuss the fact that 'new technology is expensive; therefore only the rich will have access to faster internet connection, further dividing the rich and poor' will produce a better answer, as they are discussing the sociological theme of inequality.

The content of the mass media

Factors affecting the creation and selection of content

All media is created, meaning that someone has made it. This means that all media goes through a process of **selection**. For sociologists the interest lies in whether the media presents a **biased** view. If so, who controls the bias and what are the effects of it?

Trowler listed the different ways in which we receive the media:

- a window – openly shows us other worlds and life experiences
- an interactive link – linking us to other people
- a carrier of information – a giver of knowledge
- a filter – passes on partial information that has been changed/altered to give us a certain view
- a mirror – reflects our lives
- a barrier – prevents real knowledge
- an interpreter – decides what is important information and presents it in a certain style
- a signpost – shows us what is important.

KEY CONCEPTS

Selection – the choices made in the creation of the media.

Bias – the deliberate or actual distortion or partial reporting of reality.

ACTIVITY 110

For each of Trowler's ways of receiving the media make a note of an example and draw or print out an image to help you to remember each different idea.

Who controls the media?

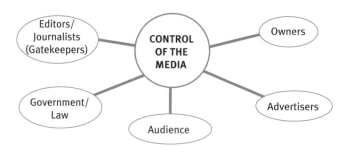

Owner? It would be difficult to deny any bias in the media, but who is controlling it? Owners clearly have some control over the content of the media. But in practical terms, how do they control it? Consider newspapers. How much do the owners actually influence the daily copy that the readers receive? The main power the owners have is that they hire and fire those within their companies who actually create media. The fact is that an owner is an investor whose interests lie in profit. However, some owners, such as Rupert Murdoch, have the reputation of being involved when they choose.

Audience? So does the main control lie with the audience? What the audience wants could be said to be the main influence over content. A look at the importance of ratings in the success or otherwise of television indicates that, to some extent, the audience does control media output. Many television shows are cancelled due to falling ratings. (Ask your teacher about the soap *El Dorado*.)

Advertising? Audiences are not the only way the media makes money for their owners. A major money-maker is advertising. A look at the many pop-ups on the internet is just one example of how advertisers use all forms of media. Even books often contain a list of other books to read. So could it be said that advertisers have the most say in content? It seems unlikely that they would have a major editorial interest. However, advertisers would not allow a programme to harm their own sales. For example, it is unlikely a company would want to advertise cosmetic surgery on television during a break in a programme showing the horrors of elective surgery. However, this does not seem to show that advertisers control the content of all media, especially media without private advertising such as the BBC.

Journalists? So does the main control lie with the **editors** or creators (e.g. journalists)? They do seem to make day-to-day choices on content. So if we look at a newspaper, for example, could we say that the editor/creator makes all the decisions on what to include? In a practical sense, this seems to be the case. They decide and act as a **gatekeeper** on what is in or out. However, they cannot print anything they like. They are restricted by laws, the audience, the owner and the advertisers.

Censorship and the law

In Britain we are said to have freedom of speech, but there are restrictions. These restrictions are known as **censorship**.

ACTIVITY 111

Imagine that you and a partner are in charge of all media. What dangers are there if all media are uncensored? Write a list of the dangers and then consider possible solutions for each. For example:

- danger – children watching sexually graphic material
- solution – not allowing young children to watch certain films/media by putting an age restriction on them.

Then report back to the class.

See Table 2.3.2 for contemporary examples on censorship. Censorship today has run into a problem. With the increased use of the internet, censorship is becoming almost impossible to implement. Self-censorship has become important. On certain websites, such as YouTube, there is an option to report offensive material, an approach which is obviously reliant on the site's users. Audiences have always played a part in the censorship of the media. A famous campaigner who wanted media to contain less swearing and sexual acts was a woman named Mary Whitehouse. Other pressure groups still exist, for example: the Christian Congress for Traditional Values, and the Press Complaints Commission (an independent body), which invites audiences to help control the media through their opinions.

KEY CONCEPTS

Editor – a person who decides on the final content of any media product.

Gatekeeper – a label for the editors and creators of media, as they are the people who decide which ideas/stories make it through to publication.

Censorship – restrictions on the freedom of speech.

SOCIALISATION, CULTURE AND IDENTITY

U2
T3

Problem	Solution
During times of war, some information on the army/military needs to remain confidential.	D Notice: all information on the armed forces has to be passed for release by the armed forces.
Some information about the government or its workings could damage society should it be common knowledge.	Official Secrets Act: an official contract signed by certain government employees agreeing not to disclose confidential material.
Media can spread some horrible lies or insults about people, ruining their reputation.	Libel/slander laws.
Children watching sexual or violent material that is inappropriate.	Certification: putting an appropriate age on material to prevent those too young from watching or using it. Watershed: ensuring media is child friendly up to a certain time, for example only allowing swearing in programmes after the 9 p.m. watershed.
Media can incite hatred based on racism, sexism, disability or other factors.	Discrimination laws: these laws apply to all walks of life, including media, and prevent inciting hatred of any group.

Table 2.3.2: Problems of unrestricted access to information and their solutions

ACTIVITY 112

Search three interactive internet sites and make a report on their censorship policies. You may need to look carefully at the terms and conditions to discover your answers.

In a democratic society that claims freedom of speech, it appears that we do not actually have this. When looking at the activity on the dangers of uncensored media, it is easy to see why we may need censorship, but are there any arguments against it?

Arguments against censorship

- No one should prevent freedom of speech.

- No one should limit what information is available to the public about the government.

- The media should report the truth, not a biased or censored version of the truth.

- The public should decide what needs censoring.

- Parents should decide what their children can and cannot watch.

- The media should remain as impartial as possible (this is known as due impartiality), presenting all the arguments for and against an issue and allowing the public to make moral decisions on the rights and wrongs of what is reported. (See also pages 117–118 on the effects of the media.)

ACTIVITY 113

The evaluation of censorship, or self-censorship, are likely topics in the exam. Practise both sides of the question in a verbal debate and as an essay. Gather examples from the media to support your arguments.

1. 'Censorship should be outlawed.' Prepare a debate for the class supporting this idea.

2. 'All censorship is necessary.' Write an essay evaluating this claim. When writing your essay remember to think about how the media is influential in the process of socialisation into the norms and roles of society.

Validity of content

Editors and other 'gatekeepers' do have legal constraints as to how they report or present information, for example it is illegal to write untruths about people (libel). However, there are other constraints as well. When considering the content of the news the following factors will be important.

- **Practical considerations such as time and space:** a news programme or paper only has a certain amount of time or a certain number of pages to fill and this restriction will affect content.

- **Practical constraints:** a media corporation with more money will be able to investigate and report on more expensive stories, such as international incidents from abroad.

- **Agenda setting:** certain subjects are considered appropriate for discussion. Marxists believe this agenda is set by the owners and may serve to distract the public from looking at the inequalities they suffer.

- **News values:** this is the idea that some subjects are newsworthy. Galtung and Ruge (1973) categorised these values into: how extraordinary a story was; whether the story was important to those in charge of society; events that are about human emotion; and dramatic events. Moore et al. (2001) stated that, depending on the type of media, certain types of news have a higher value. In a tabloid newspaper, for instance, emotional stories of human interest have the highest value, alongside stories of newsworthy celebrities. In the broadsheets, such as *The Independent*, however, the highest-value stories are the political and international ones.

ACTIVITY 114

Compare two newspapers. One needs to be a tabloid, one a broadsheet. They need to be on the same day to allow a reliable comparison.

1. Note from each:
   a. The leading story
   b. The final story (if using a newspaper with separate sections, do not include specialist sections such as sport).

2. Then count the number of stories that are:
   a. national
   b. international
   c. extraordinary tales
   d. of human interest
   e. about celebrities
   f. about crime
   g. about politics/power.

3. Write a paragraph explaining the differences between a broadsheet and a tabloid newspaper. What conclusions can you draw about how the content of each paper is selected? Use the key concepts from this section to aid your ideas.

The content of media appears to have much room for bias, whether intentional or unintentional. So does it mean that all media is untrustworthy and invalid? How can we trust the media?

KEY CONCEPTS

Agenda setting – the media deciding which subjects are appropriate for the news or for discussion.

News values – the media's decision that stories are worthy of being called news.

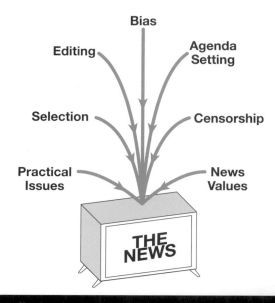

Factors affecting the creation of events and images in mass media

In a society with so much access to information, checking for validity should be possible. However, with an increasing amount of convergence and a concentration of the ownership of the media, this may be difficult.

Source 1

Tibet's ancient and fantastic civilisation and ecosystem are faced with extinction due to 58 years of mismanagement and abuse under its colonial ruler, the People's Republic of China. The ongoing destruction of Tibet will only be halted when the fate of Tibet is once again back in the hands of the Tibetans. Please contact a Tibet Support Group near you to find out what you can do to help!

Source 2

Here are some statistics about pre-1951 Tibet:

- Life expectancy was 36 years.
- 95 per cent of Tibetans were illiterate.
- 95 per cent of the population was hereditary serfs and slaves owned by monasteries and nobles.

It is because of the above facts that the Chinese believe that they are only helping Tibet. They often compare the occupation to the liberation of slaves in American history.

The above two sources show the importance of knowing where information comes from. The first source is from a pro-Tibetan website, whilst the second is from 'Everything2', an open discussion forum (posted by a pro-China supporter, who only leaves his first name). Is either source more valid? Is either more biased? The digital age allows more people to voice their opinions. However, there is no screening process for the information received. All that can be done is to acknowledge that the source may be biased and to try to find out who created the source and their background. This will give you some understanding of that bias.

Media content presentation

Having established that all media is unlikely to be a pure 'window' (Trowler), sociologists are interested in the effects of media bias and selection. In general, certain groups are consistently subject to the same bias. A look at this will show the power of the media, explaining its role as an agent of socialisation and as an agent of social control. This consistent bias leads to stereotypes.

Representations in the media

Through studies of film, television, books, music and video games, there is overwhelming evidence that certain groups are treated differently in their presentations in the media. Many argue that the effect of this is that those groups are then treated differently in society. This is known as a form of secondary socialisation. The media does this in the following ways:

- Distortion – information passes through a filter, and roles are changed to give us a certain view (Trowler).
- Repetition – the constant bombardment of the audience with one type of image makes the image seem normal.
- Socialisation – through the media we discover the desirable norms and values; otherwise known as norm-setting.
- Invisibility – not seeing certain roles makes them seem abnormal, for example househusbands.
- Role models – faced with famous examples of roles, we imitate them, hoping to gain their lifestyle.

Gender and the media

There has been much research into and discussion of the messages that the media sends out about gender. This can be looked at by focusing on:

- representations in the media
- content of 'gendered' media.

ACTIVITY 115

Using two magazines, one aimed at men and one at women, make a collage of images reflecting the content of the magazine. Then make two spidergrams showing the information you have found, the first on how women are represented and the second one for men.

Discuss and write a paragraph on your findings.

Gendered roles

The media of the 1950s to the 1970s is said to have stereotyped women's roles. However, more recent research debates whether the media still stereotypes women in the same way.

ACTIVITY 116

Table 2.3.3: The roles of women

Stereotypes in 1950–1970s:	Gender representation in 2000:
Housewife/mother Domestic servant Consumer Sex object (Tunstall 1983) Want romance/love (McRobbie 1976)	Women and men can have same skills/talents (Gauntlett 2002) Women can be strong characters (Abercrombie 1996) Women can be interested in sex (Gauntlett 2000)

1. Using the above lists, watch an episode of a television serial and decide which stereotypes of women and/or men it includes. Associate these with the relevant sociologists, for example Gauntlett (see above).

2. Use the notes from this activity and other knowledge you have gathered to write a paragraph entitled 'Gender representation in the media'. Look for the ways in which gendered socialisation exists: distortion, invisibility, role models, repetition and socialisation. Ensure you use both sociological concepts and examples in your paragraph.

Video games

Video games also have clear gender stereotypes. Provenzo (1991) did a study of video games and concluded that women are often not named, merely being someone's girlfriend or a princess. He also found that games were generally macho and that images of both genders were predominantly young and attractive.

Music lyrics

Music is another form of media that shows gender bias. Looking at the music lyrics, especially in rap, images of women are often sexist and sexual and images of men often aggressive and predatory.

All of this is evidence that the media does stereotype based on gender. These messages provide role models and then become a form of secondary socialisation.

Content of gendered media

Refer back to your findings in the activity (page 115) comparing men's and women's magazines. You should be able to see a pattern in media for men and media for women.

Ferguson (1983) researched women's magazines and found a 'cult of femininity'. She described this as a set of instructions on the norms and values of being a woman. There is now a wealth of men's magazines such as *Nuts* or *FHM* which seem to include more on how to be a man, but are also 'interest' based, with articles on men's hobbies, such as cars or gadgets. This is also socialisation on how to be man, as you will rarely find similar content encouraging women to fix cars, mend bikes or enjoy outdoor sports.

ACTIVITY 117

1. Using a weekend tabloid or broadsheet that has a women's section, write a list of subjects which the articles cover.

2. Using the list, what assumptions do these subject areas make? Consider the information you have on the stereotypes of women in the media. Is there a regular pattern? What changes do you think you would have found 20 years ago?

Evaluation of gender stereotypes in the media

It appears that the media can be sexist and does stereotype based on gender. However, an argument against this is that the media itself is not biased; it is simply a 'mirror' (Trowler, 1996) which reflects society. Another observation is that the media does not always stick to the stereotypes of femininity and masculinity. For example, in the film *Tomb Raider* the main character, Lara Croft, plays a strong female fighter who uses weapons.

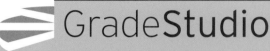

In the exam you will be expected to answer an extended question that asks you to identify and explain two sociological ideas. So when revising always ensure you revise at least two of everything!

In answer to the question 'Identify and explain two ways in which women are stereotyped in the media' a good answer would identify the ways clearly; then explain with examples. For example: 'One way women are stereotyped is in the way they are presented. Tunstall wrote that women are always portrayed as sex objects, whilst other sociologists state they are always the mother/housewife. Looking at modern soap operas such as *Hollyoaks* there is plenty of evidence of these presentations, with few unattractive women or career women. Another way in which women can be seen to be stereotyped is in the content of gendered media ...'

Race and the media

Sociologists have also researched the messages the media puts out in relation to the presentation of different ethnic groups. Many stereotypes have been in existence. Looking at the presentation of ethnic minorities in the news highlights such stereotypes. What stereotypes are present in the following headlines?

'Brother involved in honour killing'

'Increased immigration increases crime'

'Tackle crime, tackle the black gang leaders'

'Immigrants live in homes paid for by the tax-payer'

General stereotypes of ethnic minorities include: criminal, victim of crime, victim of life (e.g. starving in Africa), involved with drugs, involved in music, involved in sport. It should be easy to spot such stereotypes. However, as with gender, there are images that do not fit the stereotype and some may argue the media does not create the stereotypes – they are a 'mirror' reflecting society (Trowler).

As with gender, ethnic minorities are stereotyped through the following processes:

- distortion
- repetition
- socialisation
- invisibility
- role models.

In contemporary Britain there has been a growth of media directed at specific ethnic groups: television programmes, radio programmes, magazines and, of course, a wealth of internet sites. These may either break stereotypes or support them.

ACTIVITY 118

Stereotyping in the media is not only based on gender or race. Other areas where stereotyping is common include: age, class, region, religion, etc.

Make a class presentation based on examples of the creation of stereotypes. Choose one area to research, e.g. age. Use images in your presentation. Remember to use sociological terminology.

GradeStudio

You will need to know sociological terminology to answer mix and match questions in the exam. To aid you, write revision cards that contain the key concepts and their glossary definitions.

The relationship between audience and media

How the media shapes values, attitudes and behaviour

A major debate in the sociology of the media and in other circles is how far the media affects its **audience**. What are the effects of the stereotypes we see? Why do we have censorship? How does bias affect us?

KEY CONCEPTS

Audience – those who receive the media.

Media effects models – the different theories of how the media can affect its audience.

ACTIVITY 119

Look at the following quotes and rank them into a pyramid, putting the one most true of you at the top, working your way down to the one that is least true for you.

> When I watch violent films I laugh. They did used to make me feel sick, but now I think they are funny. I have seen so many, you cannot shock me any more. (Ahmed)

> I do watch the news, but I always wait to see what my friends think about things. They know more than I do and I usually agree with their views on the main stories. (Beverley)

> When watching a violent film I can feel my heart race. Afterwards I do feel more aggressive. (Chris)

> I will not watch violent films, I just switch them off. I think films should be for fun. I like comedies. (Ellie)

> The media creates problems. I am into rap music and wear a hoodie, but I also get A grades and have never broken the law. But the media has got me banned from public areas and labelled me a menace. (Danny)

Media effects models

Much research has been done into the possible effects of the media on its audience. The quotes in the activity above highlight four effects (covered below). There is also research that shows how the media and the audience affect each other, which will be discussed later.

Models of how the media affects its audience

1. Hypodermic syringe model

Some sociologists have argued that the media has a direct and immediate effect on its audience, like a drug being injected directly into a vein. If you watch something violent, you become violent. The following headline from *The Times* gives an example:

Grand Theft Auto withdrawn in Thailand after copycat killing

Thai distributors have pulled GTA IV after a 19-year-old killed a taxi driver while recreating a scene from the game.

(Jonathan Richards, *The Times*, 4 August 2008)

This theory relies on the idea that the audience is passive.

Do some research into the case of Jamie Bulger (1993). In what way did some people feel his death supported the idea of the hypodermic syringe model? Also research the criticisms of this death as being caused by the media.

2. Cultural effects model

This model also states that the media has an effect on its audience. However, unlike the drug analogy, it sees the effects as being much slower. Like a dripping tap, the repeated messages of the media slowly enter our consciousness and new norms are set. For example, the constant negative image of 'scrounging immigrants' leads to the public believing that all immigrants are people who take from society rather than giving to it. Certain values and behaviour are 'normalised', thus the hidden messages are a form of secondary socialisation.

3. Two-step flow model

Again, this model accepts that an audience is affected by the media, but this is seen as an indirect effect. Some people are seen as opinion leaders and they interpret the media for others. An example of this in 2008 was when comedians Jonathan Ross and Russell Brand were taken off air due to thousands of complaints, which were based not on directly hearing their show, but on media opinion of the show.

Models of how the audience affects its media

How the audience controls and uses the media

ACTIVITY 121

1. What do you use the media for? In a small group, list as many uses as possible. Use Trowler's list to aid you (page 111), but think of other uses.

   Categorise your answers into:

   Entertainment
   Communication
   Information

2. In what other ways does the audience affect the media? Think back over information previously gathered.

4. Uses and gratifications model

This model argues that the audience is not passive. The model states that the audience chooses which media to watch. The media does not change its audience and any effects of media are the desired effects of the audience. For example, people choose to watch horror films as they enjoy and are entertained by the fear which they feel. This model accepts that the media is used in different ways by its audience for different purposes.

ACTIVITY 122

Match each of the four models to one of the quotes in the Activity on page 117.

In what other ways does the audience affect the media? Think back over information previously gathered, and consider:

- pressure groups that complain about media
- interactive media such as reality television
- choice: no audience, no profit, no media.

Moral panics

Only Danny's comment (from the Activity on page 117) has not been discussed. Many sociologists of media have noted that it is too simple to state that the media has no effect on society or its audience. In fact the media often causes **moral panic**. Stanley Cohen (1972) explained this as when 'a person, situation or group is seen as a threat to society'. The media is seen to cause this in the following ways:

1. focusing on a group, person or situation
2. repeated coverage
3. sensationalisation
4. distortion
5. exaggeration
6. stereotyping and creation of folk devils
7. calling for action against the group, person or situation.

KEY CONCEPTS

Moral panic – when the media causes a group, person or situation to become seen as a threat to society.

Peter Borsay, Professor of History at the University of Wales, Aberystwyth, wrote an article in September 2007 entitled 'Binge drinking and moral panics: historical parallels?' Borsay suggests that there are historical similarities to be found between excessive drinking of the past and the modern age of binge drinking.

BEER STREET.

To provide evidence for his claim that binge drinking is not a new concept, Borsay refers to the work of Hogarth, an 18th century artist, whose prints clearly portray the negative side of excess alcohol consumption.

Borsay's article also explores the idea that the media attention surrounding binge drinking is not a new concept.

Log on to an internet search engine and find out about the issues concerning binge drinking in the past compared to binge drinking today. What do you think are the similarities and differences?

Using the information opposite, as well as the information you have found through your internet research, create a flow diagram showing how binge drinking has become a moral panic.

Use the stages/causes of a moral panic on page 118 to help. Further information can also be found in the chapter on Youth from page 167 onwards.

 GradeStudio

Candidates who are able to use sociology and show their understanding through contemporary examples will answer well. Using current news items in your exam would be beneficial.

KNOW YOUR STUFF?

The sociology of media has highlighted many sociological debates. It has shown how the media acts as an informal agent of socialisation. It has debated how the media could affect its audience, whilst countering these ideas with a discussion of how far the audience affects the media. The sociology of media has researched how the media has reflected or led change and how new media is affecting society.

Check your understanding by discussing these questions:

1. Identify and explain three uses of the media.
2. With examples, show how the media indirectly controls behaviour.
3. Define: socialisation, identity and culture.
4. Identify and explain three ways in which the audience controls the media.
5. Explain how media could be said to cause violence.
6. Define: cultural effects model; hypodermic syringe model; uses and gratifications model.

Exam**Café**

Revision

Examiner's tips

When starting revision, always break your topic into manageable chunks.

When writing about how the media affects its audience, remember to use the models. To improve your grade, always have examples for each model.

Use this table to check that you understand the key concepts for each section.

Revision checklist

Section	Key concepts
Development of individual identity and the learning of social roles The role of the media in socialisation and identity	• Identity • Norms • Roles • Values • Culture • Socialisation • Media
Definitions and types of mass media New developments and the effect of them Trends in ownership and control that discuss globalisation	• Mass media • Globalisation • Communication • Interactivity • Convergence
Media content creation: factors affecting the creation and selection of events and images in mass media Media content presentation in relation to validity Media content presentation in relation to the presentation of certain groups – looking at gender, class, age and ethnicity	• Selection • Bias • Stereotyping • Editor • Gatekeeper • Censorship • Agenda setting • News values
How the media shapes values, attitudes and behaviour How the audience use and control the media The media's role in creating deviance: moral panics	• Audience • Socialisation • Media effects models • Moral panics • Self-censorship

Exam preparation

Sample student answers

Identify and explain two ways in which the media socialises females [8]

Ethan

The media socialises people in many ways. Socialisation is the process by which people learn norms and values. One way the media socialises people is through repetition. Females constantly see certain stereotypes of women. Women are often shown as the housewife or the mother and from these repeated images they may feel that being a mother/housewife is what is normal. Repetition of 'size zero' models has socialised females into a belief that attractiveness is related to being thin.

Another way women are socialised by the media is through 'invisibility.' Media coverage of sport usually ignores women. This invisibility makes sportswomen seem 'not normal'. Girls from a young age are faced with the idea that only males achieve in certain areas as the females are 'invisible.' Another example of this is the lack of strong female characters in video games. Provenzo found that the female computer characters were either a girlfriend/relative or a weaker character. However, there are characters that go against this such as Lara Croft.

Comments

Ethan's answer clearly contains wide-ranging evidence and terminology. One good tactic is to clearly show two ways by using separate paragraphs and beginning each clearly with 'One way is...' 'Another way…' Lastly, Ethan's answer made good use of contemporary examples, showing a wide-ranging level of understanding. The critique he uses is not a necessity but gives evidence of his thorough understanding of the question.

Paramjit

The media makes women be skinny. They only show skinny women such as Victoria Beckham so all females think they must be size zero. Also women are only shown as a mum or housewife. Men are always the breadwinner and stronger than women. Also you never see female builders, so no one wants to be one.

Comments

Paramjit's answer does not have two clear ways and lacks sociological evidence. Its main problem is it lacks focus on the 'ways', really only giving common sense examples.

Toni

One way is by showing women to always be the housewife or mother. By watching this women feel they should also be a housewife or mother.

Another way is by never showing certain things. The media does not show women at the top of companies or househusbands.

Comments

Toni's answer is better than Paramjit's. It has tried to be clear about the two different ways by using two paragraphs. However, it is far too brief. It also lacks sociological terminology and evidence. One strength is that the answer is based on sociology and it shows strong but basic knowledge and understanding.

Unit 2
Topic 4: Work

The key areas you will study in this topic are:

- Different types of work
- Different experiences of work
- The link between workplace and identity
- Equality in the workplace

PAUSE FOR THOUGHT

1 What is your ideal job? Why?
2 Would you work if you didn't need to?
3 Do the most important jobs in society get the highest rewards?
4 How much will your job affect the rest of your life?
5 Who benefits from new technology at work?
6 Do we have equal opportunities at work today?
7 Do workers need trade unions?

Topic 4: Work

The workplace and identity

The development of individual identity

For adults in Britain (and for children in some other countries), their role at **work** is an important part of their **identity**.

ACTIVITY 124

Ask five adults to describe themselves in five sentences, each starting with the word 'I'. How many of them mention work? How many mention it first? (Is there a gender difference?)

In 'hunting and gathering' societies (e.g. the Australian Aborigines), work was divided by gender: men hunted animals whilst women gathered fruit and vegetables. Children learned about work **roles** from an early age. Adults of their own gender were role models and children's games often imitated adult work.

In Britain:

• work roles are achieved, not ascribed (given) on the basis of gender

• there are many different work roles, but young people have little contact with them.

How do we learn about work?

Family members influence our ideas about work; they show us how employment can affect our status, income, health, happiness and family routines.

Education prepares us for 'employment', even though it does not usually teach us how to do a particular job. The social **norms** and **values** of school usually mirror those of work.

In a typical day, we interact with many people who are at work. From them we learn what work involves and the advantages and disadvantages of different jobs.

We also learn about work through the mass media (e.g. from television, magazines or newspapers).

ACTIVITY 125

1. Identify your school's main values (e.g. respect for property) and norms (e.g. uniform rules). Would they apply at work?

2. List five work roles you meet in a typical day. What are the advantages and disadvantages of each role? (HINT: Consider enjoyment, income and status.)

The role of the workplace in socialisation and identity

Before taking on a job, you usually have to convince an employer that you have the skills, qualifications and attitude to do it well. A new recruit will then normally have a period of training to make sure they fit in and will follow the organisation's procedures and goals.

Even after this **socialisation** a new role can seem strange (remember your first day at school); it takes time for the role to become 'internalised' and part of your identity. Role symbols such as the doctor's white coat or stethoscope help to convince patients that the new doctor really is a doctor; this, in turn, makes the doctor more confident in their identity.

As well as formal training in the **workplace**, informal socialisation might take place. Colleagues might tell the employee how to get round the 'official' rules. Customers or clients might also try to influence the employee; for example, students might tell a new teacher, 'Oh, Miss Smith never set any homework'.

How people see themselves and others is affected by their experience of work. Working environments (whether coal mine, railway track, supermarket, hairdresser's, bus, office, factory, hospital or battlefield) influence people. Even though the managing director and the cleaner might enter the same building, their experiences of work will be very different.

People forced to leave work, for example through illness or redundancy, might feel their identity is damaged. Not working affects one's social status, daily routines and social relationships. Housewives and carers, for example, might feel isolated and that their unpaid roles are not really valued.

Many people look forward to retirement, but the isolation and loss of status (and income) can be a shock, particularly for those with high status jobs. The combat soldier returning to civilian life can find the adjustment very difficult.

Types of work

Increasingly people want a 'work/life balance'. For most people this means a reasonable amount of **leisure** and time with their family. To measure 'work/life balance' we first need to define 'work'.

Different definitions of work

ACTIVITY 126

How many of the following would you consider to be 'work'? Why?

- Cleaning a house
- Teaching a child to read
- Servicing a car
- Fishing
- Doing an elderly neighbour's shopping
- Cooking a meal
- Ironing your work uniform
- Gardening
- Caring for a sick child
- Selling stolen goods
- Travelling to work

The above activity shows the difficulty of dividing tasks into 'work' and 'not work'. The same task (e.g. fishing) might be 'work' for one person but 'leisure' for another.

KEY CONCEPTS

Work – a paid activity allowing people to earn money or an activity with economic value even though it might be unpaid, for example house work.

Identity – how we see ourselves and how others see us.

Roles – the parts we play in society.

Norms – rules within a culture.

Values – ideas about what is worthwhile and important in a culture.

Socialisation – the learning process in society.

Workplace – where one earns one's living.

Leisure – free time left after we have done everything we have to do.

Work (1) is earning a living

This definition says that work is a paid activity which takes place in the official or formal economy. Thus, looking after a sick child is work for a nurse, but not for a parent.

One problem is deciding where work starts and ends. Should ironing your uniform and travelling to work be classified as 'work'? They are not usually paid for by employers. These are work obligations: things you have to do to keep your job.

In some jobs it is hard to draw a line between 'working' and 'not working': a doctor might 'take work home', thinking about patients or reading about new treatments. A train driver is less likely to take work home.

Secondly, this definition leaves out paid work in the unofficial or hidden economy. Is 'selling stolen goods' work? Crime is not normally included under the heading of 'work', even if people earn a living from it.

Thirdly, this definition leaves out all unpaid work.

Work (2) is any activity that has economic value

Feminists complain that much of the work that women do is ignored, because it is unpaid. Housework, childcare and caring for elderly relatives are vital, time-consuming tasks which, in the past, were not normally counted as 'work' (even though paying someone else to do them is expensive). Similarly, growing vegetables, although unpaid, saves families money.

This second definition of work includes all unpaid work in the domestic economy, because it has economic value.

Many people do unpaid voluntary activities such as shopping for neighbours. This communal economy also counts as work according to our second definition.

An advantage of the second definition is that it gives a clearer picture of how much leisure different groups have. For example, men might have longer hours of paid work, but women, especially mothers, often spend longer on unpaid work at home.

A problem with both definitions of work is that they do not consider how the person doing the activity feels about it: their subjective view. For one person their job or cooking dinner might be activities they hate; someone else might not see them as 'work' at all, because they enjoy doing them. The section on 'People's experience of work' (pages 130–135) looks at how people feel about their work.

GradeStudio

ACTIVITY 127

1. How long did you spend yesterday on:
   a. work/school time (including any work or homework brought home)?
   b. work/school travelling time?
   c. household tasks and caring for family members?
   d. voluntary work?
   e. personal care, (e.g. eating, washing, sleeping)?
   f. leisure time?
2. Do these times vary with age or gender? (HINT: You could collect your own class data or look up the results of the Office for National Statistics Time Use Survey.)

The meaning of work

Marx thought that work was the most important activity in society (do you agree?). He also thought that all workers had a lot in common.

He thought the main division at work was between the owners of businesses (the ruling class) and the workers (or working class) who 'sold' their labour to earn a living. He believed that owners exploited workers, who would gradually get poorer and then unite to overthrow the capitalist system.

This has not happened. But do people at work have much in common?

Employment and self-employment

Most of the 29 million people in **employment** in the UK work for an employer, with four million self-employed people who work for themselves.

Public and private sectors

Most employees work in the 'private sector' for privately owned companies such as Tesco, BT or Diagio. The aim of these companies is to make a profit for the shareholders who own them.

Six million employees work in the 'public sector', for example in education, the NHS or police. The public sector does not usually charge its customers, so these employees are largely paid from taxation.

Globalisation

Globalisation affects work. Premiership football is an example. Clubs' links with the locality which gave them their names have weakened. Increasingly they are foreign-owned, employ overseas players and managers and earn their income from a global television audience, overseas tours and selling merchandise worldwide.

Many people now work for multinational companies. Multinationals operate in different countries, moving to different parts of the world as opportunities arise. For example, German-owned BMW makes Minis in Britain, whilst British-owned Tesco is expanding in India.

Sectors of employment

The economy divides into **primary**, **secondary** and **tertiary sectors** of employment.

Britain is a **service economy**, so most people work in the tertiary sector. Teachers, lawyers, nurses, bankers, tattoo artists and shop assistants all provide services.

New technology and imported goods mean that less than one million people work in the primary sector (e.g. farming, fishing or mining) and only three million work in the secondary sector (which manufactures goods from raw materials).

ACTIVITY 128

1. Do a class survey: how many adults in your households work in each sector?
2. Would students everywhere come up with the same findings as your class?

The effects of work

Adults might spend more time at work than with family or friends. Work has a major influence on the **life chances** of workers and their families.

KEY CONCEPTS

Employment – involves either working for an employer or working for oneself.

Primary sector – the sector of the economy which gathers or produces raw materials, e.g. farming, mining and fishing.

Secondary sector – the manufacturing industries, which make finished products for people to buy and use.

Tertiary sector – the service industries, such as education, retail, banking, health care, etc.

Service economy – an economy which is based on the tertiary sector.

Life chances – the chances of obtaining desirable things (e.g. good health, high income) and avoiding undesirable things (e.g. poor health, poverty).

Work and health

Marxist sociologists argued that employers might put the desire for profit before workers' (or consumers') health. However, health and safety laws and the Working Time Directive (which limits the normal working week to 48 hours) have generally improved working conditions in Britain.

However, work still affects employees' physical or mental health and life expectancy.

ACTIVITY 129

How might these factors affect workers' health? Are there other risks at work?

Machinery	Deadlines	Shift work
Low pay	Toxic chemicals	Noise
Driving	Long hours	Heavy lifting
Conflict	Working at heights	Computers

Some occupations (e.g. construction) have an above average risk of accidents and injury. Some have a risk of physical attack; Schlosser (2002) found that more restaurant workers than police officers were murdered at work in the USA in 1998.

Toxic substances are a risk in some jobs: asbestos can cause fatal illness many years after its fibres are inhaled. Until the recent smoking ban, 'passive smoking' was seen as a risk for workers in pubs and restaurants.

Some jobs might lead to an unhealthy lifestyle (e.g. a lack of exercise, rushed meals, heavy drinking with workmates). Others might have high stress levels or long working hours. Some people find shift work or night work difficult to adapt to.

Low pay might harm health if workers cannot afford satisfactory housing, heating or food for themselves and their families.

The most damaging working conditions today are generally experienced by workers in less economically developed societies who produce goods consumed in more economically developed or Western societies. Clark (2007) studied the three million workers making toys in China and suggested long hours (often 15 hours a day, seven days a week) and dangerous working conditions could seriously harm workers.

Long working hours in countries such as China can be damaging to employees

'Li Mei is worn out, so she looks older than her 18 years. Her hair is in a smooth black ponytail, but her skin is bad from too little daylight and she has many cuts on her hands. Her neck, chest and forearms are heavily mottled with the raised red patches of allergy caused by toxic chemicals, which she scratches as she speaks. She coughs a lot, has chronic aches and pains, frequent headaches and blurred vision. All these ailments have appeared during the past two years.'

Adapted from 'The Real Toy Story' by Eric Clark (Black Swan, 2007) taken from the *Daily Telegraph* Saturday magazine.

Work and income

For most people their job is their main source of income. Incomes are very unequal in Britain; there is a minimum wage but no maximum wage. Functionalist sociologists said that society uses unequal pay to make sure the most important jobs are done by the most talented and hard-working people. However, Weber, a sociological theorist, said that workers use their power to obtain higher pay.

ACTIVITY 130

Look at this list of jobs:

nurse, teacher, footballer, refuse collector, artist, soldier, hairdresser, celebrity chef, estate agent, train driver, MP, school cook, farm worker, film star, city bond dealer, managing director, checkout operator, army general, cosmetic surgeon.

1. Choose: a) the three most important for society
            b) the three most highly paid.

   Do they match?

2. Compare your answers with other class members.

When considering the link between work and standard of living, we need to ask:

- What is the weekly wage or monthly salary?
- Does income vary from week to week? (For example, sales staff might earn commission.)
- How secure is the job?
- Will it lead to promotion?
- Do extra ('fringe') benefits increase pay? (For example, John Lewis staff are 'partners' and receive a share of profits each year.)

- What about retirement? Low-paid workers usually have low incomes after retirement. Some jobs offer an occupational pension. Public sector workers (e.g. doctors, teachers) receive an 'index-linked final salary pension'. Most private sector companies have stopped these because of their cost.
- What are the family's expenses? 'Dinkies' (double income, no kids) might be better off than families with one earner and young children to support.

Earnings are linked to gender, age and qualifications. Table 2.4.1 shows average weekly gross earnings for men in the UK in 2005, by age and qualifications:

Table 2.4.1: Average weekly gross earnings for men in the UK in 2005, by age and qualifications

	25–34	35–44	45–54	55–59
Degree	£619	£810	£862	£732
A Level	£446	£545	£536	£436
No qualifications	£325	£359	£366	£335

Source: adapted from Labour Force Survey, ONS, Social Trends 36, Palgrave Macmillan 2006

ACTIVITY 131

1. How valuable are: (i) A levels; (ii) a degree?
2. The earnings figures are averages. Does this matter? (HINT: Are all degrees equally 'valuable'? Does everyone choose a job for its pay?)

The £30m man: seam of riches from miners' claims

One claimant received just 50p but lawyer made huge profit

A solicitor who specialises in claiming compensation for sick coal miners has banked a personal profit of more than £30 million from the government-funded scheme. The three-partner firm of solicitors has been paid more than £140 million from the public purse for its work on coal miner health claims.

The solicitors registered more than 90,000 claims by former British Coal workers with dust-related lung disease or a hand condition caused by vibrating machinery.

According to government figures last year, the average legal fees paid to the solicitors for their work on each settled claim was £2,264, only £25 less than the average compensation awarded to each of its clients of £2,289.

More than 760,000 claims were made by law firms across Britain. When the final payment has been made next year, it is estimated that £4,100 million will have been paid in compensation and the claimants' solicitors will have earned a total of £1,300 million.

Tens of thousands of miners were awarded less than £1,000 in compensation. The smallest award was 50p. More than 19,000 claimants died before they received anything.

During negotiations to set the solicitors' fees there seems to have been no appreciation of what the National Audit Office called 'the potential economies of scale to be gained (by individual firms) from processing large numbers of claims'. Any law firm with sufficient would-be claimants was sitting on a goldmine.

Adapted from Andrew Norfolk, *The Times*, Monday 9 June 2008

ACTIVITY 132

What does this article suggest about the life chances of different workers?

Work and family life

In what other ways might work affect family life?

- Long hours, or partners working on different shifts, affect how much leisure time families share.

- Some jobs (e.g. working on oil rigs) separate family members for long periods.

- Work affects family roles: if both partners work, they might share housework and decisions more; grandparents might help with childcare in extended families; alternatively, the wife might be left with a 'dual burden'.

- Work affects the family's status in the community.

- Work can affect how people spend their leisure time: some employers offer leisure activities and social clubs. Work colleagues might become friends outside work. Some employees enjoy work so much or have such demanding jobs that work extends into their leisure time: an 'extension' relationship between work and leisure. Other jobs might be exhausting and stressful, with leisure used to forget or recover from work: this is an 'opposition' relationship. However, many jobs might have little effect on leisure activities, giving a 'neutral' relationship between work and leisure.

- There is a link between work and family breakdown. Some jobs put extra stress on relationships: long hours, time spent apart or opportunities to meet other potential partners can lead to higher rates of divorce or separation. Not having work can be particularly damaging for family relationships.

The causes of unemployment

Many people in the UK are 'economically inactive' (18 million in 2007). Housewives, househusbands, full-time students, carers, disabled, ill and retired people are *not* counted as unemployed. Of the 31,700,000 economically active people in 2007, 29 million had a job and 1,700,000 were unemployed. For many years after the Second World War there was 'full employment' in Britain, with more vacancies than people looking for jobs. Why has **unemployment** reappeared since the 1970s? Why did it start to rise rapidly in 2008?

1. **The economic cycle:** Economies experience periods of growth during which consumers feel confident and spend money, so businesses grow and employ more workers. Unemployment falls in these periods of boom. At other times the reverse happens: consumers spend less because of worries about rising prices or debt. When sales fall, employers might make employees redundant, leading to a recession. During the 1984 and 1993 recessions, unemployment reached three million. An early effect of the 2008 'credit crunch' was unemployment among bankers, construction workers and estate agents. By the end of 2008 nearly 2 million people were unemployed and in 2009 Britain officially entered recession.

2. **New technology:** Some jobs disappear due to advances in technology. Machines such as combine harvesters do the work of many farm labourers. In automated factories, computer-controlled machines reduce the need for assembly line workers. Online shopping and banking, cash-points and automatic ticket machines all reduce jobs.

3. **Industrial decline:** Industries decline because people no longer want the product or service

KEY CONCEPTS

Unemployment – people aged 16+ who looked for jobs in the last four weeks and could start work in the next two weeks, (or are waiting to start a job in the next two weeks) are said to be unemployed (according to the International Labour Organization definition).

(e.g. typewriters, vinyl records) or because of foreign competition. Manufacturing industries such as shipbuilding have almost disappeared due to foreign competition. Many businesses operate globally and move manufacturing to countries such as China where labour is cheaper. This type of unemployment is called structural unemployment.

4. **A growing labour force:** More workers can increase unemployment. The increased employment of women, the free movement of labour through the EC and the trend for older people to work beyond retirement age have increased the UK labour force. In 1992, 28,400,000 people in the UK were economically active. What was the figure by 2007?

5. **Frictional unemployment:** There will always be some people who are 'between jobs'. This is frictional unemployment.

6. **Seasonal unemployment:** Some jobs only operate for part of the year, leading to seasonal unemployment. Exam invigilation and fruit picking are two examples. Are there others?

ACTIVITY 133

What caused unemployment in the following cases? Name the type of unemployment from the list above.

I've just finished working in a show. Next month I'm starting work as a singer and dancer on a cruise ship. I'm really excited.	It's dead here in the winter. In the summer I work in one of the hotels. I can never save any money. Maybe I should move away.
I made toys for 25 years, but they shut the factory down. It's cheaper to make toys in China. I'll never get another job now.	I used to sort out people's car insurance. I used to like meeting customers. Many people do their insurance online now, so they closed the office.
I worked as an estate agent but in the 2008 'credit crunch' people stopped buying houses and so I lost my job. My partner, a builder, lost his job too. We're struggling to pay the mortgage.	There were 800 people on the assembly line. They've put in robots now: nearly everything is automatic, including the paint spraying, which I did. They make more cars today with only 200 workers.

The distribution of unemployment

Some groups have a higher risk of unemployment than others.

Social class: Generally the working class experiences higher unemployment, especially those in unskilled or semi-skilled manual jobs. The better educated and those in middle class occupations, especially professionals and managers, usually have a lower risk of unemployment. However, the 2008 'credit crunch' has put many jobs at risk.

Gender: Male unemployment is higher than female unemployment and men are more likely to experience long-term unemployment. Unemployed men have often lost a full-time job; unemployed women are often returning to work after caring for their family.

Ethnicity: Unemployment is higher for non-white ethnic groups. In 2004, white men and women had an unemployment rate of about 5 per cent; for Indians it was slightly higher. The rate was over 10 per cent for men from black Caribbean, black African, Pakistani, Bangladeshi and ethnically mixed groups. For women, the rate was over 10 per cent for black African and ethnically mixed groups and 20 per cent for Pakistani women.

Region: There used to be a 'north/south divide' in unemployment, with the highest rates in northern England, Scotland, Wales and Northern Ireland, and the lowest in southern England. However, 2006 figures show England (5.4 per cent) has higher unemployment than Scotland, Wales or Northern Ireland.

Age: Young people are at risk because it is hard for them to compete with more experienced workers. However, the older workers are the more likely they are to be unemployed for a long time: 40 per cent of unemployed men aged 50–64 have been out of work for at least a year. Why do you think this is?

People's experience of work

Technological developments

Simple technology in traditional societies

Hunters and gatherers used simple technology (e.g. spears and bows) to meet their needs. They lacked the 'consumer goods' (cars, mobile phones, etc.) of industrial societies, but lived in balance with their environment, preserving natural resources and avoiding pollution.

Mass production in industrial societies

Before the Industrial Revolution, goods in Britain were normally produced in small quantities by skilled craft workers. The Industrial Revolution led to the mass production of goods in factories using:

- mechanisation (powered machinery)
- division of labour: jobs were broken into small parts and each worker specialised in just one part.

Businessmen like Henry Ford set up assembly lines along which the product slowly travelled; each worker completed their task until the finished product rolled off the end of the line. Ford produced 16 million Model T cars between 1908 and 1927, cutting assembly time to 1.5 hours per car. The cars were black because black paint dried fastest.

Many consumers could afford the mass-produced goods, but employees often found assembly line work noisy, exhausting, repetitive and isolating.

ACTIVITY 134

A group agree to make 200 packed lunches for charity walkers. Discuss which is better:

1. each individual producing 25 lunches
2. setting up an assembly line.

Automation

Recent developments in computer technology have transformed some manufacturing work. Modern car assembly lines like those set up in Britain by BMW need fewer workers because robots do a lot of the physical work. Employees need the skills to solve any problems that occur, but when production is running smoothly some might just be 'supervising' the machines.

Computerisation

IT developments are affecting nearly all forms of work, not just manufacturing. Office work is transformed by the use of computers; electronic communication means that those who are away from their workplace (e.g. delivering parcels, working from home or on the train) can still be in instant communication. GCSE examiners, who used to receive courier-delivered parcels of scripts, now receive scripts electronically for on-screen marking.

The advantages and disadvantages of changing technology

Advantages for employers

- Fewer geographical barriers: customers can shop online; staff can work from home (teleworking); work can be sent 'offshore' to cheaper, skilled staff in countries such as India.
- Lower staff costs: New technology (e.g. assembly lines and robots) can replace workers and might

produce more or better-quality work (they do not go on strike, get distracted or feel a bit rough after a late night). Electronic checkouts, for example, collect detailed information about sales and stock levels.
- More productivity: IT can increase the amount of work done by employees.
- More surveillance of staff: IT records what time staff log on, what websites they visit and how much work they do (e.g. where a delivery driver is). Staff members can always be contacted.
- More flexibility: businesses respond faster to changing circumstances: if ice-cream sales rise because the sun comes out, suppliers can be alerted instantly.

Disadvantages for employers

- Cost: technology is expensive to develop and breakdowns can paralyse the business.
- Risk: with so much electronic data, businesses are vulnerable to crime from employees or outsiders. Data security is a major problem: the government recently 'lost' the records of prisoners and of families who claim child benefit.
- Customer resistance: one in three households cannot access the internet and many customers prefer a 'real person' to an automated telephone line or call centre.
- Employee resistance: new technology can reduce staff morale and job satisfaction, for example if the pace of work is too fast or social relationships at work are harmed. Call centre staff, for example, often report low job satisfaction.

New technology and employees

For those who lose their job or find retraining difficult new technology is clearly harmful. But, in the long run, is changing technology good or bad for workers?

Alienation

Alienated workers might react in negative ways. (How might alienated students at school respond?)

KEY CONCEPTS

Automation – the use of automatic (or computer-controlled) machinery.

Computerisation – the use of electronic machines capable of storing and processing information and controlling other machines.

Alienation – a situation where the worker gains no satisfaction from their job.

Marx (in the 1800s) was pessimistic: he thought all work in capitalist societies was alienating. The ruling class exploited the working class in order to make a profit: they did not pay workers their real value and workers had no real satisfaction or control over their work or the products they made.

Blauner (1964) thought that worker alienation depended on the technology used. He said alienation had four features (as shown in Table 2.4.2).

Table 2.4.2: Features of alienation at work

Alienated at work	Not alienated at work
1. Feeling **powerless**: having no control over your work or working conditions	1. Feeling you have some **control** at work
2. Doing **meaningless** work: seeing no point in what you do	2. Feeling your work is **meaningful** and worthwhile
3. Feeling **isolated** from other people	3. Feeling you **belong** at work and are part of a community
4. **Self-estrangement**: feeling dissatisfied and not involved with the work	4. Being **involved**: feeling you can use your ability and achieve your potential

Blauner found high levels of alienation among car assembly line workers. When he looked at an automated chemical plant he found less alienation. Blauner was optimistic that new technology would reduce alienation.

ACTIVITY 135

Is it just technology that determines whether workers feel alienated? (HINT: Think about bullying, for example.)

New technology and skills

A positive view of new technology is that workers develop new skills (**reskilling**). Some jobs in the IT industry are highly skilled (e.g. software engineer) and computer technology gives designers, architects, photographers and film makers new opportunities for creative work.

A negative view of new technology is that it **deskills** work, leaving workers with simple, repetitive tasks. Even in the automated chemical plant, the main skill needed was the ability to read a dial.

Deskilling is seen in the fast food industry where low-paid staff have little scope for initiative: the machine, not the employee, decides how long to cook the burger and how much coffee to put in the cup. Staff might be given different jobs (job rotation) but each

one requires limited skill. Ritzer (1996) thought that these 'McJobs' were spreading to other industries.

Call centres

Many organisations (such as banks, IT companies, NHS Direct) use call centres, where staff with a computer terminal and telephone headset deal with customer calls.

Is call centre work alienating? It is often low paid and can be very stressful. Some staff complain of repetitive work, being 'tied' to their desk, having no time to recover before receiving the next call, not using all their skills (especially if following a strict script) and being too closely monitored (so they do not spend too long on calls, for example).

Call centres have an average annual staff turnover of 25 per cent (meaning that a quarter of the workforce leaves and is replaced each year). However, job satisfaction varies considerably between call centres.

ACTIVITY 136

Which features of alienation might be experienced in a call centre?

Changing patterns of work

Flexible working

'Nine to five' describes many people's idea of a 'normal' job. But how true is this today? Part-time working has increased; more jobs require people to work 'unsocial hours' to meet the demand for service '24/7'; and various forms of flexible working (such as **flexitime**) are attractive to employers and/or employees.

Some flexible working arrangements benefit employers. If businesses are much busier at certain times of the year, 'annualised hours' allow them to use staff efficiently: workers know how many hours they will work each year but their weekly hours will vary. Shops and supermarkets employ part-timers so they can match staff numbers to customer numbers at different times of the week.

KEY CONCEPTS

Reskilling – a process which increases the skill required to perform tasks.

Deskilling – a process which reduces the skill required to perform tasks. (For example, a manual camera requires the ability to focus and set the aperture and shutter speed; an automatic camera only requires one to 'point and shoot'.)

Flexitime – Employees have some choice about when they work their agreed weekly hours.

Table 2.4.3: Percentage of UK workers with flexible work patterns, 2007

	Full-time females	Full-time males	Part-time females	Part-time males
Flexitime	15	10	9	7
Annualised hours	5	5	4	3
Term-time working	6	1	11	5
Job sharing			2	1
4½-day week or 9-day fortnight	1	2		
Total	27	18	26	16

Adapted from the Labour Force Survey, ONS, in Social Trends 38, 2008, Palgrave Macmillan

Pressure for other flexible working arrangements has come from the government and workers. Balancing work and family life is difficult, especially for families with children or other caring responsibilities. The government intended that, from 2009, all parents with children under 16 would be able to request flexible working.

A recent report suggests that these 'remote workers' have longer hours than other people, perhaps working early in the morning or late at night. However, they seemed happy spending more time on their laptops and phones, because they liked the freedom to work when and where they chose. Would you be?

U2
T4
WORK

ACTIVITY 137

Look at the figures in Table 2.4.3.

1. Which are the two most common flexible working patterns for:
   (i) full-time workers?
   (ii) part-time workers?

2. Which businesses might introduce 'annualised hours'?

3. Which gender is more likely to have term-time working? Why?

4. What are the advantages and disadvantages of job sharing?

5. Speak to two people who work flexibly. What do they do? How do they feel about it?

Teleworking

New technology makes it possible for more people to work from home using a phone and computer. Teleworking has increased rapidly. In 2005, 8 per cent of people in employment were teleworkers, mainly men in professional or managerial jobs. Would you prefer working from home?

Growing numbers of people can actually work anywhere: they do not have to 'go to work' to 'do their work': home, the car, the train or the café can all be places of work.

CASE STUDY: THE MINI

Although British car manufacturers developed exciting cars such as the Mini, car assembly lines often had a poor reputation for strikes, absenteeism, low productivity and unreliable cars.

BMW bought the Mini brand and makes the new Mini at Cowley in Oxford. Their successful factory combines new ways of working with new technology.

- £230 million was invested in a high-tech production line.
- 700 cars a day are built, mainly to order.
- Parts of the plant operate for up to 134 hours a week.
- The 4700 associates (staff) are highly trained.
- Trade unions agreed a very flexible working pattern, so BMW responds quickly to changing demand.
- Associates work in small teams which can make production decisions, rotate jobs and are responsible for meeting targets.
- Regular team meetings have led to over 8000 improvements suggested by associates being introduced.
- Associates receive performance-related pay, share in profits and have facilities such as an on-site dentist, optician and counsellor.

(Adapted from www.bized.co.uk and from www.bmwgroup-plant-oxford.com)

Work satisfaction

> ### *Plenty to smile about working underground*
>
> Coal's image as a dirty, dangerous job has not changed but average earnings of £40,000–£50,000 a year means UK Coal has little difficulty in filling its handful of vacancies. Overtime and bonuses can boost earnings to £70,000 plus and compensate for a demanding job.
>
> Graham Clamp, 26, was one of the lucky candidates when UK Coal received 100 applications for 20 jobs at Daw Mill.
>
> He says: 'I enjoy the work and don't think about the dangers. There's strict safety procedures and you work in a team, helping each other. My dad's been in the industry for 30 years and he didn't discourage me. I enjoy the money of course. The job's well paid and I think I can look forward to a new career.'
>
> Adapted from R Gribben www.jobs.telegraph.co.uk, 11 September 2008

ACTIVITY 138

Read the extract in the box above.

1. What attracts Graham Clamp to his job? Would you find his job satisfying?
2. Go to *www.heinemann.co.uk/hotlinks* and enter express code 7573P. Click on the *Daily Mail website* link to find out why hairdressers are so happy at work.

KEY CONCEPTS

Intrinsic satisfaction – comes from the enjoyment of the actual job.

Extrinsic satisfaction – comes from outside the job – high pay or perks – rather than the job itself.

Intrinsic satisfaction

Some jobs are more likely to give **intrinsic satisfaction**. Jobs requiring a range of skills (e.g. teaching, designing furniture, operating on patients) are likely to be more enjoyable than jobs which are boring and repetitive. If 'McJobs' are growing, fewer workers might have intrinsic satisfaction in future.

ACTIVITY 139

1. Ask two people whether their job is more or less satisfying than, say, five years ago. Ask them why.
2. List five jobs you would really enjoy. Jot down why. Work in pairs and compare answers.

Social relationships

The relationships people have with their boss, colleagues and clients can make work enjoyable. Isolation (or stressful relationships) can reduce job satisfaction, although some people prefer working on their own.

Social status

The status which a job gives can be an important source of satisfaction and an important part of a person's identity. Phrases such as 'a good worker', 'a respected colleague' can make people feel they are valued.

Extrinsic satisfaction

For some people the main satisfaction from work comes from the fact that it gives them the time and money to enjoy their life outside work. The money might be the main reward for dangerous, boring or alienating jobs. Long holidays, a three-day weekend or cheap air travel might also give **extrinsic satisfaction**.

People who look for extrinsic satisfaction are said to have an 'instrumental attitude' to work: they just see work as a 'means to an end'.

Remember, a job can give more than one form of satisfaction. Jobs with intrinsic satisfaction are often also highly paid. People who 'only work for the money' might earn less than people who say they enjoy their work.

The 2004 British Social Attitudes Survey asked what were the most important factors to consider when choosing a career. Men and women gave very similar answers, which are shown in Table 2.4.4.

Table 2.4.4: Relative importance of different factors when choosing a career

A secure job	36%
Interesting work	25%
A good work/life balance	20%
Good pay	10%
Opportunities for promotion	8%
A chance to help others	1%

Adapted from British Social Attitudes Survey, National Centre for Social Research In Social Trends 36, 2006, ONS, Palgrave Macmillan

The recent Work/Life Balance Survey found that most people were satisfied with their job security, their work and their working hours. Their main concerns were too much work, worrying about the job outside work and not enough pay.

Work and family life

Not everyone enjoys work, but working is generally much less damaging to individuals and families than unemployment (especially long-term unemployment) as shown in Table 2.4.5.

Table 2.4.5: The harmful effects of unemployment

On the individual	On the family
Lack of social status and self-esteem: feeling useless and a burden; the stigma of having to claim benefits	Financial problems; risk of growing debts and loss of home; unable to buy treats for children
Isolation and boredom: loss of friendships from work; more free time but little money to spend on leisure activities	Family conflict; higher levels of domestic violence and a higher risk of divorce
Worse mental health, e.g. stress, depression, anxiety due to worries about family and debts	Readjustment of family roles due to the changing balance of power in the family
A less healthy lifestyle (e.g. more smoking and alcohol use, less physical activity) and worse physical health	Unable to be the sort of role model to children that you would like

Equality in the workplace

Fair treatment at work is an important social issue. Pressure groups (such as those for the disabled) and **trade unions** have campaigned for **equal opportunities**. Governments have passed laws and given the Equality and Human Rights Commission (EHRC) responsibility for equal rights.

Areas of concern

Career opportunities

Some groups find it hard to get a job in the first place. Educational achievement affects opportunities, as does the recruitment process, which can lead to **discrimination** against some workers.

Once appointed, it might be more difficult for some groups to get promoted to higher-status jobs, leading to 'vertical segregation' at work.

KEY CONCEPTS

Trade union – an organisation which represents the interests of a group of workers, especially in negotiations with employers.

Equal opportunities – a situation where people have an equal chance of success, regardless of their ascribed characteristics (e.g. gender, ethnic group, age, disability).

Discrimination – treating people unfairly, including:

- direct discrimination (e.g. saying applicants must be male)
- indirect discrimination (e.g. not giving an age limit, but saying 'applicants must have obtained their degree in the last five years')
- harassment (e.g. mocking people because of their sexual orientation)
- victimisation (e.g. picking on someone who complains of age discrimination).

Equal pay – where different types of worker (e.g. men and women) receive the same pay if they work for the same employer and do the same work (or work of similar value).

Pay

Some jobs are much better paid than others. Sociologists ask, firstly, are some groups concentrated in lower-paid jobs? Secondly, do all groups receive **equal pay** (the same pay for doing the same job)?

Working conditions

Many other factors affect equality at work, such as working hours, flexible working opportunities, holiday entitlement, health and safety at work and building layout. Might conditions which are fine for one group be unsuitable for another?

The influence of gender, ethnicity and age on employment

Table 2.4.6: Employees saying they had been treated unfairly at work in the last two years (2005–2006), by reason. (Respondents could choose more than one answer.)

Age	12%
Long-term illness	11%
Accent or way I speak	7%
Race or ethnic group	6%
Disability	6%
Physical appearance	6%
Gender	5%
Nationality	5%
The way I dress	5%
Union membership	5%
Colour of skin	4%
Religion	4%

First Fair Treatment at Work Survey, Dept of Trade & Industry, Social Trends 38, 2008, Palgrave Macmillan

ACTIVITY 143

Look at Table 2.4.6.

1. What percentage of responses might relate to: (a) gender, (b) ethnicity, (c) age?

2. Could 'the way I dress' indicate discrimination at work? Why might employers have rules about dress?

3. Do you think everyone represented in the table was actually treated unfairly? Might others have been treated unfairly without realising or without telling the interviewer?

Gender and employment

In the early 20th century, married women were a 'reserve army of labour'. They were employed when needed (especially in wartime), but otherwise were expected to play the mother-housewife role.

Women's employment has increased in recent years (while men's has fallen), and it is now 'normal' for wives and mothers to have paid work. Women with dependent children have an employment rate of 67 per cent (it is lower for single mothers).

Table 2.4.7: UK employment rates for women and men

	1971	2006
Women	56%	70%
Men	92%	79%

Adapted from Labour Force Survey, ONS, Social Trends 37, 2007, Palgrave Macmillan

There are many reasons for the increased employment of women, including:

- more service sector jobs
- more part-time jobs
- fewer births
- equal opportunities laws, such as the Equal Pay Act and Sex Discrimination Act
- changing attitudes due to women's liberation
- more financial pressure on families.

Why do women earn less than men on average?

Part-time work: Men often work longer hours. Many women work part-time, often because their family responsibilities give them a **dual burden**.

Horizontal segregation: Men and women often do different jobs; jobs traditionally done by women such as caring, catering, cleaning, clerical and retail work are often lower paid.

Vertical segregation: Men are more likely to be in senior positions at work than women. There might be an invisible 'glass ceiling' which women find it had to break through due to discrimination (**sexism**) by recruiters. Women, with greater childcare and family responsibilities, might have an interrupted career, making it harder to move up a career ladder. Some women might not be as 'work centred' as men and might want a better 'work/life' balance.

ACTIVITY 144

Does Table 2.4.8 show horizontal segregation or vertical segregation?

Table 2.4.8: UK occupations by gender, 2006

	Females	Males
Managers	11%	19%
Professional	12%	14%
Administration and secretarial	21%	6%
Skilled trades, e.g. plumber	1%	15%
Personal service, e.g. childcare	14%	3%
Sales and customer service	12%	5%
Other	29%	38%

Adapted from Labour Force Survey, ONS, Social Trends 37, 2007, Palgrave Macmillan

Many women still have low-paid routine jobs with poor promotion and pension prospects, but change is occurring. The majority of students entering medicine, veterinary science, law and teaching are female and there are more female role models in high-status jobs.

However, the 2008 EHRC 'Sex and Power' report said that many barriers still exist for well-qualified young women wanting to combine a rewarding career with family life. It suggested the 'glass ceiling' might be a 'concrete ceiling', saying that the number of women MPs, police chiefs and senior judges had fallen in the previous year.

Norway and Spain have increased the number of women in senior positions by introducing quota laws: 40 per cent of company directors must be women.

ACTIVITY 145

Go to *www.heinemann.co.uk/hotlinks* and enter express code 7573P. Click on the *Equality and Human Rights Commission website* to research the 'Sex and Power' report.
What barriers still exist for women in the workplace?

Some men (especially those with few qualifications) also face disadvantages in the job market; men have a higher unemployment rate than women.

Ethnicity and employment

Illegal immigrants and migrant workers employed by 'gang masters' might be especially at risk of exploitation at work, facing long hours, dangerous working conditions, low pay and often large deductions, for example for accommodation. The government is attempting to tackle this problem through the Gangmasters Licensing Authority.

Other members of minority ethnic groups appear to be at a disadvantage in comparison with the white population. For example, unemployment rates for men are significantly higher for black Caribbean, black African, Bangladeshi and Pakistani men. The lowest rates are for white and Indian men.

Racial discrimination has been illegal since the 1968 Race Relations Act, but could still be an important explanation for these figures. Certainly, many people believe they have been refused a job because of discrimination (although this might be difficult to prove).

Social class background and educational qualifications are also important factors: for example, relatively few Pakistanis and Bangladeshis have degrees when compared with Indians. Where different groups live might also affect unemployment rates.

Change is occurring, but there are still relatively few members of some minority ethnic groups in highly paid, high-status occupations; discrimination, social class background and educational achievement remain important factors.

High-profile campaigns such as 'Kick **Racism** out of Football' highlight the need to make sure people can carry out their job without fear of harassment or discrimination. Many call centre operators in India say they experience racial abuse from callers in the UK.

Age and employment

Britain's ageing population (with a growing proportion of elderly people) makes age discrimination (**ageism**) a pressing issue. There are now more pensioners than under-16s in Britain. In future many people will work beyond the current retirement age of 65 – the economy will need the workers, the government will need their taxes and older people will need the income and other benefits of working.

KEY CONCEPTS

Dual burden – a situation where women combine the responsibilities of paid work with the mother-housewife role.

Sexism – discriminating against or expressing negative views or stereotypes about a gender.

Racial discrimination – treating people unfairly because of their ethnic group or race.

Racism – discriminating against or expressing negative views or stereotypes about an ethnic group or race.

Ageism – discriminating against or expressing negative views or stereotypes about an age group.

Some companies are keen to employ the 'over 50s'. John Harvey still worked at Sainsbury's Islington store at the age of 87. Asda introduced 'grandparents' leave' for older workers, and other flexible working arrangements (e.g. part-time work) make it easier for older people to stay in employment.

The 2006 Age Discrimination Act should also help. Under this act, workers cannot be forced to retire before 65 (and they can ask to carry on working beyond 65). When making staff redundant, employers cannot simply select the oldest workers.

Age discrimination legislation also protects young people; an employer would have to justify setting a minimum age (e.g. 25) for a vacancy.

ACTIVITY 146

1. Why might employers discriminate against older workers?
2. Why do companies such as B & Q value older workers?
3. Should age discrimination protection end at 65?

How workers gain rights

In 2007, the Equality and Human Rights Commission (EHRC) took over the job of promoting equal rights and tackling all forms of discrimination at work.

Employees have many other legal rights, including:

- a contract of employment
- the right to join a union
- a safe working environment
- protection from unfair dismissal
- protection for 'whistleblowing' (speaking out about suspected wrongdoing at work).

Employees who have been unfairly treated (e.g. unfairly dismissed or discriminated against) can take their case to an employment tribunal. If successful, they can obtain compensation and/or get their job back.

Employees also have responsibilities at work, for example to work safely and to follow their contract of employment.

ACTIVITY 147

Go to *www.heinemann.co.uk/hotlinks* and enter express code 7573P. Click on the *Directgov website* to find out about your employment rights and responsibilities.

Employers also have rights, for example to dismiss workers for unsatisfactory conduct or if they cannot do their job properly.

Trade unions

Trade unions represent workers' interests. They give workers more power than they would have on their own. Unions:

- negotiate with management, for example about pay and working conditions
- support members who are treated unfairly by their employer
- provide services to members such as training, legal advice or financial support
- put pressure on the government to introduce laws and policies that benefit members.

For example, in 2008, Unite launched a campaign for restaurant staff being paid below the minimum wage by employers (who said diners left them tips).

Unions have a close relationship with the Labour Party and contribute to party funds. The Conservative government (1979–1997) introduced laws to limit union power. For example:

- a secret ballot of members was required before calling an official strike
- union members could not be forced to take part in industrial action
- picketing (standing outside a place of work to discourage other workers from entering) was limited.

Strikes are one method of 'industrial action' used by unions to put pressure on employers if negotiations have failed. 'Go slows', 'overtime bans' or 'working to rule' also put pressure on employers by reducing the amount of work done.

Employers might respond by asking managers to carry out the tasks normally done by striking workers or might 'lock out' the employees.

Union membership has fallen: just 30 per cent of employees now belong to a union. Workers have not united as a single group, as Marx predicted, to challenge capitalism. The rising living standards of most workers and the divisions (e.g. of income and status) between workers might explain this.

Many workers in the global economy have poor working conditions, so unions have an important role in helping the most vulnerable. Schlosser (2002) said:

> 'Some of the most dangerous jobs in (USA) meatpacking are performed by late-night cleaning crews. A large proportion of these workers are illegal immigrants. Their work is so hard and horrendous that words seem inadequate to describe it. "It takes a really dedicated person," a former member of a cleaning crew told me, "or a really desperate person to get the job done."'

KNOW YOUR STUFF

In this chapter we defined 'work', discussed how we are prepared for work and looked at how work (and unemployment) can affect our lives. We examined the changes taking place at work (e.g. the growth of automation, call centres and flexible working) and considered their effects on job satisfaction. We also saw how gender, ethnicity and age, in particular, affect our opportunities at work.

Check your understanding of this topic by discussing the following questions:

1. How does society prepare us for work?
2. What is 'work', and how does work affect our life chances?
3. What are the effects of new technology at work?
4. What makes work satisfying?
5. Do people have equal opportunities at work?

ExamCafé

Revision

Key concepts

'I always get confused over words such as "automation" and "alienation", or "intrinsic" and "extrinsic" satisfaction.'

You need to learn all the key concepts for this topic so find the method that suits you best and start early. You could put them on revision cards, stick them round your room or classroom and test each other whenever you get a chance e.g. before your lesson starts.

You need to explain your points fully in the 8-mark and 24-mark questions; examples and studies are always useful, so when you make your revision notes make sure you add them in. Up-to-date examples are good, so keep your eye on the news in the weeks leading up to the exam and add anything interesting to your revision notes.

Make sure you have understood the following issues and related key concepts:

Revision checklist

Workplace and identity	Key Concepts
Learning about work	• Work
Socialisation at work	• Identity
Types of work	• Roles
What is work?	• Norms
Earning a living	• Values
Unpaid work e.g. housework	• Socialisation
The meaning of work	• Workplace
The effects of work	• Leisure
– on life choices e.g. health, income	• Employment/Unemployment
– on family life	• Primary/Secondary/Tertiary sector
Unemployment	• Service economy
– causes	• Life choices
– patterns	• Automation
People's experience of work	• Computerisation
Changing technology	• Alienation
– advantages	• Reskilling/Deskilling
– disadvantages	• Flexitime
Changing patterns of work	• Intrinsic/Extrinsic satisfaction
Work satisfaction	• Trade union
Equality in the workplace	• Equal opportunities
Influence of:	• Discrimination
– gender	• Equal pay
– age	• Sexism
– ethnicity	• Racism/Racial discrimination
Employee rights	• Ageism
Role of trade unions	

Summarising content

The 24-mark question always asks you to look at both sides of an issue to do with work. Try to make a list of the most likely issues, and prepare some points for both sides of the debate. Possible topics could include:

- whether work has much effect on peoples' lives
- who benefits and who loses from new technology
- what the main cause of unemployment is
- whether work is satisfying or unsatisfying today
- whether or not people have equal opportunities at work today
- who has more power at work: employers or employees
- whether trade unions are needed today.

Exam preparation

> 1. 'Changing technology benefits workers.' Evaluate the arguments for and against this claim. **[24 marks]**

Understanding exam language

The instruction 'evaluate' means that you must debate the statement in the question. As well as explaining how 'changing technology' might benefit workers, you must show how it could harm workers (or benefit employers or consumers more). To answer this question you need knowledge: how has technology changed? What are the effects of the changes?

Sample student answer

Jack

Comments
Jack starts to answer the question immediately by naming and defining a change in technology; an important advantage for workers is clearly explained and the paragraph is improved by also pointing out a disadvantage.

One change in technology is mechanisation: the use of machinery. An advantage for workers is that it can make jobs much easier physically: a fork lift truck can lift heavy weights, a digger can dig up the road much quicker than a worker with a shovel. This reduces the risk of injury and means workers might be able to carry on with the job even when they are older. However, a disadvantage for workers is that more machines might mean fewer jobs: for example, loading and unloading ships used to provide work for many 'stevedores'.

Comments
A very good paragraph: assembly line technology is explained and Blauner's study is used to explain alienation. The paragraph has good evaluation because it finishes by mentioning a benefit of assembly lines for workers.

Mechanisation led employers like Henry Ford to set up assembly lines (e.g. manufacturing cars). Division of labour is used, with each worker responsible for a small part of the production process. Blauner said assembly line technology alienated workers. They couldn't control the speed of the assembly line, so they were powerless; they could not communicate with other workers because of the noise, so they were isolated; the work they did was very repetitive, so it was boring and meaningless. Blauner said assembly line workers were 'self-estranged': they felt dissatisfied and not involved in their work. Therefore assembly line technology might not benefit workers. However, some assembly line work was well paid compared to other jobs, so this benefited workers who had an instrumental orientation to work and just wanted the money.

Assembly line technology might have benefited employers more than workers: they could mass produce goods quickly and cheaply; this gave higher profits to shareholders who owned the businesses. However, a problem for employers was that assembly lines were often affected by strikes, absence and poor-quality work. Assembly line technology might have benefited consumers more than workers: for the first time many people could afford products like cars.

A more recent change in technology is automation: the use of computer-controlled machinery. Car production is now much cleaner and involves fewer but highly skilled staff. Workers might find working in an automated factory like BMW's at Cowley much more satisfying than working on an assembly line. However, BMW have introduced many changes apart from the new technology (e.g. team working, profit sharing) which might also make workers more satisfied.

Employers, not workers, introduce automation; they see advantages like higher productivity (production per worker), better-quality products and higher profits. Customers might also see benefits: modern cars are much more reliable than cars built 30 years ago.

Computer technology can have disadvantages for workers. Jobs can disappear (e.g. as more people shop online or use cash machines). Many print workers lost their jobs when newspapers adopted computer technology. Jobs can be deskilled as computers take away the workers' skills (e.g. checkout operators do not need to add or subtract or identify products); Ritzer says this has happened in the fast food industry and it is spreading to other jobs: he calls these jobs 'McJobs'. Deskilling can reduce intrinsic job satisfaction.

Comments
This paragraph is good because it moves the question beyond 'workers', by asking whether employers or consumers benefited most from new technology.

Comments
The answer needs to look at recent changes in technology, and it does. Continuing with the example of car production makes a good link between mechanisation and automation.

Comments
Again this paragraph develops the question beyond a narrow focus on 'workers'.

Comments
This paragraph shows excellent knowledge: it shows understanding of concepts such as 'deskilling', 'McJobs' and 'intrinsic satisfaction'; it also uses good examples (e.g. print workers, checkout operators and fast food workers).

ExamCafé

Comments

These two paragraphs show knowledge of two important changes resulting from computer technology: call centres and teleworking. In each case advantages and disadvantages for workers are mentioned, which keeps the answer focused on the question. The answer has moved away from car manufacturing, which is good because most workers now work in the service sector of the economy.

Comments

A conclusion is essential for this type of question. This one is good: it makes three points which round off the argument. It supports the rest of the answer by showing that changing technology has advantages and disadvantages for workers.

Call centre work has grown due to new technology. This gives employment, but many call centres have a high staff turnover, suggesting workers are not very satisfied. This might be due to low pay or stressful working conditions. Employers benefit from call centres because they can operate from one place instead of having branches all over the county. Some customers find call centres convenient, but others find them frustrating and expensive.

One advantage of electronic technology is teleworking. Some jobs can now be carried out from home (or places like trains or cafés). Employees might like the freedom this gives and not having to commute to work. However, it might lead to working longer and feeling isolated.

In conclusion, employers have the power to introduce changes in technology at work, so it is usually introduced when employers see a benefit. New technology can benefit workers (e.g. through easier work, teleworking or reskilling) but it can have disadvantages too (e.g. unemployment or deskilling). However, it is not only technology that determines whether workers are satisfied with their jobs: friendly colleagues, a good boss, enjoyable work, feeling appreciated and a fair salary are also important.

Exam tips

This excellent answer shows an example of how to write well on a 24-mark question.

- Read the question carefully.
- Focus your answer on the question; you can do this if you link the first sentence of each paragraph to the question.
- You do not need *all* the paragraphs shown in this answer, but you should include at least four main paragraphs.
- Make sure your paragraphs present a debate: points for the statement in the question and points against it.
- In a debate, phrases such as 'however', 'on the other hand' and 'a different view is' are very useful.
- Include sociology, not just common sense: you need some sociological concepts (e.g. automation), studies (e.g. Blauner) or examples (e.g. call centres).
- Practise writing paragraphs that are detailed. You do need to explain your points and define the terms you use.
- Always write a conclusion.

Unit 2
Topic 5: Crime and deviance

The key areas you will study in this topic are:

- Definitions of crime and deviance
- Controlling crime and deviance
- Patterns of crime
- Explanations of crime

PAUSE FOR THOUGHT

Which of the following are legal?

1 A pregnant woman urinating in a policeman's helmet
2 Skateboarding in a police station
3 Naming a pig Napoleon
4 Getting a fish drunk
5 16-year-olds drinking alcohol
6 Placing a stamp upside down
7 Dying in the Houses of Parliament
8 A man wearing women's clothing
9 Driving whilst talking on a mobile phone without hands free
10 Dropping a sweet wrapper out of a car window

Topic 5: Crime and deviance

Definitions of crime and deviance

> **ANSWERS TO PAUSE FOR THOUGHT:**
> 1. Legal in the UK; pregnant women can urinate wherever they want
> 2. Illegal in Miami, Florida
> 3. Illegal in France
> 4. Illegal in Ohio, USA
> 5. Legal in the UK if with someone over 18 who bought the alcohol
> 6. Can be prosecuted under treason laws
> 7. Illegal in the UK
> 8. Legal in the UK
> 9. Illegal in the UK; punishable with a fine and points on your licence
> 10. Illegal in the UK; in some places punishable with an £80 on-the-spot fine

From doing the Pause for thought activity, you should now realise that what is legal and illegal is not always what we might expect. Some things we might regard as strange are legal and some we might think of as normal behaviour are actually illegal.

Actions that are against the law are known as **crimes**. Actions that seem to be 'abnormal' or go against the **norms** and **values** of society are known as **deviance**. Not all that is illegal is deviant and not all that is deviant is illegal. Thus you can have legal and illegal deviance.

What is deviant largely depends on the situation. Therefore, it is situational or relative, meaning that it is only deviant in certain places, at certain times or in certain cultures.

ACTIVITY 148

Copy and complete the following table:

Action	When deviant	When not deviant
Eating with your hands		
Kissing someone of your own gender		
Singing in the street		
Drinking alcohol		
Punching someone in the face		
Being 16 and driving a car		
Marrying someone who is 14		
Wearing a veil		
Killing another person		

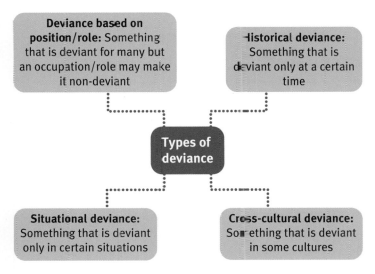

Deviance based on position/role: Something that is deviant for many but an occupation/role may make it non-deviant

Historical deviance: Something that is deviant only at a certain time

Types of deviance

Situational deviance: Something that is deviant only in certain situations

Cross-cultural deviance: Something that is deviant in some cultures

- Member states should criminalise and impose penalties of a certain level for sexual exploitation of children and child pornography, as well as establishing their own jurisdiction and granting protection and assistance for children, as particularly vulnerable victims, and their families.

- All member states shall not subject anyone to torture or to cruel, inhuman or degrading treatment or punishment.

- All member states shall ban smoking in enclosed premises open to the public, which form part of a public or private establishment.

These rulings are evidence that there is some attempt to standardise what is deviant.

ACTIVITY 149

Copy out the above spidergram and for each type of deviance, add an example. You will notice that some examples may fit more than one type of deviance, but try to use a different one for each.

ACTIVITY 150

List three reasons which show that deviance is relative and three reasons which show that it is sometimes not. For each reason include examples as evidence.

So alongside legal and illegal deviance, there are many different types:

- **cross-cultural deviance**
- **situational deviance**
- **historical deviance**

Although deviance is usually relative to the culture, situation and time frame you are in, there have been attempts to standardise moral codes through the legal system. For example, all people in Britain are subject to the same laws, which define what is acceptable and unacceptable behaviour across the country. There have also been attempts to define deviance and make it illegal across different cultures, for example through European law and United Nations rulings. By requiring that such moral codes become law in member countries, they become more universal.

The following are some examples of rulings by the European Union.

 Grade**Studio**

A common exam question is: '"All deviance is relative". Evaluate the arguments for and against this claim.' The activity above should help you to plan and write this essay as timed practice. Remember to include a conclusion, as missing this out will effect the quality of your answer.

KEY CONCEPTS

Crime – an action that is against the law.

Norms – a set of unwritten social rules.

Values – beliefs of right and wrong in society.

Deviance – actions that go against the norms and values of a society or group.

Cross-cultural deviance – something that is deviant in some cultures but not in others.

Situational deviance – something that is deviant only in certain situations.

Historical deviance – something that is deviant only at a certain time.

A 'metric martyr' will appear in court after being charged with using imperial measures on her market stall

Janet Devers, 63, is due to appear at Thames Magistrates' Court to face 13 charges including two alleging that she used imperial weighing scales without an official stamp.

Mrs Devers, from Wanstead in east London, had her imperial weighing scales seized from her vegetable stall in Dalston, north London, last year.

She has been dubbed the new 'metric martyr…'

The case, brought by Hackney Council, is proceeding despite plans to scrap imperial measures being abandoned by the European Commission.

Thoburn, from Sunderland, was fined for selling bananas by the pound and Dove, from Mevagissey in Cornwall, was ordered to pay court costs for selling mackerel at £1.50 per pound.

Harman, also from Cornwall, was ordered to pay costs for selling Brussels sprouts by the pound, while Hunt, of east London, was given a 12-month conditional discharge for pricing pumpkins by the pound.

Staff reporter, *The Sun*,
18 January 2008

Steven Thoburn, who was convicted for selling goods in only imperial measures in 2001, was the original 'Metric Martyr'.

ACTIVITY 151

1. What is the European law that is being discussed in the above extract?

2. How does the article show that attempts to standardise law or deviance sometimes bring about related problems?

3. Research and make notes on two other examples of problems with attempts to standardise law and deviance. (Research the United Nations or European Union.)

The article highlights the difficulty of standardising ideas of 'deviance' in different countries. What works in some countries or cultures will not automatically apply in others. However, there do seem to be some extremes of behaviour that will always be considered deviant and which are not relative to the culture or time. Can you think of any examples?

GradeStudio

It is important that your answers include evidence. This can take a variety of forms: sociological studies, sociological terminology, relevant contemporary examples and relevant laws and media references. For a discussion on the relativity of deviance and crime, contemporary examples will be very important. So you should watch out for relevant examples in the news and keep a note of them to use in the exam.

Controlling crime and deviance

Agents of social control

Understanding how to behave in society can be complicated. Think about your behaviour today. Why have you attended school? In truth there is more than one answer to this, as we **conform** to rules for many reasons. Your attendance could be due to personal choice, such as loving school or being with your friends, or it could be due to a number of other reasons.

ACTIVITY 152

Discuss with a partner why the following groups and institutions might influence whether you go to school:

Family   School   Peer group   Mass media   Prison

Workplace   Government   Police   Court

Individually decide which group or institution has the greatest influence over whether you go to school.

Our behaviour is controlled by many groups of people and institutions. These are known as **agents of social control**. But there is a difference in, for example the way the family controls us compared with the police. Sociologists refer to this difference as the divide between **formal social control** and **informal social control**. Agents of formal social control (e.g. the police) exist to maintain control of society. Agents of informal social control (e.g. the family) also control individuals, but this is not their sole purpose of existence.

ACTIVITY 153

Divide the agents of social control mentioned in the previous activity into two lists: formal and informal agents of social control.

GradeStudio

Students sometimes find it difficult to divide the agents of social control into formal and informal. As a school may have a 'formal' discipline policy, this might seem different to family discipline. But remember that the main purpose of a school is not to control people, but to educate them. It is important that you know which agents are which, as questions in the exam may distinguish between the two, and you may write an incorrect answer should you get it wrong.

Formal social control

Table 2.5.1: Agents of formal control and their methods of control

Formal agent	How they control society
The government	Through the Houses of Parliament, the government legislates (makes laws) to control behaviour.
The police	The police force enforces the law.
The judiciary (court system)	Courts decide how to punish law-breakers.
The penal system (prisons and other sanctions)	These are the different ways law-breakers can be punished and controlled.
The army	The army defends a country, but may also be called in to prevent large-scale law-breaking.

ACTIVITY 154

Copy out Table 2.5.1 and add a third column which gives examples of how the agent may control behaviour. For example, for the government you may add the fact that they have introduced laws against people under the age of 18 purchasing a knife.

Informal social control

It is more difficult to list how informal agents of social control may control behaviour. Largely this is done through social pressure, although there may also be sanctions that follow a list of guidelines. A good example of this mixture of approaches can be seen at school.

School rules are often written down and sanctions will be agreed through policy. Sanctions may include: detentions, letters home, writing lines, a 'hard stare'. However, behaviour may also be controlled by giving positive reactions to good behaviour, such as merits or house points and rewards such as trips, prizes or certificates. However, our behaviour at school is not only controlled by the school itself, but also by the relationships we have with individual teachers; you may not want to disappoint a teacher whom you like. Our behaviour at school may also be controlled by other agents, such as our peer group or our family.

But *how* do informal agents control us, if not through agreed guidelines? Consider what would happen if you broke a social norm, for example by coming to school with no clothes on. How would you learn that this deviant behaviour was not acceptable? Often it is merely the reaction of others that teaches us to conform. They may laugh at us, exclude us, mock us, withdraw us from lessons (exclusion); they may consider it a sign of mental illness and ensure we see a doctor. Even a simple scowl or smile can help us decide whether our behaviour is appropriate.

The study *Learning to Labour* by Paul Willis (1977) on working-class boys at school argued that there was a counter-school subculture. He researched 12 boys and found that they chose not to conform to the norms and values of the school. He felt that their behaviour was not only due to peer group pressure, but actually had more to do with the influence of the workplace and the family. In 1977, Willis felt it was clear to the boys that working-class children got working-class jobs and that, therefore, their school life was not important. Because of this they did not conform and did not care about the middle-class norms and values the teachers were trying to force upon them. Willis' findings confirm that our behaviour is controlled in a variety of ways.

RESEARCH LINK

Research methods – Willis used qualitative methods in his research.

For more information on these look at pages 21–22 in Sociology basics: Part A.

ACTIVITY 155

These comments show how complex our decisions about behaviour are. For each comment, discuss in a small group which agents of social control are being discussed. Decide which agent of social control has the most influence over each child's behaviour.

I want to do well in Maths, as I like it, but my friends call me a geek if I tell them I want to get on. (Adam)

I'm good at PE so I always bring my kit. I have loads of friends that hate PE, but I love it. They don't bring their kit on purpose. (Lucy)

I love reading – my Mum and I think Harry Potter books are great. But I'd never tell any of my friends that. They think reading is for girls. (Ben)

My friends are all good at English and writing. They all get really good grades, but I hate it. I'm in different sets from them and dread going to English. Writing is just boring! (Ahmed)

I work hard in school because I want to be a doctor, like my dad. Without good grades I can't get into university and I'll never become a doctor. (Sarah)

I bunk school most days. I'm in Year 11 and can't wait to leave. Me and my friends just hang around in the high street and try not to get caught by the police. (Katie)

GradeStudio

Whilst it seems quite easy to discuss the work of formal agents of social control, students often find it hard to describe *how* informal agents actually control our behaviour. Examples of control are not enough on their own.

Solutions to crime

Preventing crime is difficult, as there can be many reasons why a crime is committed, and to stop the crime you first need to understand the causes. (These are discussed later in the chapter.)

However, the penal system does not only prevent crime. Its functions are:

- to prevent crime
- to deter others from committing crime
- to reform offenders
- to punish criminals
- to keep the public safe.

Due to its many functions, the penal system needs to consider its choice of action carefully for each criminal.

Table 2.5.2: Methods of punishment

Punishment	Definition
Antisocial behaviour orders (ASBOs)	Individual social orders, e.g. banning someone from an area
Community service	Offenders ordered to work in a community, e.g. clearing graffiti
Corporal punishment	Physical punishment, e.g. whipping
Curfews	Often part of an ASBO, limiting the time the offender may be allowed out in public
Death penalty	Known as capital punishment; illegal in Britain
Electronic tagging	Attaching a tag to the offender to control and monitor where they are
Fines	Financial punishment
Mental health orders	Granted if the crime is due to mental illness
Prison sentencing	A loss of freedom for a set amount of time
Probation	Being offered supervision instead of prison to ensure that offending stops

Most media coverage focuses on the need for longer prison sentences. However, with prisons becoming full, alternative punishments are becoming increasingly important. Read the following interview.

ACTIVITY 156

In small groups, decide on a fitting crime for each punishment above. For example, you may decide that community service should be the punishment for a crime against the local environment such as graffiti.

WHAT ARE PRISONS?

Interviewer: What is a prison?

Respondent 1 (prison warden): It is a way to take away people's freedom as a punishment for crimes committed. But it does more than just that. It helps society by keeping them safe. It also helps the offender. They are able to improve skills, which will hopefully help them when they re-enter society.

Interviewer: How?

Respondent 1 (prison warden): They can receive education and even take academic exams. Others choose to build on career skills.

Interviewer: (Question to respondent 2, a prisoner) What is a day like in prison?

Respondent 2 (prisoner): I sleep in a cell with one other inmate. I have a couple of my things, a couple of pictures and my radio, but there is not much else. The prison gives us a bit of furniture, but there is not much. Every day we have to clean our cells. We are allowed to buy cigarettes and snacks in the shop in the prison, but we are told how much we can spend, and it does not buy much.

Interviewer: (Question to respondent 2, a prisoner) So what is your favourite part of the day?

Respondent 2 (prisoner): I miss going outside, so my favourite time of day is the 30 minutes we get to go to the exercise yard. But they cancel it if the weather is bad. I hate that! Meal times are OK too. We all eat in the canteen and can hang out with each other.

ACTIVITY 157

Using the information in the above interview:

1. What are prisoners allowed to do?
2. What are prisoners not allowed to do?

Which of the functions of the penal system do you think prisons carry out? Give reasons for your answer.

In the exam you may be asked to evaluate the use of prisons. Prepare for this by ensuring you can discuss both the positive and negative issues of prisons. A good answer will consider both the functions of the penal system and alternative punishments. A good way to prepare might be through a class debate.

KEY CONCEPTS

Official statistics – numbers and percentages to show what crimes are being committed and who is committing them, taken from government sources. Information can be supplied by such agencies as the police, the courts and the prison system.

ACTIVITY 158

RESEARCH TASK

Official crime statistics are produced every year, so there is a wealth of information out there just waiting for you to find it! Using the internet, try to find out the answers to the following questions. Work either on your own or in a pair. The following websites may prove useful for your search:

- www.homeoffice.gov.uk
- www.direct.gov.uk
- www.statistics.gov.uk
- www.bbc.co.uk
- www.crime.org
- www.statistics.gov.uk/socialtrends/
- www.police.uk

1. What were the top three crimes committed in the UK last year?
2. Which crimes have decreased in the last five years?
3. Which crimes have increased in the last five years?
4. Which crimes have very low figures in the statistics?
5. How does the official picture of crime differ from the view of crime presented in the media?
6. Did any of the statistics you saw surprise you? If so, which ones and why?

Patterns of crime

Crime is something that everybody has an opinion on. We see shocking reports on television and in the newspapers, leaving us fearful and anxious about the impact crime may have on our lives. Many of us also have personal experiences of crime, either as victims or as criminals, and this, too, cannot help but impact on our lives in some way. But how do we actually know how much crime is being committed in society? Can we really believe the media reports of gangs on every corner, credit card cloning when we make a purchase and evil villains waiting to pounce as we walk home at night? Let's hope not or we would never leave the house! Sociologists use a variety of different methods to try to provide as accurate a picture as possible of how much crime there actually is and who is committing this crime. They then use this information to consider the ways that crime may impact on a community and on an individual's behaviour. So let's start by seeing how sociologists go about measuring how much crime there is in society.

Measurements of crime

The government's Home Office department publishes statistics every year about the number and type of crimes committed and the people who have been convicted of these offences. They are a cheap, easily available and up-to-date source of secondary data. These **official statistics** on crime are what we see reported in the media and what the government typically bases its policy decisions about crime on. They are, therefore, clearly a good starting point for any sociologist who wants to find out information about crime. Or so you would think. But do the crime figures actually give us an accurate and full picture of crime? Read on and see.

It seems that you can get a pretty full picture of what is going on regarding crime from close examination of the crime statistics (see Table 2.5.3 opposite). Sociologists, however, treat such statistics with extreme caution, as they are only really a record of the number of crimes recorded by the police. So for a crime to actually make it into the official statistics, the following has to happen.

1. Firstly, somebody has to realise that a crime has taken place. This sounds obvious, but do we really always know that a crime has been committed? Imagine the case of a homeless person being murdered. Would anyone necessarily know this crime had taken place?

Table 2.5.3: Number of crimes recorded by the police in 2006/07 and 2007/08

Offence group	2006/07	2007/08	% change
	Number of offences[1] (000s)		
Violence against the person (VAP)	1,046.2	961.2	−8
Most serious VAP [2]	*19.2*	*16.9*	*−12*
Other violence against the person – with injury [3]	*437.4*	*435.5*	*−11*
Other violence against the person – with no injury [4]	*539.6*	*508.8*	*−6*
Sexual offences	57.5	53.5	−7
Most serious sexual crime [5]	*43.7*	*41.5*	*−5*
Other sexual offences	*13.8*	*12.1*	*−12*
Robbery	101.4	84.7	−16
Domestic burglary	292.3	280.7	−4
Other burglary	329.8	303.0	−8
Offences against vehicles	765.0	656.5	−14
Other theft offences	1,180.8	1,121.1	−5
Fraud and forgery [6]	199.7	155.4	−22
Criminal damage	1,185.0	1,036.2	−13
Drug offences	194.2	229.0	18
Other offences	75.7	69.3	−8
Total recorded crime	**5,427.6**	**4,950.7**	**−9**

1. The figures given in the table are the latest available. Therefore they may differ slightly from figures published in previous bulletins.
2. Most serious violence against the person includes homicide and serious wounding.
3. Other violence against the person – with injury comprises less serious wounding and causing or allowing death of a child or vulnerable person.
4. Other offences against the person – with no injury comprises threats or conspiracy to murder, harassment, endangering railway passengers, possession of weapons, other offences against children, procuring illegal abortion, and assault without injury.
5. Most serious sexual crime comprises rape, sexual assault, and sexual activity with children.
6. These offences were modified by the Fraud Act 2006 which came into force on 15 January 2007. For cheque and credit card fraud counting changed from a per fraudulent transaction to per account basis from 15 January 2007. From 1 April 2007 these offences were reported to a single point of contact within each police force by financial institutions.

Source: http://www.homeoffice.gov.uk

What about a smashed car window – accident or criminal damage? Who can say? What about the child who steals a ten pound note out of their dad's wallet – will dad realise he's been a victim of crime? If a crime has not actually been detected, then it is not going to get reported to the police and so it will not appear in the crime statistics.

2. Secondly, the crime has to actually be reported to the police to appear in the statistics. Now we all know that, as good citizens, we should report any crimes we see or any crimes committed against us to the police, so they can solve them for us and punish the criminal involved. But for many reasons this does not always happen.

ACTIVITY 159

1. Have you ever reported a crime to the police? What was it? Have you or anyone you know ever seen or been a victim of a crime and not reported it? What reasons were there for this? Discuss your thoughts as a class.

2. Working in a small group, make a list of all the crimes that you think would not be very likely to be reported to the police. Make sure you have reasons for everything you have written down.

3. Now think of those crimes that are likely to be reported. What are they and why do the police frequently get to know about them?

Hopefully, what you have discovered from doing the last activity is that the police do not get to find out about a lot of the crimes that are being committed. You may have mentioned that people sometimes do not think the police can do anything about the crime so feel there is no point in reporting it. Perhaps your discussion covered the idea that a lot of witnesses and victims actually know the criminals and so do not report the crime because they do not want them to get into trouble. Ideas about embarrassment (sexual crime), fear (of consequences) and privacy (a family matter) may have also cropped up. You may have come to the conclusion that crimes involving insured articles are the most likely to be reported, as without a crime report the insurance companies will not pay up. So really what we are seeing in the official crime statistics is not a true picture of crime at all – it is only the tip of the iceberg. Many of the crimes that are affecting people day by day are referred to by sociologists as the 'dark figure of crime'. They are the crimes we know little about as they do not feature in the official figures.

As well as a crime having to be reported to the police to make it into the statistics, it also has to be *recorded* by the police. Not every crime that is reported actually gets recorded, because the police are able to use their discretion at this stage of the process. They may feel that the crime is not serious enough to record (someone riding a bike without lights may just get a warning) or that they do not really want to get involved, for example a family matter, such as an argument between husband and wife. If there is a lack of evidence, this can be another reason why the crime may not be recorded. If someone reports a stolen passport, for example – without evidence that it has actually been stolen – there is always the possibility of it just having been lost. So the police may choose not to record it as a crime. Remember, if it does not get recorded then it does not get into the official statistics.

A final thing to consider is how the police operate. There are a lot of different police forces out there, and this can have a big effect on how things are done. Just think of your teachers in school for a moment. Even though your school will have rules and codes of conduct, not all your teachers will deal with things in the same way. Do something in one class and you'll get detention, in another you'll be told off and in another absolutely nothing will happen. It is a similar scenario when it comes to the police – each force and even each officer will do things differently. This can really effect the validity of the crime statistics, as what will be recorded as a crime in one force will not necessarily be recorded in a different one.

RESEARCH LINK

Remember that you studied official statistics as a source of secondary evidence when you were learning about research methods. For more information on this look at pages 20–21 in Sociology basics: Part A.

Some forces, for example, do not record thefts of items below a certain value, whereas others will record these. Some forces will have been told to prioritise certain crimes (e.g. smoking marijuana), meaning that these crimes are very likely to be recorded by that force but not necessarily by others. The end result of all this is that the 'dark figure' of crime increases and the accuracy and usefulness of the official statistics becomes questionable.

GradeStudio

To do well in a question about the official crime statistics you need to make sure that you know what they are, how they are produced, their good points and their bad points. Have a go at the following question, then swap your answer with a classmate and see who has answered the question best. Try to identify what it is that makes the difference between a good and a basic answer – your teacher will help you with this.

'Evaluate the usefulness of official statistics on crime.'

ACTIVITY 160

RESEARCH TASK
Try to organise an interview with a member of your local police force to see what else you can find out about the realities of day-to-day policing. In groups of three or four, prepare ten questions that you would like to ask. Think carefully about how you word these. Remember that your relationship with the interviewee will determine the quality of data that you receive. Write your findings up as a research report and submit it to your teacher for marking. Tip: see the Research Link at the top of the opposite page.

To try to tackle these weaknesses in the crime statistics, sociologists have developed other ways of measuring crime that they feel are likely to result in a more accurate picture. The main methods they have used are **victim surveys** and **self-report studies**

KEY CONCEPTS

Victim survey – people are asked what crimes have been committed against them.

Self-report study – a questionnaire that asks people what crimes they have committed.

Victim surveys

These have proved a popular method of trying to discover just what the true picture of crime is in society. They are typically done with a large-scale sample where people are interviewed about what crimes they have been a victim of in the last year. This is thought to be a better way of uncovering a more valid picture of crime than the official statistics, because it removes the problem of the non-reporting and non-recording of crime. Probably the best-known victim survey is the British Crime Survey, which is carried out every year on a national sample of people. Results from this are often shown in the media and are used by politicians to help with crime policy decisions. Indeed, they have become almost as well known and used as the official statistics.

Although they are widely thought of as a useful source of data on crime, victim surveys are not without their problems. For example, there are no guarantees that information given in interviews is actually accurate. The process relies on memory – notoriously unreliable – and on people telling the truth. There are likely to be lots of cases where the respondent feels embarrassed and so does not admit to all the crimes that have been committed

against them. Sexual abuse, rape and domestic violence are all good examples of this. Another issue is that people under the age of 16 are not interviewed – this may prove problematic as clearly children are also victims of crime. Finally, some sociologists question how useful a national crime survey actually is. Problems associated with crime are different across the country and in different communities and cultures. A generalised picture such as that produced by the British Crime Survey may, therefore, only have limited uses. To counter this, some sociologists have carried out local victim surveys. These have been done in Islington and Merseyside, for example. At a localised level, these can give a real idea of the frequency and types of crimes committed in a particular area. Results from these local surveys, of course, cannot be generalised to the whole of the UK.

ACTIVITY 161

1. Imagine you have been asked to take part in a victim survey. How likely are you to tell the truth? Explain your reasons.

2. Would the gender, age and ethnicity of the interviewer affect how truthful you were? Consider each factor in turn and discuss with your classmates.

3. Do you think a structured, semi-structured or unstructured interview would work best for a victim survey? Or perhaps you think a questionnaire would be better? Work with a partner and compare your answer with others in your class to see what people think.

Self-report studies

A final method used by sociologists to try to produce an accurate picture of crime in the UK is that of self-report studies. This time people are asked what crimes they have committed, usually by having them tick off from a list what they have done. Everything is anonymous and confidentiality is assured. This is thought to encourage respondents to be more truthful. Truthfulness is also encouraged by the fact that the human element of an interviewer is removed from the process. This encourages people to tell the truth and not to feel embarrassed by what they have done. This method increases validity because, as with the victim surveys, whether the crime has been reported and the criminal convicted becomes irrelevant. It allows researchers to measure the amount of crime committed by those people who have never appeared in the official statistics. Below is an example of the types of questions you might be asked in a self-report study. Have a go at this by copying the list and ticking off any of the crimes listed that you have committed.

1. 'Have you ridden a bike without lights in the dark?' □
2. 'Have you trespassed onto someone else's land or property? □
3. 'Have you bought cigarettes underage?' □
4. 'Have you stolen items worth less than £5?' □
5. 'Have you stolen items worth more than £5?' □
6. 'Have you written graffiti on something that doesn't belong to you?' □
7. 'Have you carried a weapon?' □
8. 'Have you used a weapon?' □
9. 'Have you downloaded music illegally?' □
10. 'Have you bought goods from someone knowing them to be stolen?' □
11. 'Have you used public transport without paying for a ticket?' □
12. 'Have you truanted from school?' □
13. 'Have you broken into a building such as a shop or garage?' □
14. 'Have you taken illegal drugs?' □
15. 'Have you had sex with someone for money?' □

As with any research method, however, this too has its problems. Reflect on your own experience of answering the questions for a moment. Were you completely honest? Why or why not? Sociologists have raised the following concerns about self-report studies:

• Many people are reluctant to take part as they do not want to be asked about their criminal activity.

• Those people that do take part may not tell the truth. They may be reluctant to admit to certain crimes or may exaggerate their criminality in order to impress others.

• These reports are usually completed with young people – they are, therefore, not representative of all crimes committed.

• The reports often focus on delinquent (see page 156) rather than criminal behaviour and so are limited in their usefulness.

So, as you can see, there are several different ways of measuring the crime rate. Victim surveys and

self-report studies have been developed in order to try to reveal more of the dark figure and so get a more valid picture of crime and criminals than that produced by the official statistics. None of the methods are perfect, however, and we must, therefore, be careful when coming to any conclusion about who is actually committing crime in society and how much crime is going on.

Crime and its impact on the community

The picture of crime that we get from the media and the methods discussed above inevitably have an impact on what we think about crime and how it affects our actions. Many people believe that it is the fear of crime, rather than the reality, that controls our behaviour and thoughts. Obviously this is closely linked to the sensationalist and often stereotyped reporting in the media.

ACTIVITY 162

1. Have a think about your own fear of crime. What crimes are you most afraid of? Why? Where does this fear of crime come from?

2. Who do you think of as committing these crimes that you are afraid of? Do you think your ideas are actually true?

3. What kinds of things do your parents/carers do to protect you from crime? Do you think this is effective? Why or why not?

This fear of crime does not just affect us as individuals; it also affects neighbourhoods and communities. On a positive level, some communities may benefit from punishments for criminals that require them to do community work such as removing graffiti or tidying up public gardens. More commonly, however, the effects of crime on a community are negative: people living in fear, homes armed with every security device available and neighbourhoods where people do not know their next-door neighbours, let alone others down the street.

We are living in a culture of fear, where social control has become an acceptable norm. Just think of some of the neighbourhoods near to where you live; you might have a cluster of houses displaying 'neighbourhood watch' stickers in their windows and, your own house might be part of such a scheme. You walk down a street or go on public transport and the likelihood is that you will be picked up on CCTV; 'Big Brother' is able to track your movements should he so wish. We have increased security checks at airports, retina scanning, more DNA testing than ever before and photo identification built into many devices. Our society has never been so controlled, yet crime is still a big problem for many of us. We only have to look at the many police initiatives to cut the crime rates in our communities to see that current thinking is that we have a problem with crime that we need to tackle.

So we now have community police officers and members of the public acting as a formal agent of social control, as well as antisocial behaviour orders and curfew systems telling people what they can and cannot do, what time to be home, where they can and cannot go and who they can mix with. The state is increasingly adopting the socialisation roles of parents and schools, all in the name of making us safer. How successful this has all been, however, is debatable.

ACTIVITY 163

1. Using the internet, your own knowledge of your local community and media resources, produce an annotated collage of images or a PowerPoint presentation to illustrate how crime and the fear of crime has impacted on society. Work in small groups on this task and share your finished work with your teacher and classmates.

2. Prepare for a whole-class debate on the topic: 'The fear of crime is more of a problem than crime itself.' If you are not one of the main speakers, make sure you get involved by preparing questions for each team.

3. If you were up for election tomorrow, what would you do to make communities feel safer? Write your campaign speech to convince others that your ideas will work. Good luck!

Patterns of crime by class, gender, ethnicity and age

It is time now to take a look at who, according to the official statistics, commits crime in society. In the next section we will look at reasons to explain these trends and patterns. A word of warning, though – do not forget the dark figure of crime. How true the 'facts' derived from the official statistics on crime actually are remains to be seen.

Social class and crime

It seems that there is a strong link between a person's position in the social class hierarchy and their likelihood of committing a crime. In simple terms, the lower their class position, the higher their criminality. Indeed, working-class young people

have a crime rate that is about eight times higher than that of upper- or middle-class youth. When you look at the prison population, it is a similar story, with working-class people being hugely over-represented. Crime rates in inner city areas and council estates are also typically higher than in rural areas or the suburbs. These areas, of course, are largely working class.

ACTIVITY 164

1. List all the reasons you can think of to explain why members of the lower class groups in society may commit the most crime.

2. There is always the possibility that the statistics are inaccurate, meaning that the working class might not actually commit the majority of crime in society. If this is true, then what reasons can you think of to explain why the working class are more likely to be stopped and searched, arrested, convicted and sent to prison than other classes? Consider the role of the public, the police, the media, schools, peer groups and the courts in your answer.

Gender and crime

Statistics show that males are far more likely to offend than females. Take a look at the 'facts' below that illustrate this trend.

- In 2005, there were 30.7 million females compared with 29.5 million males in the UK population.

- However, male offenders in England and Wales outnumber female offenders by more than four to one.

- In 2002, only 19 per cent of known offenders were women.

- Of the population born in 1953, 34 per cent of men but only 8 per cent of women had a conviction for a serious offence by the age of 40.

If you are interested in the links between gender and crime, the website referenced above contains plenty of easy-to-read and fascinating facts that you might want to check out. It will certainly make you think, so is highly recommended. Interestingly, despite females' relatively low levels of involvement with crime, statistics suggest that the number of female offenders is rising. You may have personal experience of this yourself, or have read about or seen such claims in the media.

In September 2008, former politician, Ann Widdecombe, was so worried by this growing trend that she made a television social documentary to try to discover why so many young girls were increasingly becoming attracted to gang violence and crime. Her findings shocked viewers with the images of drunken female violence, regular antisocial behaviour and discussions of being 'tooled up'. Carrying knives and, to a certain extent, using them was seemingly a norm amongst the girls featured and, even more worryingly, the girls claimed that guns were also easy to get hold of.

ACTIVITY 165

1. What reasons can you think of to explain why males commit more crime than females?

2. Why do you think female crime in the 21st century is on the increase? Discuss your ideas with a partner and then debate with your classmates.

RESEARCH TASK

1. Visit any of the well-known websites that provide statistics on crime (see the list on page 150) and see if you can get hold of up-to-date figures on the amount of male crime compared to female crime. Do the types of crimes that males and females commit differ? Why do you think this is? Check recent figures with crime statistics from a few years ago. Has the female crime rate gone up, stayed the same or gone down?

2. See if you can find information on Widdecombe's female crime documentary on the internet. You may even be able to download the programme to watch yourself.

Ethnicity and crime

Links between ethnicity and crime are quite complicated to summarise, as any trends depend largely on the specific ethnic group under consideration. As our multicultural society continues to change with the arrival of people from a wide variety of ethnic groups, so any links between a person's ethnic group and their likelihood of committing a crime will also change. According to the statistics, Afro-Caribbean people are over-represented in the UK's prison population as compared to their numbers in society. It could be concluded from this that Afro-Caribbean people commit more crime than other ethnic groups.

However, the social prejudices of our society must also be considered here in terms of how they may have affected Afro-Caribbean people, especially young males.

The proportion of British Asians in prison is roughly equivalent to their proportion in the population. This ethnic group, it would seem, is relatively law-abiding. Remember, though, that statistics can often be deceptive.

Age and crime

You probably will not be surprised to hear that it is people in your age category who are the most likely to commit a criminal offence, specifically those aged 14–20. This age category represents approximately a third of all those found guilty of crime. However, most young people do not continue with their criminal behaviour into adulthood. Young people are also involved in delinquent behaviour. This may not be criminal activity but is certainly antisocial and so attracts negative sanctions from the authorities, parents and schools. Typical examples of **delinquency** are truancy, resisting authority, vandalism, foul language, underage sex and drug taking.

ACTIVITY 166

Study the age–crime curve graph below and answer the questions that follow.

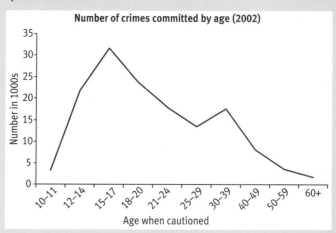

1. According to the graph, at what age do most offences take place?

2. When are people least likely to commit a criminal offence?

3. How many offenders aged 18–20 were cautioned for their criminal behaviour in 2002?

4. How would you explain the trends seen in the age–crime curve?

Most sociologists believe that all of these social factors (age, gender, class and ethnicity) work together in determining a person's likelihood of offending. It is unlikely that any factor on its own will be a reason or an explanation for crime. There are no easy answers here.

SOCIALISATION, CULTURE AND IDENTITY

U2 T5

Explanations of crime

From what we have seen in the last section on patterns of crime, we know that *statistically* those people most likely to be convicted of criminal acts are young, working-class, black males. So what are the reasons for this?

Age

Why do young people commit a disproportionate amount of crime in society?

- **Peer pressure.** Young people can come under a lot of pressure from their peer group to fit in with the group's norms and values. This can be either positive or negative, but is typically associated with antisocial or delinquent behaviour in young people. **Peer group pressure** can occur in a lot of different ways, ranging from subtle hints to physical force. For a lot of young people, this is one of the main reasons why they commit crime – they want to be like their friends or gain status in the peer group. Committing acts of crime or deviance is one way of doing this.

- **Subcultures.** Some sociologists have taken the idea of peer group pressure a bit further and developed the idea that small numbers of young people have norms and values so different to mainstream society that they can be referred to as a subculture. Evidence for this can be found in their high levels of antisocial behaviour and delinquency. This might be seen in gang violence, intimidation and alcohol and drug misuse. Clearly, if the norms and values of the subculture do not class criminal and deviant acts as wrong, then these are likely to become typical, normal behaviour for the young people involved and are thus another reason for their increased criminality.

- **Boredom.** Many young people claim that one of the key reasons why they get into trouble is boredom; having nothing to do and nowhere to go. In these circumstances, crime may occur simply because it is something different to do and is a way of adding thrills and excitement into an otherwise dull existence. Research does seem to prove that this 'adrenaline rush' is actually a key reason to explain young people's involvement in crime.

- **Lack of social control at home and in education.** Another reason often given for why young people have high rates of offending is that there has been a general decline of social control in society. Families imposing few, if any, rules on their children, the reduction in the powers of control given to schools and an increasing street culture have all been said to be contributory factors. We all know that young people push the boundaries imposed on them and, if social controls are not in place to counter this, then criminal behaviour may well be the end result.

- **Labelling theory.** Another sociological theory often used to explain the criminal behaviour of young people – and of other groups in society – is the **labelling** theory. A researcher called Cicourel (1976) found, from his observations of the police and probation officers in the USA, that how a young person presented themselves and behaved directly affected their likelihood of arrest and conviction. So if the young person acted as authority figures imagined a 'typical delinquent' would act, then they would be labelled as a criminal and so become more likely to be convicted and to get a harsher sentence. Interestingly, they pictured young delinquents as coming from a low-income, broken family, being male, not having done well at school and often from an ethnic minority. It is clear, therefore, that labelling does not just apply to the age of the offender, but also to other social characteristics.

In short, if the police and the courts believe that large numbers of offenders are young people, then young people will be labelled as potential criminals and so are likely to be watched, stopped and searched regularly. This will obviously mean that they are more likely to be caught in a criminal act than other groups of people. Just think about the suspicion that the authorities and, indeed, older generations generally, have about 'hoodies' in today's society. We are so suspicious of their behaviour that some shopping centres have gone so far as to ban young people wearing hoods from entering the building!

KEY CONCEPTS

Delinquency – the undesirable, antisocial behaviour of young people.

Peer group pressure – pressure applied to a person by a group of the same age to try to get them to fit in with the group's norms and values; often applies to young people.

Labelling – thinking of a person or a group of people in a particular way, often negatively, presuming that all of the group are a particular type of person.

ACTIVITY 167

1. Discuss in a small group examples of peer pressure that have happened to you or your friends. What methods have been used? Why do you think they work? Do you think males and females are affected in the same ways by peer pressure? Explain your thoughts and then discuss with your class.

2. What facilities are there for young people in your local area? Do you think there are enough? Do you think that with more to do young people would be less likely to commit crime?

3. Flick through a selection of tabloid newspapers and see what examples you can find of the labelling of young people. What subcultures are more likely to be labelled? Why do you think this is? Do you agree with Cicourel that the social class, gender and ethnicity of a young person all affect whether they are negatively labelled or not?

Gender

Why do men commit more crime than women?

- **Differential gender socialisation.** If you think back to Unit 1, you should remember studying

differential gender socialisation. The main idea is that from birth girls and boys are socialised very differently by all the agents of social control. Do you remember Ann Oakley's (1981) study of family socialisation where she discovered that manipulation and canalisation was going on (see pages 35–36)? Many sociologists have used ideas such as these to help explain why males commit more crime than females.

ACTIVITY 168

Working with a partner, create an annotated poster to illustrate the main ways that the agents of socialisation socialise girls and boys differently. This should not be difficult – evidence can be found all around us!

What you should have seen from this activity is that our expectations of what females and males do are very different. If girls are, from an early age, trained to be in the home, passive and caring, whilst boys are encouraged to be outside in public spaces, being active and aggressive, then it is hardly surprising that males commit more crime than females. Many sociologists have even gone so far as to say that criminal behaviour is actually just a natural extension of masculinity. Whether you believe this to be the case or not, it is true to say that when we imagine a criminal it is typically a male image that we get. Males are somehow 'allowed' to be criminal, whereas for females this is still unexpected and 'abnormal' behaviour.

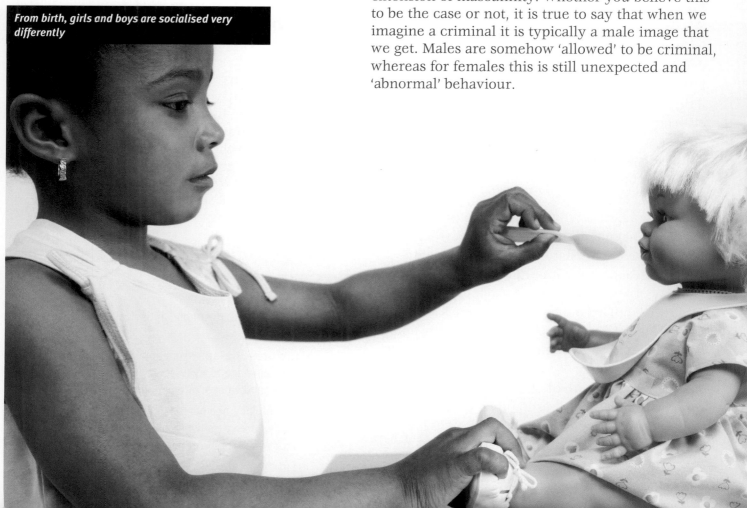

From birth, girls and boys are socialised very differently

SOCIALISATION, CULTURE AND IDENTITY

U2 T5

- **Different levels of social control.** Another reason that helps to explain the different levels of criminal behaviour between males and females is the different ways that both genders are controlled. In a society consumed by fear, girls are protected and shielded from danger in a way that boys are not. Just consider your own experiences of this for a moment, particularly if you have siblings of the opposite gender. In many families, the female child is not allowed to walk home at night, has a strict curfew for when to be home and is picked up or given money for taxi rides home. Most boys, however, have far greater freedom. They are usually allowed to return home later, walk everywhere and get home under their own steam. This is typical of a society that still views males and females very differently. It may be that the fact that boys have greater freedom than girls gives them greater opportunity to commit crime and could be a key reason to explain their higher levels of criminality.

- **Gender stereotyping.** A final factor to consider with regard to gender and crime is closely linked to the ideas of differential opportunities discussed above. Sociologists believe that our society still operates with a wide range of gender stereotypes in place, meaning that how we think about and react to males and females is very different. The implication of this for criminal behaviour is that those involved in the criminal justice system will also have different expectations of and reactions to males and females. For example, police officers, judges and juries may all be operating within accepted societal stereotypes of women that make it harder for them to believe that they are really criminal. This is not the case with males, however, and may be another reason to help explain why males are convicted of crimes more frequently than females. It should be noted, however, that as women get increased freedom and equality in society, thanks to the work of feminism, so their criminality is increasing. They are less likely to be at home, more likely to be in public and social situations and have a far wider range of powerful female role models to look up to.

KEY CONCEPTS

Gender socialisation – teaching males and females the expected patterns of behaviour for their gender in society.

Police targeting – where the police focus on a particular group of people in society, believing them to be more likely to be involved in criminal behaviour than other groups.

ACTIVITY 169

RESEARCH TASK
Using relevant internet sites on criminal statistics (see the list on page 150) and books such as *Social Trends*, investigate whether female criminality is increasing in society. Compare trends over time and produce graphs to represent any key findings. You could also research victim surveys and self-report studies and see if similar findings can be found there.

Ethnicity

Why are black men over-represented in the criminal statistics and prison population?

- **Poverty and unemployment.** If you believe the trends in the criminal statistics that state that certain ethnic minorities are more likely to commit criminal acts than others, then one possible explanation for this is the higher levels of poverty and unemployment that these groups experience in UK society. In a consumer society like ours, we are bombarded by advertising for material goods and so those without the means to buy these are under considerable pressure to fit in with the rest of society. One way of getting the products, of course, is to turn to crime. This, however, is certainly not the only explanation and many sociologists believe that the criminal statistics actually exaggerate black criminality. They think that the statistics are a reflection of our racially biased criminal justice system.

- **Police targeting.** One explanation that fits well with such ideas is that of **police targeting**. In the same way that young people are negatively labelled and stereotyped by society, so it can be argued, are certain ethnic minorities. This will mean that the police focus more of their time and efforts on those people in society that they believe are committing the majority of crime. The same kind of assumptions will be in operation in the court room. It may be that these prejudices are the reason that so many black people are found in our prison system, rather than that they are actually more likely to be criminal. Explanations such as this, of course, are closely linked to labelling theory that we looked at in the 'Age' section on page 157.

- **Discrimination and racism in the criminal justice system.** Some sociologists have gone so far as to say that the British justice system – the police, courts and prison system – are racist. They believe that **discrimination** and **racism** are integral to all aspects of law and order in Britain and so some ethnic minorities, such as Afro-Caribbean people, get a raw deal. This discrimination leads to them being more prominent in the criminal statistics and creates a stereotype linking black people with criminality. Believing that they are not treated equally in the criminal justice system may also result in some ethnic minorities feeling **alienated** from society. This could lead to further deviant behaviour via a **self-fulfilling prophecy**, as people see no point in following norms of acceptable behaviour in a society that has basically rejected them. They may, therefore, become involved in deviant or criminal behaviour as a result of the seemingly racist society they live in.

- **Different norms and values.** Sometimes different cultures have different norms and values to those of mainstream society. This may result in criminal or deviant behaviour being committed as a part of that culture. For example in the Rastafarian religion, smoking marijuana is perfectly acceptable as a way of getting closer to Jah (God). In Britain, however, this practice is illegal.

KEY CONCEPTS

Discrimination – treating people differently because of their social characteristics, e.g. not giving someone a job because they are female.

Racism – a form of discrimination; treating someone differently to others in society because of their ethnicity.

Alienation – not feeling part of the wider society or culture; feeling separate and cut off from it.

Self-fulfilling prophecy – a way of thinking about a person or group of people, usually negative, that causes that person or group of people to behave in a way that makes the belief reality.

ACTIVITY 170

RESEARCH TASK

There has been a lot of focus in sociology and society generally on the alleged racism in our criminal justice system. Your task is to find out a little more about this by using a selection of appropriate research methods, both primary and secondary. Working in small groups will probably work best.

- Use the internet, sociology journals and magazines and textbooks to investigate the Stephen Lawrence murder case and the Macpherson Report.

- Think of relevant people in your local community who may be able to help you discover whether racism is a factor in explaining the disproportionately high levels of black people in the prison population.

- Put a research plan together that will allow you to gather as much evidence and information as possible.

- Make sure you allocate tasks appropriately in your group and organise yourselves effectively to meet your deadline.

Present your findings as a piece of journalism for your teacher to assess. This could be a piece for a school or local newspaper, video footage for local television news or a documentary, or a podcast to be accessed online.

Note: This is a sensitive topic for investigation so remember all of the ethical guidelines you learned about in Unit 1 (pages 19–20) when you prepare your research plans. Make sure you approach the task without prejudice and avoid any leading or potentially offensive questions. You need to act as a real sociologist would here – be professional and free from bias at all times.

Social class

Why are the working class, particularly those from inner city areas, more likely to be convicted of crimes than other social classes?

- **Socialisation and subculture.** Some sociologists believe that different social classes in society are socialised differently. If a child has not been adequately socialised into the norms, values and morals of society then there will be little to stop them committing acts of crime and deviance.

Indeed in some communities it may be the case that criminal behaviour is an accepted part of life. For these sociologists it is the culture and way of life of the working class that helps to explain a higher involvement with crime and deviance. This is a good example of a cultural explanation of crime.

- **Lack of opportunities.** Other sociologists do not agree with the cultural view, believing instead that working-class criminality is more to do with inequalities in society than anything else. This is known as a structural view of crime, meaning that the unfair structure of society, rather than a working-class subculture, is to blame. For a variety of reasons, such as having a poorer education, fewer qualifications, a worse-paid job and less spare cash, crime may be a real temptation for some working-class people.

- **Status frustration.** Another theory of crime which also considers things from a structural point of view is that of status frustration. This is closely linked to the ideas of a lack of opportunity in the paragraph above. Statistics all show that working-class youth does less well in education than do other social classes. This could be due to such factors as lower aspirations, teacher labelling and lack of money. The end result, however, is that for many of the working class, education becomes a time in their life when they are made very aware of their lack of status and power in society. This is further emphasised when they later find it difficult to gain a good job with clear promotion possibilities.

This is all said to result in them feeling frustrated and angry with an unfair society which has condemned them to failure. One way to get their own back and to rebel against this society is to resort to criminal and delinquent behaviour. It must be noted, however, that most working-class people are not criminal, something that explanations such as this one fail to explain!

- **Marxism.** This final explanation also looks at the structure of society when trying to explain the higher levels of criminality in the working class. British society, like most societies in the Western world, is a capitalist one. This means that profit, money and material possessions are highly valued and we often find ourselves in competition with others to have the latest clothes, gadgets and cars. To make matters worse, this message is also reinforced by the media. We are constantly bombarded by advertisements trying to persuade us to part with our hard-earned cash, and having money to spend has become a norm.

But what do you do if you do not have the money to join in with all this spending? Well, Marxists believe that crime is one alternative. They also think that our legal system is biased in favour of those at the top of the class structure who have the most money. This means that a working-class person is far more likely to be targeted and prosecuted for criminal behaviour than, say, a member of the upper class. Labelling theory and stereotyping could also be used to help explain the apparently higher levels of criminal behaviour in the working class.

ACTIVITY 171

1. Some people argue that crime is committed because people do not have enough money. What are the problems with this argument?

2. Is there any evidence of working-class status frustration in your school, college or local community? Discuss as a class.

3. Do you agree with the Marxists that the higher your social class the less likely you are to be convicted of a criminal offence? Why or why not?

4. Prepare your evidence and ideas to persuade others either for or against the statement 'more social control in society would reduce crime'.

You should now be clear on all the important definitions and key concepts such as delinquency, situational deviance and crime. You should also understand the role of social control and be able to see the difference between formal and informal agents in terms of their role in reducing crime and deviance in society. In the topic you have also considered patterns of crime by age, gender, ethnicity and social class. Here we looked at how crime is measured and the inherent problems with these methods. We also considered how crime can impact on a community. Finally, we looked at key explanations for crime, including an understanding of structural and cultural causes. Make sure you cover all of these topics when you are preparing and revising for your final examinations.

 # GradeStudio

Remember in the exam that students who perform well are those that can use sociological theory and concepts accurately. You have been introduced to a wide range of these in this section of the Crime and deviance chapter, so make sure you use them!

Have a look at the following two introductions to the question:

'Identify and explain two explanations for why the working class commit more crime.'

Decide which one works best and why.

GEORGIA: 'Sociologists have identified a wide range of ideas to explain why certain social groups in society are more likely to be convicted of criminal behaviour than others. The working class are a good example of one such group. The two factors that I shall be discussing in this answer will be status frustration and subculture.'

ALEX: 'The working class commit more crime because they are lazy and haven't got a job and so have no money.'

KNOW YOUR STUFF?

Check your understanding by discussing these questions:

1. What is the difference between a crime and an act of deviance? Give examples of both.

2. Identify and explain two formal agents of social control.

3. Which method of measuring crime is likely to produce the most valid picture of crime? Explain your answer.

4. What are the links between social class, gender, ethnicity, age and crime?

5. What is the difference between a cultural and a structural explanation of crime?

6. Outline and assess three different sociological explanations of why people commit crime.

ExamCafé

Revision

To start revision: always break your topic into manageable chunks. When you revise an area, use your knowledge of exam structure to invent possible questions. For example, for each area consider what evaluative questions could be asked.

When writing about why crime is committed, remember to revise both the structural and cultural causes.

Use this table to check that you understand the key concepts for each section.

Revision checklist

Section	Key concepts
1. Definitions of crime and deviance	
The social nature and relativity of deviance; the standardisation of deviance; normality and conformity	deviance crime delinquency
The relationship between crime and deviance	norms values beliefs historical deviance situational deviance cross-cultural deviance
2. Controlling crime and deviance	
Types of social control (formal/ informal)	informal control
Agents of social control (family, school, peer group, mass media, workplace and formal agencies, including police and courts)	formal control conformity agents of social control
Solutions to crime: the effect of prisons; community service; mental health orders; ASBOs, etc.	
3. Patterns of crime	
Measurements of crime	official statistics
Crime and its impact on the community	self-report studies victim surveys
Patterns of crime by class, gender, ethnicity and age	
4. Explanations of crime	
Knowledge of the different explanations of why people commit crime	socialisation peer-group pressure
Understanding the structural versus cultural nature of causes	opportunity structure labelling sociological explanations

ExamCafé

Exam preparation

Sample student answers

> 'To solve crime we need longer prison sentences.' Evaluate the arguments for and against this claim. **[24]**

Finley

Comments

Finley's answer does contain some terminology and shows clear understanding of it. He has also shown application and explanation. What is there is relevant, but only answers the question in part. However, he has neglected to evaluate the claim.

Criminals are in need of longer prison sentences. The punishments now are too easy. You can commit a crime and just get a probation order, which means that you do not really pay for your crime. Some people go in and out of prison often, which proves they should not have come out in the first place. Some criminals get community service orders which means they have to help out in the community. Examples of this include cleaning up public places. This hardly seems harsh enough if you have raped someone. Some criminals receive mental health orders. This may mean they have to take medication and receive counselling. In the media some who receive this have killed or tortured people. That does not seem fair.

So I do believe that we need longer prison sentences.

Austin

To discuss whether longer prison sentences would help solve crime you need to look at two things: why people commit crime and what other punishments are available. The media does seem to think we need longer prison sentences, but there is a lot to think about. However, there are also other ways to solve crime, perhaps by prevention.

Prison sentences are good for solving crime as they offer several of the functions needed. If you commit a crime then you should lose your freedom. It is a punishment for whatever you have done. However, there are other reasons that prisons are good. For most people it acts as a deterrent: people do not commit crime, because they do not want to lose their freedom. Another good thing about prisons is that they try to reform the criminals. They offer education programmes and career training and often even counselling to help the criminal build a better future.

However, there are two main problems: there are not enough spaces in prisons any more and they cost the taxpayer a lot of money, and not all criminals should be imprisoned. For example, if you commit a petty crime such as shoplifting maybe going to prison is not suitable. Also when there you may meet worse criminals and become socialised into a criminal lifestyle. For shoplifting you may need to discover the cause of the crime. If it is a mental health issue such as kleptomania maybe counselling would be a better punishment.

Another crime that may not be best punished with prison is graffiti or criminal damage to public property. A more suitable punishment may be community service as it shows the criminal the effects of their crime.

However, it seems that all punishments available to solve crime may ignore a better idea, preventing crime in the first place. Informal agents of social control such as the family have their part to play. For example, a family as the primary agent of social control should teach their children right from wrong. This would solve more crime than any prisons. Other informal agents of social control such as schools and peer groups could also help prevent crime. Of course the police could also do more to prevent crime such as setting up more CCTVs or working with young people on how to stay out of trouble.

The main reason I do not feel that prisons are the best punishment is because of the very high reoffending rate. This alone shows that, no matter how long the sentence, prisons are not reforming their prisoners. Whilst it may feel like revenge is served if you lock criminals away longer, it is costly and does not change the criminal. So it appears that to stop crime you need to look at the cause to work out the punishment — for some prison sentencing is not the best option, whilst for other crimes it may be.

Comments

This response clearly shows a good level of knowledge. It discusses different forms of punishment as well as using good terminology to discuss the function of criminal punishments. This response clearly discusses the claim with relevant information. It explains all ideas fully, giving good examples. Finally, this response has a good, clear, evaluative style. It argues for and against the claim. It links all ideas and offers a good introduction and conclusion.

Unit 2
Topic 6: Youth

The key areas you will study in this topic are:

- How 'youth' is defined
- The peer group as an agent of social control
- What is youth subculture?
- What are gangs?

PAUSE FOR THOUGHT

- At five you can drink alcohol in private.
- At seven you can open your own bank account.
- At ten you are criminally responsible (eight in Scotland).
- At 13 you can get a part-time job.
- At 16 you can have sex, buy a lottery ticket, buy fireworks, get married with your parents' permission, fight for your country, leave school and enter a brothel legally.
- At 18 you can buy alcohol, buy cigarettes, get a tatoo, bet, vote and get married without consent.

1 What do you think of these laws?
2 What do they say about the term 'youth'?

Topic 6: Youth

Defining youth

What is childhood?

When do you think someone is a child? Sociologists such Philippe Ariès (1962) believed that the concept of **childhood** was only invented in the Middle Ages. He stated that before that, at about the age of six, children became miniature adults.

The invention of childhood

RESEARCH LINK

Go to *www.heinemann.co.uk/hotlinks*, enter express code 7573P and click on the *BBC website* to find out more about Victorian children.

Childhood is often regarded as the age after infancy and before **adolescence** (which is the period between childhood and adulthood – the **teenage** years). However, the United Nations rules that a child is anyone under the age of 18. What is clear is that childhood has changed through the ages.

1700s: At a young age children learnt a trade or craft, often through an apprenticeship. Girls didn't learn to read or write and, depending on how rich their parents were, some girls were married by the age of 12.

Early 1900s: Due to the 1870 Education Act children all had to go to school from the age of 5 to 10. They learnt a curriculum based on their gender and were given the cane if they behaved badly. Due to employment acts children under 8 no longer worked in the mines, up chimneys, or in factories.

Late 1900s: Due to the Butler Act of 1944 children stayed at school until they were 15 (raised to 16 in 1973). Due to the 1988 Education Act boys and girls all learnt the same curriculum (introduction of the National Curriculum).

21st Century: Since the Children's Act 2004, children can't be hit by a family member if it leaves bruises!

2009: Children have to go to school until they are 16 (planned to increase to 18 by 2015). Children can work, but not during school hours. Children can't marry until they are 16 (if their parents agree) but they can fight for their country!

ACTIVITY 172

Pick a time period from the flow diagram, do some further research and write a diary of a day as a child at that time.

KEY CONCEPTS

Childhood – the age after infancy but before adolescence.

Adolescence – the period between childhood and adulthood.

SOCIALISATION, CULTURE AND IDENTITY

U2
T6

Teenager – someone between the ages of 13 and 19.

Disappearance of childhood – Postman's view that the innocent age, in which the young have little responsibility or worry, is being eroded.

Loss of innocence – the belief that children grow up fast and become aware of adult issues early.

Youth – the period between childhood and adulthood.

Social construction of youth – the belief that the age of youth is not the same everywhere; that social factors affect both age and the norms surrounding that stage.

Some sociologists such as Neil Postman (1983) believe that there is currently a **disappearance of childhood**. Because of the adult messages children see every day in the mass media, they become 'confused little adults'. He called these children 'tweenagers' and used the examples of underage drinking and smoking as evidence. Results from a survey by MINTEL found that by 14 years of age, 90 per cent of girls are wearing some kind of make-up (2004). Other contemporary evidence can be seen in girls' magazines such as *Bliss* and *Cosmo Girl*, which have given away vouchers for free tanning spray and contained articles on how to get a boyfriend. Such evidence has led to a debate over whether children are going through **a loss of innocence**. This is a world where children grow up fast, are aware of their own bodies and are worried about adult issues such as sexuality. However, not all agree that childhood has been eroded, especially when comparing life now to the 1800s.

GradeStudio

You need to be able to debate whether childhood is disappearing to ensure you can write an essay on this subject. At GCSE, students often struggle with evaluation. Ensure you use words such as 'in agreement' and 'similarly' or 'however' and 'in disagreement' to link your ideas appropriately.

GradeStudio

Revise using your key concepts as answers in the exam that lack sociological evidence do not score highly. For example, an answer that states 'childhood is disappearing because young girls are having sex' would be weak. A better answer would be: 'Some feel childhood is disappearing, for example Postman, who used examples such as underage sex to evidence a loss of innocence.'

Do a search of images in the media and make a collage to illustrate Postman's 'disappearance of childhood' theory. Using your key concepts, write a presentation to explain your collage.

Youth

Youth is a term that people define in different ways and apply to different age groups. This can be seen when looking at the laws for young people (see Pause for thought on page 167). For ease, many define it as the period between childhood and adulthood. Sociologists are interested in whether youth is actually a specific biological stage or something that society creates and defines (a **social construction of youth**).

Evidence for youth being a biological stage

- Biologically, all youth go through hormonal changes at puberty.
- At this time, young people experience changes in both their attitudes and behaviour.
- Many young people go through times of being irritable and unsure of themselves.

Evidence for social construction of youth

- **The law:** in each society the rights and responsibilities of young people differ greatly. Laws are very different in various societies. For example, in England you must be 17 to drive, whereas in many American states you can drive at 16.
- **Social norms:** customs also vary. In England the average age for a female to marry is just over 27, whereas in Niger it is just over 17.
- **Emotional/behavioural norms:** whilst it is often believed that for all youth life is confusing and emotional, some sociologists such as Margaret Mead (1927) argue that this is not the case in every society. Mead claimed that Samoan young people did not have this period of turmoil.

U2
T6

YOUTH

Find examples of the different arguments for youth as a biological stage and youth as a social construction. Copy and complete a table as below:

Arguments for biological stage	Other examples	Arguments for social construction	Other examples
Physical differences.	Girls begin their menstrual cycle.	Law is different in different societies.	In England you may buy cigarettes from the age of 18; in Bhutan it is illegal for anyone to buy tobacco products.

GradeStudio

The activity you have just completed is a good example of a possible debate topic for a 24-mark question. Try writing an introduction and a conclusion for the question:

'Youth is just a biological stage.' Evaluate this claim.

Remember, a good conclusion is necessary to write a complete answer!

ACTIVITY 175

Create your own life stage timeline showing the appropriate ages for each stage and using the following terms: Childhood, Adolescence, Toddler, Teenager, Middle aged, Elderly, Youth.

Transition

It appears that youth may be more related to change and **transition**, than to biological age. It could be seen as a time that allows a young person to leave behind childhood ideas and behaviour and become an adult. In some cultures it is a time of experimenting with adult roles, such as beginning part-time work. In the contemporary UK this transition may include learning to drive, whereas in other cultures it may be marked very differently. The ceremonies and proceedings used to mark the transition from childhood to adulthood are often known as either **rites of passage** or initiation rites.

Coming to secondary school is a transitional stage. Did your school have any initiation procedures? What were they? What was their purpose? Can you think of any they should add?

Examples of rites of passage

Suri life: to become initiated into adulthood, Suri boys become 'rora', which includes acts of violence, insults from the elders of the tribe, having to complete menial tasks, being whipped and sometimes being starved. Through this process a boy becomes a man.

Dassanech life: to become initiated into womanhood, girls from 10–12 years of age are circumcised. This ceremony is conducted by the elder females in the tribe. Once this has been done, the girl becomes recognised as a woman and is able to marry.

RESEARCH LINK

Go to *www.heinemann.co.uk/hotlinks*, enter express code 7573P and click on the *BBC website* for pictures and further information on the Suri and Dassanech tribes.

Debutantes: in England upper-class girls used to become women when presented to society at a 'coming out ball'. In rich American families this tradition is often marked with a large ceremony (debutante ball), where the girls wear white gowns and gloves and are individually introduced to the society or audience of the ball. For further information or ideas about debutantes see the film *She's the Man*.

Bar/Bat Mitzvah: Jewish boys and girls attend classes to learn about their religious heritage along with their future role as a Jewish mother or father. When they are 12 (for girls) or 13 (for boys), the young person is expected to show they have enough knowledge to take on their personal religious responsibility. At this stage a ceremony marks their transition to adulthood.

Having looked at these four rites of passage, what is different in the ways they mark the transition from childhood to adulthood? Why do you think they are different?

KEY CONCEPTS

Transition – a period of change from one stage to the next.

Rites of passage – initiation into the next stage of life.

Agents of social control – the various groups, both formal and informal, that control our behaviour.

Conformity – following the rules.

Formal agents of social control – agents that only exist to control society, such as the police.

Informal agents of social control – agents that control society, although control is not their primary function, such as schools.

Peer group – others of the same age, interests and social status.

It makes sense that different societies have different norms and values. Therefore, all rites of passage will be different in order to match the particular society's requirements for socialisation. In a society where men hunt, obviously a boy needs to learn to hunt!

GradeStudio

Remember that you will be tested on your key concepts. Think about what each concept means and, to help you remember, write down an example of each.

Control through peer groups

As a young person you are socialised and controlled in a number of ways. Sociologists refer to the different groups that control you as the **agents of social control**. Some of these exist with the sole purpose of controlling you and making sure you **conform** (follow the rules). These are known as the **formal agents of social control**. Others also control you, but this is not the only reason they exist. These are known as the **informal agents of social control**.

ACTIVITY 176

Using your knowledge of agents of social control, which of these do you think are formal and which are informal?

Family	The police	The courts
School	Mass media	Peer group
Religion	Prisons	Workplace

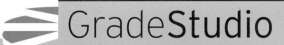

GradeStudio

You will be expected to know the different agents of social control. Often students are unclear on the difference between informal and formal agents. Make sure you revise the difference.

ACTIVITY 177

Copy the pyramid below and use it to arrange the agents of social control in order to reflect the influence you think they have on your life.

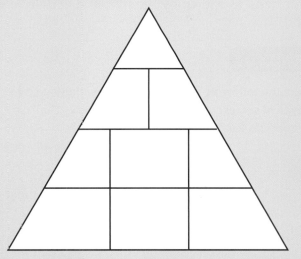

1. Discuss and compare your answers in a small group. Explain why you have chosen your order. Did you find there were many similarities? Why do you think that is? Survey your class to find out the number one agent. Was there much agreement?

2. Imagine you are a child of five. Would the pyramid change much? Why? Imagine you are 35 years old. Would the pyramid change much? Why?

The peer group as an agent of social control

A simple definition of **peer group** is 'others of the same age, with the same background, interests and social status'. Many young people feel that their peer group is a main agent of social control. Although it is an informal agent, the influence of a peer group when we are 15 can be very strong.

So how does our peer group actually control us?

Often it is fear of rejection or being laughed at that controls our behaviour. However, sanctions can also be verbal or physical. It is the pressure to conform from our peers that make us decide to follow this agent of social control rather than another. For example, you might have to decide whether to go home on time, as dictated by your family, or to stay out longer, as dictated by your peer group. **Peer group pressure** is often stronger at different points in our lives, as shown by the pyramid activity on page 171.

In the media, peer group pressure is commonly associated with negative behaviour, but it can be positive. Your peer group can convince you not to break the law, remind you to help others in trouble or even get you to do your homework! This is known as *positive* peer group pressure, as it helps you to conform to society's norms and values. Whilst the peer group is seen as an agent of social control that conflicts with many others, this does not have to be the case (as will be discussed in the following section on subcultures).

Youth escapes charges over 'happy slap' attack

The youngster attacked Becky Smith, 16, so friends could film the assault for fun on their mobile phones in a youth craze known as 'happy slapping'.

But the police have decided Becky's attacker should only receive a caution for the assault.

Becky was left with a black eye, bruises and cuts in the attack launched by a fellow school pupil in Blackley, Manchester. She was jumped from behind by a youngster, also 16, who knocked her to the ground and she had to then spend two days in hospital.

A gang of five boys filmed the attack and the video clip was passed around school via mobile phones, and was shown to Becky's brother Craig, 13.

The victim's mother, Georgina Smith, 39, described the incident as 'sickening' and said her daughter had been left terrified and did not want to go back to school because other pupils had watched the video of the attack.

The attack on Becky was the latest in a string of violent 'happy slapping' incidents – including the alleged rape of an 11-year-old girl. It involves children attacking other youngsters or random passers-by and recording the attacks on their mobiles. Videos of the 'slaps' are then exchanged between phones and posted on the internet as a joke.

Last month, two 18-year-olds were jailed for six-and-half years each after setting fire to a stranger and filming the attack on a phone. Victim Matthew Kitchen, 41, had fallen asleep in a bus shelter in Bury, Greater Manchester, when Benjamin Mortenson and David Smolinski set him alight. Mr Kitchen nearly died. The video footage was shown at Bolton Crown Court, and features the pair shouting: 'This is the funniest thing I have ever seen ... We're gonna kill him ... He's on fire.'

Adapted from: *Daily Mail*, 20 June 2005

Youth subculture

Defining the different types of youth culture

Consider every other young person in the UK of your age. What similarities are there to yourself? The idea that all young people have a similar set of norms and values, which is different to that of other age groups, is known as **youth culture**. As discussed earlier in the chapter, youth is defined in many ways, which makes it hard to find a single set of norms and values for all young people.

Young people are connected by norms that are created by:

- the legal position of young people – e.g. the norm of attending school
- the biological changes that young people go through – e.g. the norm of mood swings
- society's expectations of young people – e.g. the norm of not being a parent.

An example of Goths.

U2
T6
YOUTH

ACTIVITY 181

Copy and complete the following table about yourself:

Daily activity	
Leisure activity	
Favourite music	
Favourite sport/hobby	
Favourite possession	

Compare your answers to the activity above in a small group. Were there many similarities? Why? If your group contained your friends then it is possible that some of the answers were similar. This is because we often mix with friends who have similar norms to ourselves. For example, if you love horses you will spend time with others who love horses. These groups are known as **youth subcultures**. A subculture is a culture within a culture. In school these different groups are often easy to spot.

KEY CONCEPTS

Peer group pressure – the feeling that you should conform to the expectations of others your age.

Youth culture – a set of norms and values that connect all young people.

Youth subcultures – different cultures that are within youth culture.

Relationship between youth subculture and identity

The youth subculture we choose to mix with partly defines our identity. The spidergram below shows the different features of identity.

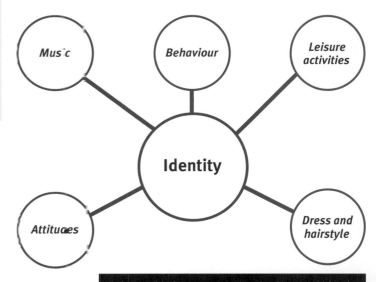

Relationship between youth subculture and identity

Since the 1950s, sociologists and the media have written about many different types of youth subcultures. In the 1950s it was the Teddy boys; in the 1960s it was Hippies, Mods and Rockers; in the 1970s it was Skinheads and Punks; in the 1980s it was New Romantics later followed by the Goths; in the 1990s it was Hip Hop and in the 2000s Chavs and Emos. Can you think of any other major youth subcultures that are around today?

Table 2.5.1: Elements of two youth subcultures

Subculture	Goths – 1980s	Punks – 1970s
Attitudes	A sense of themselves as being different to the rest of youth. Saw themselves as 'outsiders.' Important values: individualism, tolerance, creativity.	A sense of themselves as being anti-establishment; angry and out to shock.
Behaviour	Non-violent, pro-tolerant behaviour to the marginalised. Creative activities, e.g. creating art.	Antisocial. Spitting at gigs. 'Expressing their anger' through violent acts such as vandalism, squatting, anything that showed their anti-establishment attitude.
Leisure activities	Getting pierced, going to gigs, hanging out with friends.	Going to gigs. Hanging out with friends. Direct action against anything they disagreed with.
Drugs	Not a specific drug as such. Associations with the drink Absynthe.	Lots! Sniffing glue was a famous favourite.
Dress/style	Black clothes, often based on gothic style. Lots of make-up.	Ripped drainpipe jeans, lots of safety pins (including through the face), tartan skirts over trousers (both genders).
Hairstyle	Black, usually back-combed.	Mohican; extreme and individual styles that involved lots of hair spray and long spikes and bright dyes.
Music	Gothic macabre music, e.g. Bauhaus and Marilyn Manson.	Angry music made by bands that confessed to having no musical talent, such as the Sex Pistols. It was very punk to be proud of not being musical.
Sociological research	Hodkinson (2002) The subculture is formed based on actual shared interests, not just a need to rebel.	Frith (1978) The subculture was a reaction to high unemployment, a music industry full of teenage clean-cut pop bands and politics they did not agree with.
Websites/ Films for further information	Go to *www.heinemann.co.uk/hotlinks*, enter express code 7573P and click on the *Goth website*. *The Crow* Vampire films generally	Go to *www.heinemann.co.uk/hotlinks*, enter express code 7573P and click on the *Punk77 website*. *Sid and Nancy* *Punk: Attitude*

ACTIVITY 182

Research one of the subcultures in the list below:

1950s Teddy boys
1960s Hippies or Mods and Rockers
1970s Skinheads or Punks
1980s New Romantics or Goths
1990s Hip Hop
2000s Chavs or Emos.

Pick a subculture of your own choice. Then make a presentation showing how it affects the identity of its members. Use the spidergram on page 173, to help you plan your presentation.

 GradeStudio

You will need to understand, and give examples of, how any two youth subcultures create an identity. To gain a good grade you need to ensure your answers include sociological evidence. When researching the different subcultural groups, try to gather knowledge of any relevant sociological research where possible. To ensure your answers remain sociological, also use key concepts. If a student writes '*Goths all wear black and like make-up*', they will not score highly. However, if they write '*the Goth subculture is linked by their obvious style: clothing, hair and make-up being black and their core values: tolerance and creativity*', they will demonstrate usage of key concepts of subculture, style and values.

Youth subcultures can link people with similar interests and create identity, but some youth may choose to join based on their biological or social characteristics.

Think about the communal areas of your school or college. Do you think that class, race or gender affect the groups young people choose to be in?

Class

Some subcultures seem to unite young people of similar economic status. J Clarke (1976) researched Skinhead culture and wrote that it united members of the working class, allowing its members to release their frustration at being poor and unemployed. It has been stated that their anger was targeted at immigrants and that they were a patriotic but also a racist subculture. However, many others believe that the Skinhead subculture did not start out this way, but that it had its roots in Ska music, a fusion of Jamaican and British and American rock.

Ethnicity

Ethnicity clearly links some groups of young people. Look around the public areas of your school or college. Do you see evidence of this? Studies of Bhangra claim that this music from the Punjab has created a youth subculture. It incorporates music, style and dance which have now spread to a wide audience. This subculture has crossed over to mainstream culture, as seen through fusion music such as Apache Indian which combines Bhangra and hip hop.

Gender

In the 1970s, some sociologists argued that young teenage girls were part of a gendered subculture. McRobbie and Garber (1976) referred to this as a **bedroom subculture**. They wrote that it existed separately from boys, who were hanging out in public. They interviewed a group of girls and found that their culture was led by the media and involved experimenting with hair and make-up and discussing boys in their bedrooms.

More recently, further studies of girl power have looked at whether this has changed girls' subcultures.

KEY CONCEPTS

Bedroom subculture – a subculture of young teenage girls.

Growth of affluence – an increase in wealth.

Manipulation by the media – this is the idea that the media has invented youth culture in order to make money.

RESEARCH LINK

McRobbie and Garber got some of their research from a group interview. For more information on this form of interviewing look at page 7 in Sociology basics: Part A.

GradeStudio

It is really good practice to use the sociological studies in your work. Find ways to revise and learn the different studies (such as McRobbie and Garber). Making revision cards can help you memorise the different names.

Reasons for the development of youth culture and subcultures

If, as suggested previously, youth is a social construction, then the development of youth culture can also be said to be a social construction. Research has concluded that youth culture came to Britain after the Second World War. Many reasons have been given for this.

- In the 1950s, Britain experienced a **growth of affluence**. This meant that British people had some money to spend, as they were richer.
- Young people who were leaving school at 15 had jobs and, therefore, had money to spend on their chosen subculture, its music and fashion.
- As time went on and the school leaving age rose, young people had even more time to spend on their chosen subculture.
- Business owners and advertisers wanted the young people's money, so they started making products and marketing them to the young – known as **manipulation by the media**.

ACTIVITY 183

Draw a spidergram to help you to revise the reasons why youth subcultures grew in Britain. Add examples or drawings to help you remember these reasons.

The reasons individuals join subcultures are varied. Consider a subculture you know something about. Why would someone join?

Reasons to join a subculture

- **Shared interests:** such as music, style and fashion.
- **Rite of passage:** all young people, before they become adults, experiment and try to be their own person through different subcultures.
- **Solution to problems:** for example, if you are facing racism, you may choose to join others and, therefore, share your problems.
- **Peer group pressure:** this may make you feel you have to join in.

Law breaking	Friendship
Family	Loyalty
Leadership	Well organised
Territory	Girls
Boys	Violence
Drugs	
Peer group pressure	

KEY CONCEPTS

Solution to problems – join a subculture to share problems.

Gang – a group that has some form of membership, some form of hierarchy and is often involved in criminal activities.

Territory – a gang's area which they claim as their own.

Delinquent subculture – groups that commit illegal activities.

GradeStudio

It will be important in the exam to illustrate your understanding. This is easily done through relevant examples. Practise by thinking of further examples of the reasons to join a subculture.

Gangs

Defining different types of gang

When you think of the term **gang**, what does it mean to you? Many of our ideas are based on the images we see in the media, whether in the news or in fictional films. Which of the following terms would you associate with gangs?

In this section, you will see that all of the above can be associated with *some* gangs. Gangs differ in why they exist, how they came together and how they are organised. However, a gang can be broadly defined as a group that has some form of membership, some form of hierarchy and, often, is involved in criminal activities.

Key aspects of being in a gang

Territory: gangs are often associated with an area. Recently the media have highlighted the growth of signature graffiti, which includes the use of a post-code. The gang will feel some ownership over an area and see any uninvited entry by other gangs as an aggressive act. Tag wars using graffiti are an example of this.

Delinquent subculture: gangs are bound by different norms and values from those of other young people, usually associated with law breaking. Whether through drug selling, violence or tagging (graffiti), membership of these groups is often about taking risks and committing crime.

Loyalty: gangs are bound together by the rule that membership means you must pledge allegiance to the gang. A member must be prepared to do anything for the gang when asked.

Hierarchy: gangs often have a clear hierarchy with a known leader or leaders. They are often seen to be well organised, although some studies show this is not the case for all gangs.

Twisted World of Britain's Gang Kids

EXCLUSIVE As lawless young savages bring casual murder to our cities.

By Jon Kirk

THE deadly world of Britain's ultra-violent street gangs is exposed by *The People* today. Hoodlums as young as SIX roam the streets carrying pistols, sawn-off shotguns, knives and baseball bats. These child savages think nothing of shooting, stabbing, stomping and maiming innocent people who stray on to their 'turf'. And rival gang members will be murdered for simply looking at them 'the wrong way'.

Our investigators discovered that INITIATION rituals include attacking innocent people or 'nonnies' – non-gang members. Knives are carried all the time but members can obtain guns and ammo in just one hour. Members are often illiterate, unemployable school drop-outs – dealing in drugs, stolen cars and guns. Sex between underage gang members is common. An SMN (South London gang: Shine My Nine) 'elder', 18-year-old 'Sarge' who has been involved with gangs since he was 13, told us: 'Gangs are a dangerous and scary place to be. There's murders, stabbings, shootings and beatings on a daily basis. But youngsters keep joining up, and more gangs keep appearing. There's no stopping it.'

There are dozens of reasons youngsters are flocking to join. Members told us they gain protection from rival gangs – essential in parts of Britain where 'nonnies' are attacked for fun. Being part of a gang is also a lucrative move, with earnings of up to £500 from crime. And they can fund their drug addiction with constant access to illegal substances. A high proportion of the kids are from broken homes and being part of a close-knit group is like having a 'family'. Others simply want to experience life in the fast lane.

Each gang is made up of 'elders' – leaders with a string of convictions – and raw recruits known as 'youngers'. New members must pass a chilling initiation which includes robbing passers-by, or 'boying' (humiliating) non-gang members. Anyone who dares fight back faces being stabbed with meat cleavers, craft knives or chisels. They listen to gangsta rap music, and idolise the heroes of violent films like *Boyz in the Hood*, *Goodfellas* and *Menace II Society*.

Other gangs have bases in more than one city, such as the Paki Panthers and the Tamil Tigers. Religion is also said to be a defining factor, with some gangs comprising solely Muslim or Catholic members. A 16-year-old member of SMN told our reporter: 'There are risks to joining a gang like getting robbed, shot or beaten by rivals. But the benefits are totally worth it. It's a big family where we earn loads of money, do exciting things, and gain protection.'

Adapted from *The People*, 22 July 2007

ACTIVITY 184

Using the adapted secondary source above, write a list of all the features and key aspects of being in a gang.

RESEARCH LINK

The information above is an example of a secondary source. For more information on these look at pages 20–22 in Unit 1, Sociology Basics.

ACTIVITY 185

Looking at the quotes opposite, discuss in a small group the different reasons for joining a gang.

Reasons for joining gangs

- *'I hang out with the others for something to do. There is never anything to do round here.'*

- *'My boys are all I have. They look out for me when no one else does. They are like brothers to me.'*

- *'The gang as you call it, are just my mates. We hang out together, make each other laugh. What else do friends do?'*

- *'All my life I have been a loner, I never fitted in anywhere. But now I fit in. Now in the gang I have somewhere I belong.'*

- *'In my gang I am important. The other girls see me as hard. At school I am just the dumb one, but in the gang I am the one they all look up to.'*

- *'I don't see myself as a gang member. Some idiots on my estate sometimes make me do stuff. I don't like to talk about it. But no, I am not one of them.'*

Boredom: for many, joining a gang is relief from **boredom**. It is little more than 'something to do.' Because of this, many youth workers feel that the way to stop young people getting into gangs is by providing activities and groups for them to get involved in.

Family: fictional presentations of gangs in the media often focus on the idea that young people who join gangs are lacking in family and/or role models. This image is one of boys with no fathers turning to gang leaders to replace their missing dad. What films can you think of that portray this image?

Friendship: for some, the people they 'hang out with' are merely their friendship group rather than a gang. The media sometimes reports normal youths' behaviour as gang behaviour. Their uniform appearance is due to shared tastes and their behaviour is just related to friends having fun. The supposed hierarchy, with a known leader, is just the norm of a group where some take on the role as leader, whilst others take on the role of followers. The strong loyalty of the group results from the value we have for friends.

Status frustration: Albert Cohen (1955) stated that some working-class children in the USA fail to succeed in school and have little social status. Due to this he noted that some, out of resentment (**status frustration**), join a group which has different norms and values to the society in which they are a failure. In this new group or gang, the young person can gain a new, higher status due to the different (often delinquent) norms and values.

Sense of belonging: Walter Miller (1958) felt that adolescence is a time when young people often feel lonely and unsure of themselves. As a result they feel the need to belong, to fit in. For this reason gang membership is popular as it offers a **sense of belonging**.

Peer group pressure: in some films, gang membership is presented as a rite of passage in the area depicted. It is not optional. Joining the gang is what you have to do to or you will be picked on as a 'nonnie' (non-gang member). For an example look back at the article on page 177.

Social networks: In Howard Williamson's study *Milltown Boys* (1997), after observing a delinquent gang for some time, he concluded that it was not organised. Although the gang cared about territory and hierarchy, they were not focused on illegal activities – it was more about having a **social network**.

Later in this chapter we will investigate the idea that gangs are partly a creation of the media.

So who joins a gang?

Now you have looked at the reasons why young people join gangs, it should be easy enough to draw up a list of the kinds of people who join gangs. But what about your gender, your class and your ethnicity? Do you think these affect the likelihood of becoming a gang member?

Gender

We sometimes seem to forget that girls join gangs too. They even start their own gangs. As girls are being socialised differently to their grandmothers, their behaviour is changing too. There are many media reports of girls leaving their 'bedroom culture' (see page 175) and being involved in gang life. Ann Widdecombe explored this in her documentary *Ann Widdecombe Versus Girl Gangs* (2008). Whilst she concluded that there had been a rise in girl gangs and female delinquency, there was no evidence of the existence of as many female as male gangs.

Ethnicity

As mentioned in the media article on page 177, religion and ethnicity are often factors in whether young people join gangs and which gangs they do join. If you think about the reasons to join a gang, which ones would lead a young person to join a gang with shared ethnicity?

Class

Howard Williamson (1997) found class to be an important factor in his study of the Milltown Boys of Cardiff. However, as mentioned previously, from his study he felt that the group he observed were more a social network than a gang.

ACTIVITY 187

Research and make a presentation of a gang and/or a social network which is based on class, gender or ethnicity. Try to explain why the members join. Also include examples of as many of the key aspects of a gang as you can.

GradeStudio

Remember that contemporary examples are a good source of evidence. The case study examples from your presentations will make useful and memorable evidence for the exam. However, you will not need to write a project on one group for the exam. To write a good answer, just use examples of the main features to show how and why members join gangs.

Media and gangs

Having discussed how gangs are defined and why young people join gangs, this final section will be looking at the media treatment of gangs. After comparing the reasons why people join gangs with why you choose to hang out with your own friends, the similarities may make you question the media's treatment of gangs. Whilst it would be difficult to deny the existence of violent gangs with brutal initiation rites, some media coverage has been said to exaggerate other delinquent behaviour. This causes audiences to become interested in the subject, which in turn encourages the media to

report more on that topic, often resulting in the public feeling frightened. Stan Cohen (1972) called this a moral panic (see also page 118 in the chapter on Mass media). The flow diagram which follows gives an example of this.

Moral panic

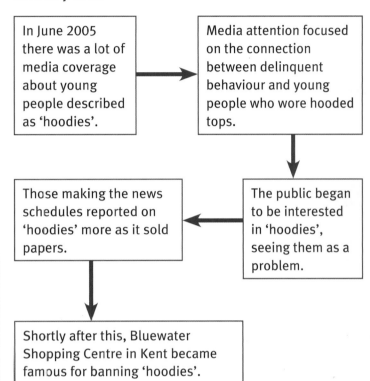

In June 2005 there was a lot of media coverage about young people described as 'hoodies'. → Media attention focused on the connection between delinquent behaviour and young people who wore hooded tops. → The public began to be interested in 'hoodies', seeing them as a problem. → Those making the news schedules reported on 'hoodies' more as it sold papers. → Shortly after this, Bluewater Shopping Centre in Kent became famous for banning 'hoodies'.

An example of media creation of a moral panic

Sociologists such as Cohen argue that gangs are partly the media's creation. They have **labelled** young people as delinquent and the media's exaggerated coverage of them often becomes self-fulfilling.

ACTIVITY 188

Can you think of a current moral panic? Collect examples of articles from newspapers and the internet. Then, write out your example in a flow diagram (as above) showing the media treatment of a group or subject.

Some sociologists feel that the media is creating these moral panics on purpose. They feel that these groups of young people are often used as a **scapegoat**; the media blames them instead of looking at society to see why they are in gangs. These sociologists believe that to stop gang culture, you have to look beyond the individuals involved and find out who is vulnerable to gang membership and how to help them.

Grade**Studio**

You will need to be able to evaluate whether only lonely young people join gangs. Practise by planning your response and the evidence you would cite. Remember to argue for and against the claim and consider the conclusion you would write. Be careful not to just give your personal opinion. For example, 'I think people in my area join gangs because they have no dads' does not include evidence. The following answer would score highly: 'Some young people do join out of loneliness. This was discovered by Walter Miller who said gangs offer a "sense of belonging"'.

KNOW YOUR STUFF?

In this chapter we have looked at how society defines youth; both in the law and through an agreed understanding of what the term means. We have also looked at how peer groups can control individuals, sometimes with their consent and sometimes under pressure only. When individuals join a group and become, for example a 'chav' or an 'emo', the characteristics of these groups or subcultures can be studied by sociologists. A 'gang' is an example of a more aggressive subculture.

Check your understanding by discussing the following questions:

1. Identify and explain three ways in which childhood could be said to be disappearing. Use evidence such as key concepts and examples to explain your ideas.

2. Explain three ways your subculture can affect your identity.

3. Using examples, show how your peer group can affect your behaviour. Remember to use evidence in your answer.

4. Identify and explain three types of informal control.

5. Using one example, show how an initiation ceremony can help an individual to be socialised into the norms and values of their society.

SOCIALISATION, CULTURE AND IDENTITY

ExamCafé

Revision

Examiner's tips

When writing about youth subcultures, ensure you include evidence. To revise for this use the table on page 174.

Use this table to check that you understand the key concepts for each section.

Revision checklist

Section	Key concepts

• knowledge of the biological stage versus social construction views of youth
• knowledge of cross-cultural rites of passage/initiation
• knowledge of the debate over whether childhood is being eroded.
	• youth
	• rites of passage
	• adolescence
	• childhood
	• transition
	• social construction of youth:
	  – loss of innocence
	  – disappearance of childhood
	  – teenagers.

• types of social control (formal and informal) • agencies of social control (family, school, peer group, mass media, workplace and formal agencies including police and courts) • the role of the peer group in controlling the behaviour of young people.	• informal control • formal control • conformity • agents of social control • peer-group pressure.
• defining the different types of youth culture • relationship between youth subculture and identity • reasons for the development of youth culture/youth subcultures.	• youth culture • youth subcultures • bedroom subculture • growth of affluence • solution to problems • peer group pressure • manipulation by the media.
• defining different types of gangs • reasons for joining gangs.	• gangs • territory • delinquent subculture • social network • scapegoat • labelling • sense of belonging • status frustration • boredom.

Exam preparation

Sample student answers

> 1 Identify and explain 2 examples of how youth subculture can affect your identity. **[8]**
>
> 2 'The term youth is just a social construction.' Evaluate the arguments for and against this claim. **[24]**

Answer to question 1

Rashid

One example of a subculture that can be seen to affect your identity is the Goth subculture. It affects several parts of your identity. It affects your dress and image. Goths wear black and lots of make-up. It also affects your attitudes; Goths often feel that they are outsiders and care about creative activities. Lastly, being a Goth affects your identity through behaviour. They spend their time going to gigs, getting pierced and listening to Marilyn Manson.

Another example of a subculture that affects identity is the Punks. They wore outrageous clothes, safety pins and had brightly coloured hair. The punks all listened to the Sex Pistols and believed in anarchy. Being a punk meant not caring about the rules of life.

Comments
Rashid's paragraph is good because it thinks sociologically about the ways in which identity is affected by subculture. It logically looks at dress and image, attitudes and then behaviour. It gives the answer a good structure and ensures it is not just common sense. However, the answer could be further improved by noting that the research on Goths is from Hodkinson's work.

Comments
The second part of the answer is not as good as the first. It begins well with a clear second idea. It is good practice to begin your second idea with a separate paragraph and a clear starter such as 'Another idea/ way...' However, the second idea lacks sociological structure. Rashid needed to focus on the features of identity affected by subculture.

Comments
Overall, the answer has several ideas, which is good as it is wide ranging. However, it lacks the use of sociological evidence through either key concepts or studies.

Answer to question 2

Sarah

Comments
This is a good introduction. It outlines a partial plan for the essay. However, it could be improved by mentioning the other side of the debate and defining social construction.

Comments
This is a good paragraph. It includes evidence – a contemporary example based on law. It then successfully uses a relevant example. It could be improved further by the student then relating the point back to the question: 'This shows that …'

This statement is arguing that the term youth is a social construction. This can be seen if you look at the law, emotional and behavioural norms as well as social norms.

Over time and in different societies the law surrounding youth changes. An example of this is the law in 2008 stated you have to be 18 to buy cigarettes, but before that you could buy them at 16. The fact that the law has changed shows opinions about when young people are old enough to choose to smoke have also changed.

Comments
This paragraph starts well. The use of 'however' is important and leads into the next section clearly. Again, there is some good sociological evidence in the accurate and relevant use of key concepts.

However, many people would argue that youth is a biological stage not a social construction. They would argue this by looking at hormonal changes all young people go through, known as puberty. They would also discuss the emotional changes that lead all young people to be irritable and aggressive.

Margaret Mead felt that youth was not a biological stage because in her studies of Samoan youth, they did not go through a period of turmoil. In different societies there are different social norms surrounding young people. For example, in some societies girls are expected to marry at 17, like in the Niger, whereas in British society girls get married at around 27.

So from this evidence it is clear that youth is a mixture of a biological stage and social construction. It involves biological changes but the social norms and expectations of youth in different times and places do change.

Comments
In this section, Sarah uses a good study, but she does not link it to the debate. She just drops it in. Instead, she should have linked it to the paragraph before. It is a good evaluative point against the biological stage, but has not been presented in that way. Sarah could have begun the paragraph with a phrase such as: 'In disagreement with this view is …'
The second point, about social norms also needs a link, for example 'Another way of proving that youth is a social construction is to look at social norms…'

Comments
This is a good conclusion. It does not choose one final right answer, but it does briefly sum up and give an explanation.

Comments
Overall, this is a good response. Its strength is in its use of relevant sociological evidence. It offers key concepts, contemporary examples, studies and legal changes. Its weakness is its lack of link words and there need to be more explicit links back to the question title.

Applying sociological research techniques

Look at the lists below and match each definition to the correct term.

1. Data made up of charts and graphs	a)	secondary
2. Data made up of words and description	b)	sample
3. When care has been taken to look after the people taking part in the research	c)	covert
4. Truthful or accurate information collected by a researcher	d)	primary
5. Doing the research again gets the same results	e)	quantitative
6. Studying people without them knowing	f)	ethical
7. Information collected first hand by the researcher	g)	objective
8. Information already there and not collected directly by the researcher	h)	qualitative
9. Data not influenced by the researcher's own views	i)	valid
10. A group of people chosen to collect data from	j)	reliable

Question 3a: Evaluate the **secondary source** referred to in Investigation 1. Was it useful in meeting the aims? Give reasons for your answer. [3]

Response: This question is to test your skills of evaluation. That means how well you can work out the strengths and weaknesses of a part of the research. You should look for both good points and bad points and explain them.

You need to be aware that the secondary source in the investigation is an article from *The Times* newspaper, but you will have discussed this when you studied the investigation material in your lessons.

If you do not show in your answer that you know the aims of the research, you will not be able to argue whether they have been met or not and it is unlikely that you will get any marks! Therefore, stating the aims clearly would be a good idea.

A possible example could be:

- *Aim* – To see what the police think of 'hoodies'.
- *Relate to the source* – In *The Times* article, information was collected from a number of areas, including the Greater Manchester Police, West Yorkshire Police and police on Merseyside. From all, there were comments which took the view that people who hide their faces with hoods or similar are likely to be criminal.

- *Now evaluate* – The evidence from the police gives their view of young people who hide their faces with clothing. It is useful as it fits with the aim to see what the police think of 'hoodies'.

Note: The question says **aims**, i.e. more than one! This means that referring to only one aim will not be enough.

GradeStudio

Evaluating

This is the most difficult of the skills you will need, but with practice you will learn to use it!

Try evaluating something in your everyday life such as a party you went to. List the good things about it, then the bad things. Now decide whether, overall, it was worth going to.

Words such as 'on the other hand' and 'however' are useful, as they show you have considered both sides.

Question 3b: Was it useful in proving the hypothesis? Give reasons for your answer. [3]

Response: This is an evaluation question similar to question 3a, so you need to follow the same guidelines.

A possible example:

- *Hypothesis* – The researcher is trying to prove that the police are more likely to stop teenagers if they dress in a particular way.

- *Evaluate by selecting evidence from the source* – The *Times* article is useful in proving the hypothesis, as it states that a man in Stockton-on-Tees was imprisoned for wearing a hooded top in a car park. It also says that an ASBO given in Manchester banned someone from wearing a glove on his right hand and this also proves the hypothesis.

Note: You should try to find more than one piece of evidence.

Section B

The instruction in your exam paper will be set out as below:

> **Section B: Using *Investigation 2* and your sociological knowledge answer the following questions**
>
> Answer **all** questions.

Questions and examiner's advice for Investigation 2

Question 4: Identify a possible hypothesis for Investigation 2. [2]

Response: For this question you will need to use the title or aims of the investigation to work out a hypothesis which could apply. It must relate to the topic and must be written as a statement or claim rather than question.

Some possible examples:

'Computer games have an effect on teenagers' behaviour.'

'Computer games have no effect on teenagers' behaviour.'

Note: A hypothesis is what a researcher *thinks* might be the case, but it has not yet been tested. Although the two hypotheses above say the opposite, either could be applied to the investigation.

ACTIVITY 192

Below is a list of research studies. For each one, decide whether it is a hypothesis or not.

1. 'A study to find out what young people think of gangs.'
2. 'Families today are smaller than in 1950.'
3. 'Why is marriage less popular today?'
4. 'I think that most criminals are young males.'
5. 'An investigation into gender and education.'
6. 'What are the reasons for the increase in unemployment?'
7. 'Middle-class people enjoy their jobs more than working-class people.'
8. 'Boys are more likely to play sport than girls.'
9. 'Why do magazines stereotype people?'
10. 'The media is not the main cause of violence.'

Question 5: Identify **one** aim of Investigation 2. [1]

Response: This should be a straightforward question, as the aims are listed. All you need to do is copy one of the three listed aims onto your answer sheet.

Remember that there is no need to describe or explain the aim as you are not asked to do so.

Question 6a: Describe what is meant by the term 'sampling'. [2]

Response: You studied the techniques sociologists use to choose their samples in Part A. You should be aware that researchers have an idea of the type and number of people they want to collect data from.

This question asks you to *describe*, so a simple answer which refers to researchers 'choosing people to study' may not gain both of the marks.

ACTIVITY 193

Remembering the word CASTLE can help you with sampling. A representative sample should reflect the following:

Class
Age
Sex
Time
Location
Ethnicity.

Draw a poster to show how CASTLE relates to sampling.

Question 6b: Describe the sample that was used in Investigation 2. **[2]**

RESEARCH LINK

For more information on sampling types and size see pages 16–18, and on ethics see pages 19–20 of *Sociology basics: Part A.*

Response: For this answer you need to apply your knowledge about sampling to the investigation. Again, this question asks you to *describe*, so an answer which simply says 'the researcher asked some people' will not gain the 2 marks.

You need to find from the investigation the type or size of the sample used. In this investigation the sample was made up of teenagers (mostly 16–19) who were the friends of the researcher and also their friends. You should try to use sociological terms such as 'snowball sample'.

Question 7: Identify and explain **two** ethical issues associated with 'doing covert observation on criminal friends'. **[4]**

Response: For this answer you will need to apply what you have learned about the right way to go about research in order to protect people.

As you are asked to *explain*, you will only get one mark if you simply state one ethical issue. You must also explain what makes it an ethical issue and how it relates to the investigation and 'doing covert observation on criminal friends'.

Some examples:

1. *Ethical issue* – It is wrong to spy on people without their permission.

   Explanation – Covert observation means that the researcher will watch his friends without them knowing.

2. *Ethical issue* – A researcher might witness illegal behaviour.

   Explanation – The researcher has criminal friends. He might want to tell the police about law breaking but this will put him into a difficult position if he witnesses it.

 GradeStudio

To ensure that you do not run out of time in the exam, make sure that you are very familiar with the pre-release material. To help you, some questions will direct you to specific numbered lines of the investigations.

ACTIVITY 194

Look at the lists below and match each definition to the correct term.

1.	Face-to-face discussion used to collect information	a)	random
2.	Small study use to test the main study	b)	data
3.	List of questions given to people to collect data	c)	representative
4.	Type of interview	d)	participant
5.	Information collected by a sociologist	e)	interview
6.	Statistics from the government	f)	questionnaire
7.	Type of observation	g)	pilot
8.	Research which has not been influenced by the views of the sociologist	h)	unstructured
9.	A sample chosen by picking names from a hat	i)	official
10.	A sample made up of all types of people	j)	objective

Question 8a: Identify and explain **two** ways the researcher could have tried to ensure that data from the questionnaires was accurate. **[4]**

Response: To answer this question you first need to think about the word 'accurate'. This refers to the data as being **valid** or truthful. Data should accurately reflect the views or behaviour of the people being studied. You need to think of the ways or techniques that a researcher could use to try to make sure the data is accurate.

If you simply state two ways, you will gain only 2 marks. The question asks you to *explain*, so to get all 4 marks you will need to correctly state two ways, then for each one you will need to explain how it might have helped to produce accurate data. You should refer back to the investigation, as this will make your explanation clearer.

Some possible examples:

Way 1 – Make sure the questionnaires are not filled in by the friends in a group.

Explanation – Their answers may be affected by their mates so they do not tell the truth, for example it may not seem 'cool' to admit to liking school in question 4.

Way 2 – Ask open questions rather than closed.

Explanation – Open-ended questions allow the person answering to be able to respond freely and develop their answer in an accurate and honest way. All the questions in the questionnaire are closed.

Question 8b: Identify and explain **one** improvement the researcher could have made to the questionnaire. **[2]**

Response: For this question you will need to relate closely to the questionnaire. To get both marks you will need to identify the improvement and then explain how the improvement you have identified would make the questionnaire better.

Your answer could focus on a problem with the questionnaire itself, such as the wording or design of the questions.

KEY CONCEPTS

Validity – the truthfulness and accuracy of the data. The more accurate something is, the more valid it is.

Reliability – means that findings can be checked by another researcher. If another researcher can do the research in the same way and get the same results, then the research is reliable.

Some possible examples:

Improvement 1 – Increase the number of answers for people to choose from in question 4.

Explanation – Question 4 gives a choice of only two answers, yes or no, but for some people the answer might be 'sometimes', as the person filling in the questionnaire might like some aspects of school but not others.

Your answer could focus on something missing from the questionnaire and you could suggest what could be added and explain why.

Improvement 2 – Make the questionnaire longer and add questions about the effects of music on behaviour.

Explanation – The aim of the questionnaire is to find out how the media affects teenagers, but it does not ask about this

Note: There are many ways of answering this question, as the questionnaire is not very good and has lots of weaknesses! You only need **one** improvement and explanation.

Question 9a: Evaluate the **results from the questionnaire** referred to in Investigation 2. Do the results meet the aims of the Investigation? Give reasons for your answer. **[3]**

Response: Remember that this is an evaluation question, so you need to think about how good or useful the results are. If you do not show in your answer that you know the aims of the research and what the results show, you will not be able to say whether or not the aims have been met, and it is unlikely that you will get any marks. Therefore, stating aims and results clearly would be a good idea.

Some possible examples:

Aim 1 – To find out if computer games affect the way teenagers act.

Result – All liked fighting games.

Relating aims and results (evaluate) – The results show that they like games with fighting, but do not show that they copy the fighting, so the aim has not been met.

Aim 2 – To find out if teenagers are labelled as criminals.

Result – None of the results showed other people's attitudes to teenagers.

Relating aims and results (evaluate) – No data was collected to show labelling, so the aim has not been met.

Note: The question says 'results' *and* 'aims', i.e. more than one! This means that referring to only one aim and one result will not be enough.

> **Question 9b:** Do the results prove the media has an effect on how teenagers act? Give reasons for your answer. **[3]**

Response: This is another evaluation question, similar to 9b. If you do not show in your answer that you know what the results show, you will not be able to say whether or not the statement above has been proven, and it is unlikely that you will get any marks!

Some possible examples:

Result 1 – Two-thirds of the teenagers favoured hip-hop music and many liked reggae.

Relating aims and results (evaluate) – The results show that they like music associated with gangs, violence and drugs, but this does not mean that the teenagers belong to gangs, behave violently or take drugs. Therefore, the statement that teenagers' behaviour has been affected by the media has not been proven by the research.

Result 2 – They all liked fighting (computer) games and football.

Relating aims and results (evaluate) – The results show that they like fighting in games, but there is no data which shows whether they fight. Therefore, again, the statement that the media affects teenagers' actions cannot be proven.

Section C

> **Question 10:** Using **one** of the Investigations and your sociological knowledge evaluate how you could **improve** the research. What were the weaknesses and how could you overcome them? You could focus on the following:
>
> * the hypothesis
> * the aims
> * sampling
> * methodology
> * secondary evidence. **[12]**

Response: This is a tough question, as you need to use all the skills you have learned. You need to know and understand research techniques and you also need to make links to the investigation and evaluate it.

First decide which investigation you are going to use and state this clearly at the start of your answer.

Sample approach

To evaluate

You need to think about:

* The *weaknesses* of the investigation. The list in the question might help you, but you can get full marks without using all the points in the list.
* The ways you might overcome the weaknesses of the research – *changes* you would make to improve the investigation with an explanation of *why* you think the changes are needed.
* Any *good things* about the research, for example any method or technique which you think has been used well and *why* you think this.

A possible example:

Hypothesis – You might think that because of the results, the hypothesis could have been different, for example (Investigation 1): 'Teenagers wearing hooded jumpers are more likely to commit crime.' This is more appropriate because it is what the newspaper article shows.

Aims – You might say that different aims would have been more suitable. For example, none of the research relates to the aim 'To find out if teenagers are labelled criminal' (Investigation 2). This could be changed to: 'To find out if teenagers who watch violent computer games commit violent acts'. This would fit better as the focus of the research is on media effects.

You might think about how the study could be developed further by identifying related areas or social problems, for example focusing on gender and having the aim 'To find out if one gender is stopped by the police more than another gender'.

Sampling

You might consider how the sample could be improved to make it more representative, for example by making it bigger, having equal numbers of males and females or having a wider geographical area. In Investigation 2, the male researcher gave the questionnaires to his friends, who may have been mostly males, so the sample would not represent the views of females.

APPLYING SOCIOLOGICAL RESEARCH TECHNIQUES | U3

This activity aims to help you to understand about *representative* samples. The more boxes you make, the wider the range of different types of people in the sample.

1. Draw a flow chart as shown below and write in examples and numbers. For a study of teenagers you could use your sociology class, sports team, church group or any other group you know.

2. Divide the groups again, for example by age, cultural group or a different characteristic.

3. Is your sample representative of the *sample population* (the group you wanted to study)? Give reasons for your answer.

4. Identify ways in which you might make your sample more representative. (You should revise the different sampling types explained in Part A.)

5. Draw another flow chart to show a *representative* sample of one of the sample populations below. Show the sample type or method you would use.

    *   Primary school teachers in Britain
    *   Working women in Leeds
    *   Music fans

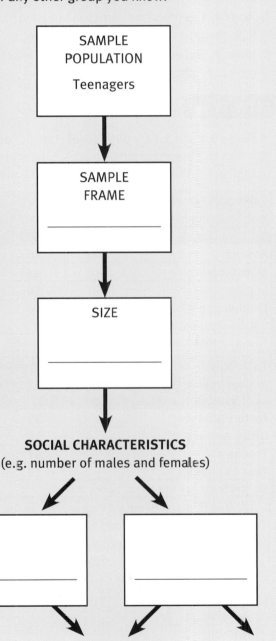

Methodology

You may suggest that a different method would have been useful to meet the aims or prove the hypothesis. For example, in Investigation 2 unstructured interviews with young people who play violent computer games could be used to find out how they feel when they watch the violence and whether they are likely to copy the violence. In Investigation 1 non-participant observation might be useful to see what type of people the police stop in the street and whether or not they are 'hoodies'.

Secondary sources

You could consider alternative secondary data which might help to meet the aims or prove the hypothesis, for example (Investigations 1 and 2):

- television documentaries showing police activity
- official statistics on youth crime.
- studies published by other sociologists.

GradeStudio

Check the question – are you told to use only **one** of the investigations or can you use both?

If you are told to **compare** the investigations or part of the investigations, you must use both of them and look for ways in which they are the same and ways in which they are different.

Test your knowledge and understanding

Practise your skills

This part of the chapter is made up of tasks which you can do to help you revise the research methods. It will help you to check your understanding of them, and to evaluate the techniques used and the evidence collected. The later tasks are based on extracts from research investigations and these will show you how the pre-release material can be studied before the exam.

When Patrick worked in an approved school (borstal), he got to know a gang member who got him into the gang. He studied the gang in the 1960s by pretending to be one of them. He had to dress and act exactly like a gang member, remembering to button his coat in a particular way and talk like them. He made notes on the speech and ways of the gang but not until he had stopped his research and left the gang.

He witnessed extreme violence by the gang and Patrick became frightened when he refused to carry a weapon and the gang became suspicious. After four months, the threat of violence became too much for him and he had to leave Glasgow quickly.

Patrick waited until 1973 before he published his study. This was partly because he was afraid he would be found but also to protect the identity of the gang members. James Patrick was not his real name.

ACTIVITY 196

In the box above is a description of an investigation by James Patrick, who used covert participant observation to study gangs in Glasgow. Read the description then answer the questions.

1. What type of data would this research method produce?
2. Identify and explain **one** way in which:
   a. the data would be valid (accurate/truthful)
   b. the data would not be valid.
3. Identify **two** problems Patrick might have had in getting into the gang.
4. Identify and explain **two** ethical issues which this research raises.

ACTIVITY 197

In Tables 3.1 and 3.2 are two sets of statistics about attitudes to smoking in public places. Study the data (including the titles), then answer the questions.

Table 3.1: Percentage of adults in the UK who agreed with smoking restrictions in certain places.			
	2001	**2003**	**2005**
At work	86	86	86
In restaurants	87	87	91
In pubs	50	56	65
In other public places e.g. banks, post offices	85	90	92
Source: Omnibus survey, Office for National Statistics			

Table 3.2: Percentage of people in Manchester in favour of the smoking ban 2008 (random samples of people from a factory, an office, a school, a class)	
Factory workers	35
Office workers	55
Teachers	85
Year 11 pupils	30
Source: Study by a freedom to smoke group	

1. Identify the type of data which makes up the statistics as either *primary* or *secondary*.
2. Identify the type of data which makes up the statistics as either *quantitative* or *qualitative*.
3. Identify which one of the sources is *official statistics*.
4. Identify **one** conclusion which could be drawn from:
   a) Table 3.1
   b) Table 3.2.
5. Identify and explain **two** ways in which Table 3.1 is more useful than Table 3.2.
6. Identify and explain **two** ways in which Table 3.2 is more useful than Table 3.1.
7. Decide which source is the most useful overall. Explain your answer (you should try to use the terms *valid* and *reliable*).

Analysing extracts from two investigations

In this section you will need to use the extracts from two investigations. These will be similar to (but shorter than) the ones in the pre-release material for your exam. The activities should help you understand how to use the pre-release material to help you prepare for the Unit 3 exam.

Investigations – 'Gender and Sport'

Investigation 1

Extract 1a

Study by a 20-year-old female football player:

'The media represents sport as of interest only to males.'

Aims:

- to find out how two different newspapers report sport
- to find out what women think of media reports of sport.

Investigation 2

Extract 2a

Study by a 16-year-old male Chelsea Football Club supporter:

'Women and football'

I want to find out what people think about women playing football. I also want to find out whether women go to football matches. I think that if football is on the television in a home, it is because the men want it on and I want to see if this is true.

ACTIVITY 198

Look at extracts 1a and 2a.

1. Identify the hypothesis for Investigation 1.
2. Identify **one** aim for Investigation 1.
3. Identify a possible hypothesis which could be used for Investigation 2.
4. Identify the **three** aims of Investigation 2.

Investigation 1

Extract 1b

For my primary research I decided to do a content analysis of the sports pages of *The Sun* and *The Times* newspapers for six days. To do this I will count up and record the number of times the things listed below appear in the sport sections of the newspapers:

- pictures of men
- pictures of women
- stories by men
- stories by women
- reports of men's sports
- reports of women's sports.

I will also carry out a survey by sending out questionnaires to 100 women who play football. I will do this by using a snowball sample and sending questionnaires to ten teams around the country.

Investigation 2

Extract 2b

To collect my primary data I am going to talk to 20 people in my street and ask them some structured questions. I will record their answers onto sheets. I will do this tomorrow as I am off school with a cold. I will knock on doors until I find 20 people who are in.

I will also carry out an observation of people who go to football matches. I work at a burger bar in the football ground on a Saturday. While I am there I will watch out and see if the women who go are interested in the game or whether they are only there because they are taking their kids or going to be with their boyfriends. I can take photos with my mobile phone.

ACTIVITY 199

Look at extracts 1b and 2b on the previous page.

1. Identify the **two** primary methods used in Investigation 1.

2. Identify the **two** primary methods used in Investigation 2.

3. Identify the sampling method used in Investigation 1.

4. Compare the samples used in the two investigations. Which do you think will produce the most useful data? You could consider:

   a) size

   b) method used

   c) representation of different types of people.

5. Draw a spider diagram to show the strengths and weaknesses of each of the four primary methods you have identified.

Investigation 1

Extract 1c

The Questionnaire

I play football for a women's team and think the media ignores women in sport and only reports on men. I want to find out if other people think this. Please answer the questions below.

1. What social class are you?_____

2. What age are you? 18–20 ☐
   20–22   ☐
   22–25   ☐
   over 25 ☐

3. Do you watch sport on television?
   yes ☐ no ☐

   If yes, is this only because your husband wants to watch it?

4. Do you read about sport in newspapers?
   yes ☐ no ☐

   If yes, do you read it in
   a) *The Sun* ☐ or b) *The Times* ☐?

5. Don't you think that women in sport are ignored in the media? yes ☐ no ☐

6. Do you play sport?
   a) sometimes ☐ b) occasionally ☐
   c) rarely ☐ d) never ☐ e) often ☐

ACTIVITY 200

Look at extract 1c above.

1. Identify a question which is 'open'.

2. Identify a question which is 'closed'.

3. Identify and explain **three** problems with the questionnaire in producing accurate data.

Investigation 1

Extract 1d

Results of the content analysis of newspapers

	Men	Women	Both men and women
Pictures of ...	20	3	2
Stories written by ...	10	1	N/A
Reports of sport played by ..	25	5	1

ACTIVITY 201

Look at extracts 1d (on the previous page) and 2d.

1. Identify and explain one conclusion which could be made from the results of the content analysis in extract 1d.

2. Identify and explain for Investigation 1:

   a) **one** way in which the primary results prove the hypothesis

   b) **one** way in which the primary results do not prove the hypothesis.

3. Identify and explain **two** conclusions which could be drawn from the results for Investigation 2 in extract 2d.

Investigation 2

Extract 2d

Results of the survey of my neighbours

People's views of women playing football

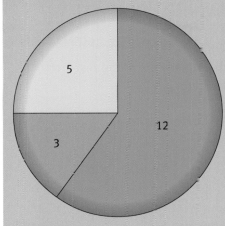

Attitudes to watching women's football

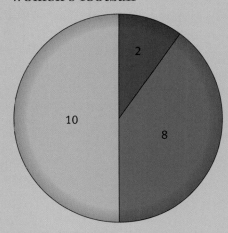

- It is ok for women to play football – 12
- It is wrong for women to play football – 3
- Don't care if women play or not – 5

- It is just as exciting as men's football – 2
- Men's football is better – 8
- Keep all football off the TV; it's boring – 10

Investigation 1

Extract 1e

Case study from a women's health magazine, 2009

> Megan, 29, from a small town in the North of England worked as a reporter on a local paper. She had always been keen on sport in school, was captain of the girls' football team and played hockey for the county. When she trained as a journalist she was eager to report on sporting events but felt the male reporters were not happy about this.
>
> When Megan asked them why, they replied with comments such as 'Women can't understand the rules of football so how can they write accurate stories for the paper'? She asked if she could write an article on the England women's football team, and had a really good photograph to put in the article, as her friend was a team member. However, she was disappointed when the male editor of the paper said there was no space for the photo and her article was made into a very short report and put into a corner of the sports page.
>
> Finally, Megan felt she had had enough. She left her job as a journalist because she was sick of the attitudes of the men. Megan is now training to be a nurse.

Extract 1f

From a Published Study (2002) by a Professor of Media Studies at a University in Scotland

> The research found that broadsheet newspapers such as the *Guardian* and *The Times* were less likely to present stereotypes of men and women than were tabloid newspapers such as *The Sun* and the *Mirror*. Also, the broadsheet papers were more likely to include features which are of interest to women and had a higher percentage of articles written by women than the tabloids.

ACTIVITY 202

Look at extracts 1e and 1f.

1. Identify the **two** secondary sources used in Investigation 1.

2. Identify and explain **two** ways in which the results from the secondary sources support the primary results in Investigation 1.

3. Evaluate the secondary sources used in Investigation 1.

   a. Were they useful in meeting the aims? Give reasons for your answer.

   b. Were they useful in proving the hypothesis? Give reasons for your answer.

Look back at all the extracts for both investigations.

1. Choose one of the investigations and explain how you might develop the research in the future. You could refer to:

    - aims and hypothesis
    - primary data
    - secondary data
    - sampling.

2. Compare the two investigations and evaluate which is the best research. You could refer to:

    - the primary methods
    - the sample
    - the results
    - the objectivity of the researcher
    - ethical issues.

Conclusion

You need to make sure that before the exam, you have studied the pre-release materials of the two investigations in depth.

1. First make sure you know and understand the research methods and techniques explained in Unit 1.

2. Then make sure you have identified all the **aims and hypotheses** and thought of others which could be used.

3. Be clear about which **primary methods** have been used and the strengths and weaknesses of each one. Also make sure you can identify other primary methods which could have been used and can explain why they would be useful.

4. Be clear about which **secondary sources** have been used and the strengths and weaknesses of each one. Also make sure you can identify other secondary sources which could have been used and can explain why they would be useful.

5. Make sure you understand which **sampling** techniques have been used in the investigations. Be able to explain any problems with the sample and evaluate how representative it is.

6. Understand which data in the investigations is **quantitative** and which is **qualitative** and the strengths and weaknesses of each.

7. Be clear about the terms **validity** and **reliability** and be able to evaluate the results

in terms of whether or not they are valid and reliable.

8. Study all the **results** (primary and secondary) in the investigations and make sure you can recognise the results which support each other and those which oppose each other. Also match the results with the aims and hypothesis and be able to recognise where they help to prove the hypothesis *or* where they disprove the hypothesis.

9. Understand any tables or charts in the investigations and the **conclusions** which could be drawn from them

10. Be aware of any **ethical** issues and ways in which the investigations have made sure that the research is ethical and any ways in which they have not.

11. Check that you understand ways in which the investigations are similar and ways in which they are different. Also consider the **strengths and weaknesses** of all the techniques (as above) in the investigations, so that you can suggest possible **changes** and evaluate them.

12. You need to be able to **compare** the two investigations, so that for each part you can see how they are the same or different.

13. Think about how each of the investigations could be **developed** if the researcher wanted to add to it in the future or extend it to gain a better understanding.

Read the following passage. On a separate piece of paper, match the correct word from the list below for each numbered space. For example, 1 = b).

Sociology is not just common sense but is exciting and practical, as researchers try to prove the _____1_____ they form at the start of the study. They do this by collecting evidence or _____2_____. The methods they use are either _____3_____, used to collect first-hand information, or _____4_____, which has already been collected. A popular method is to conduct a _____5_____ using a questionnaire. This is sent out to a _____6_____ of people and this should include different social classes, ages and cultural groups (black, white, goths, chavs, etc.) so that it is _____7_____ of the population being studied.

Before sending out questionnaires, a good researcher should carry out a _____8_____ study to see if the questions can be understood by everyone. This will also test out whether the _____9_____ type of questions have a big enough choice of answers, and find out if people will be happy to write long answers for the _____10_____ type of questions.

Sociologists want their data to be truthful or _____11_____ and also to be like science – do it again and get the same results! This means their research will be _____12_____.

The internet is great for getting data; the government put their _____13_____ statistics online. These numbers and charts are _____14_____ data, and are different to words and description, which are _____15_____ data. Which is best? _____16_____ _____17_____, who studied gangs in Glasgow, wanted in-depth information so he used _____18_____ observation. Great stuff, but was he right to pretend to be a gang member by using _____19_____ research? Also, he knew about violent, criminal acts but didn't tell the police, so some people would say his study was _____20_____. It would be good if someone had gone back to the gang every few years and done a _____21_____ study to see if the lads changed their behaviour as they got older!

Gangs are really interesting and a detailed _____22_____ _____23_____ of one gang member's life story might help us to understand what gangs are all about. Some sociologists say this is no good, as it would not help us to understand how *most* people act so that researchers can make a _____24_____.

So, sociologists do not agree with each other! That means you have to be able to _____25_____ by looking at all sides of an argument, understanding the strengths and weaknesses, and then deciding which is best. If you can do this you will do really well in your sociology exam! GOOD LUCK!

a) reliable, b) hypothesis, c) data, d) evaluate, e) open, f) primary, g) unethical, h) pilot, i) sample, j) case, k) study, l) secondary, m) official, n) qualitative, o) generalsation, p) survey, q) representative, r) James, s) Patrick, t) quantitative, u) longitudinal, v) participant, w) valid, x) closed, y) covert

Adolescence – the period between childhood and adulthood.

Ageism – discriminating against or expressing negative views or stereotypes about an age group.

Agenda setting – the media deciding which subjects are appropriate for the news or for discussion.

Agents of social control – the various groups, both formal and informal, that control our behaviour.

Alienation – a situation where the worker gains no satisfaction from their job.

Anti-school subculture – a small group of pupils who do not value education and behave and think in a way that is completely opposite to the aims of a school.

Audience – those who receive the media.

Automation – the use of automatic (or computer-controlled) machinery.

Beanpole family – a tall, narrow extended family often containing four (or five) generations.

Bedroom subculture – a subculture of young teenage girls.

Bias – the subject is presented in a one-sided way which favours one point of view more than others.

Boomerang family – a family in which non-dependent children return home to live with their parents.

Boredom – joining a gang is something to do when there is nothing else to do.

Canalisation – parents give children gender-specific goods that are considered the norm for their gender – dolls for girls and not boys, for example.

Case study – a detailed and in-depth study of one particular group or situation.

Censorship – restrictions on the freedom of speech.

Child abuse – harm caused to a child or young person under 18 by an adult (NSPCC definition).

Childhood – the age after infancy but before adolescence.

Closed questions – respondents are presented with either a list of options or a two-way choice and have to select the response with which they most agree.

Cohabitation – living together as partners without being married.

Communication – any form of dialogue, either written or verbal, between people.

Compliance – to do what is wanted and expected of you, to follow orders and rules.

Computerisation – the use of electronic machines capable of storing and processing information and controlling other machines.

Conform – to accept what you are told and so behave and think in the way that is expected of you.

Conjugal roles – the roles of husbands and wives or a couple who are living together as partners.

Convergence – the coming together of different forms of media.

Covert observation – where the researcher does not let the group being studied know that they are being observed.

Crime – an action that is against the law.

Cross-cultural deviance – something that is deviant in some cultures but not in others.

Cross-sectional – if a sample is cross-sectional, then it will be made up of a range of different people to best represent the research population.

Culture – the way of life of a group of people; it is learned and shared. The main parts of culture include knowledge, skills, social norms, values and beliefs.

Dark side of the family – a situation in which family life damages its members.

Delinquency – the undesirable, antisocial behaviour of young people.

Delinquent subculture – groups that commit illegal activities.

Deskilling – a process which reduces the skill required to perform tasks. (For example, a manual camera requires the ability to focus and set the aperture and shutter speed; an automatic camera only requires one to 'point and shoot'.)

Deviance – actions that go against the norms and values of a society or group.

Disappearance of childhood – Postman's view that the innocent age, in which the young have little responsibility or worry, is being eroded.

Discrimination – treating people unfairly.

Divorce – the legal termination (ending) of marriage, leaving the couple free to remarry if they wish.

Domestic violence – threatening behaviour, violence or abuse (psychological, emotional, physical, sexual or financial) committed by a family member against another.

Dual burden – a situation where women combine the responsibilities of paid work with the mother-housewife role.

Editor – a person who decides on the final content of any media product.

Employment – involves either working for an employer or working for oneself.

Equal opportunities – a situation where people have an equal chance of success, regardless of their ascribed characteristics (e.g. gender, ethnic group, age, disability).

Equal pay – where different types of workers (e.g. men and women) receive the same pay if they work for the same employer and do the same work (or work of similar value).

Ethics – ideas about what is morally right and wrong.

Extended family – any family larger than a nuclear family. There are different types of extended family.

Extrinsic satisfaction – comes from outside the job – for example, high pay or perks – rather than the job itself.

Family – consists of people we are related to by ties of blood, marriage, adoption, civil partnership or cohabitation. There are many different types of family.

Femininity – the quality of acting in a way that a society deems is typically female behaviour.

Feminist – someone who thinks that women are disadvantaged in society and wants to make them equal with men.

Flexitime – employees have some choice about when they work their agreed weekly hours.

Focus group – several respondents are interviewed at once and are allowed to discuss the questions being asked of them.

Formal curriculum – subjects that are studied and examined in schools and colleges; sociology, media studies and history, for example.

Formal social control – written rules and laws enforced by powerful agents such as the police and courts.

Functional sociologists – sociologists who believe that each part of society has roles to fulfil in order that society can survive as a whole.

Gang – a group that has some form of membership, some form of hierarchy and is often involved in criminal activities.

Gatekeeper – a label for the editors and creators of media, as they are the people who decide which ideas/stories make it through to publication.

GCSE – the General Certificate of Secondary Education is the name of an academic qualification awarded in a specified subject to students typically aged 14-16.

Gender socialisation – teaching males and females the expected patterns of behaviour for their gender in society.

Generalisations – results from a study can be applied to the whole of the research population.

Globalisation – the opening up of the world economically through production and consumption.

Growth of affluence – an increase in wealth.

Hidden curriculum – what schools teach students through day-to-day school life, i.e. this is not part of the formal timetable. This will reflect society's attitudes and values and prepare students for their future role and place in that society.

Historical deviance – something that is deviant only at a certain time.

Household – one person living alone or a group of people who have the same address and share either one meal a day or their living accommodation.

Househusband – a man with the main responsibility for domestic tasks and childcare, whose partner is the main breadwinner.

Housewife – an unpaid role which makes wives financially dependent on their husbands.

Identity – how we see ourselves and how others see us.

Inequality – not everybody in society has the same chances of success.

Informal education/learning – non-directed learning that occurs outside the classroom and does not have a curriculum to follow.

Informal social control – controlling people's behaviour using informal methods in everyday situations.

Interactivity – audience participation in the creation of media.

Intertextuality – media that is about other media.

Interview questionnaires – questions are read out to the respondent by the researcher, who then records the respondent's answers.

Interviewer bias – where the interviewer influences the answers that the respondent gives.

Intrinsic satisfaction – comes from the enjoyment of the actual job.

Labelling – thinking of a person or group of people in a particular way which then determines how you behave towards them.

Leisure – free time left after we have done everything we have to.

Life chances – the chances of obtaining desirable things (e.g. good health, high income) and avoiding undesirable things (e.g. poor health, poverty).

Lone-parent family – a mother or father living without a partner, and their dependent child(ren).

Longitudinal study – a study completed over a long period of time.

Loss of innocence – the belief that children grow up fast and become aware of adult issues early.

Low response rate – not everyone that you want to participate in your research may do so, meaning that your respondents may no longer be typical of the population under study.

Manipulation – parents encourage children to behave in a way that is seen to be appropriate for their gender.

Manipulation by the media – the idea that the media has invented youth culture in order to make money.

Marriage – a legally recognised tie between a husband and wife.

Masculinity – the quality of acting in a way that society deems is typically male behaviour.

Mass media – any form of communication, either written or technological, that is invented to allow transmission to many people.

Material deprivation – not having the money needed to buy items that can help children succeed in education.

Matrilocal – living with or near to the wife's family.

Media effects models – the different theories of how the media can affect its audience.

Meritocracy – a society where a person's ability determines how well they do in life in terms of their social status and wealth.

Mixed ability – students of various abilities are taught together in the same class.

Moral panic – when the media causes a group, person or situation to become seen as a threat to society.

National curriculum – subjects and tests that the government has decided must be done in all state schools.

Negative sanctions – punishments used to prevent unacceptable behaviour.

Neolocal – the couple set up their own home.

News values – the media's decisions that stories are worthy of being called news.

Non-participant observation – where a researcher watches a group without getting involved in what they are doing.

Norms – the unwritten rules of society that determine acceptable behaviour.

Nuclear family – a two-generation family, consisting of parents and their dependent children (i.e. children until 16, or under 18, if in full-time education).

Objectivity – studying topics and people with an open mind and not allowing your own views and opinions to influence the findings.

Observer effect – when the presence of an observer affects the actions of the group under study, preventing the observer from seeing natural behaviour.

Official statistics – numbers and percentages to show what crimes are being committed and who is committing them, taken from government sources. Information can be supplied by such agencies as the police, the courts and the prison system.

Ofsted – the Office for Standards in Education, Children's Services and Skills inspects and reports on educational institutions to monitor performance, care and standards.

Open questions – respondents are free to answer the question in any way that they like; there are no preset options.

Operationalise – to define exactly what is meant by any terms used for categorisation.

Overt observation – where the researcher tells the group under study that they are being observed or does not attempt to hide their presence from them.

Participant observation – where a researcher joins the group being studied and acts as they do whilst completing the observation.

Patriarchy – a society dominated by males, where they have more power than females.

Patrilocal – living with or near to the husband's family.

Peer group – others of the same age, interests and social status.

Peer group pressure – pressure applied to a person by a group of the same age to try to get them to fit in with the group's norms and values. Often applies to young people.

Pilot study – a small-scale study completed before a piece of research to identify any possible problems.

Police targeting – where the police focus on a particular group of people in society, believing them to be more likely to be involved in criminal behaviour than other groups.

Positive sanctions – rewards used to encourage acceptable behaviour.

Primary data – information that researchers have gathered themselves.

Primary sector – the sector of the economy which gathers or produces raw materials, e.g. farming, mining and fishing.

Private school – any school that charges a fee for pupils to attend

Public school – higher-status private schools with very high fees. Members of the Royal family and the very wealthy are usually educated in these schools.

Qualitative data – in-depth data, usually presented in a written form.

Quantitative data – numerical data, often presented as statistics.

Racial discrimination – treating people unfairly because of their ethnic group or race.

Racism – discriminating against or expressing negative views or stereotypes about an ethnic group or race.

Random sample – the sample group is chosen completely at random.

Reconstituted family – a family in which one or both partners has been married or cohabited before, and has a child or children, creating step-relationships.

Relativity – specific to a particular situation, social group or society, i.e. not general.

Reliability – means that findings can be checked by another researcher. If another researcher can do the research in the same way and get the same results, then the research is reliable.

Representative – when the data can be said to accurately represent the research population in terms of, for example, gender and age composition.

Research device – the research method that you will use for your investigation, such as a questionnaire or interview questions.

Research population – the group(s) of people relevant to the study being completed.

Reskilling – a process which increases the skill required to perform tasks.

Rites of passage – initiation into the next stage of life.

Sample – a small group of people, usually cross-sectional, on whom research will be carried out.

Sampling frame – the source from which a sample is drawn.

SATs – standard assessment tests taken at the end of Key Stage 2. (The government stopped the SATs at KS3 in 2008.)

Scapegoat – someone to blame to avoid dealing with the true problem

Secondary data – information that has been collected by somebody else and then used by the researcher.

Secondary sector – the manufacturing industries, which make finished products for people to buy and use.

Secular society – a society that is not ruled by religious beliefs.

Segregation – separating students, often males and females, and so giving them different experiences and opportunities in school. This could be through single-sex schooling or through keeping them apart within a mixed gender environment.

Selection – choosing students to attend a school because of their ability.

Self-censorship – when the audience is expected to police and monitor all necessary restrictions on the freedom of speech.

Index